T0330397

Re-examining Monetary and Fiscal Policy for the
21st Century

Re-examining Monetary and Fiscal Policy for the 21st Century

Philip Arestis

University of Cambridge, UK and Levy Economics Institute, USA

Malcolm Sawyer

University of Leeds, UK and Levy Economics Institute, USA

Edward Elgar

Cheltenham, UK • Northampton, MA, USA

Published by
Edward Elgar Publishing Limited
Glensanda House
Montpellier Parade
Cheltenham
Glos GL50 1UA
UK

Edward Elgar Publishing, Inc.
136 West Street
Suite 202
Northampton
Massachusetts 01060
USA

A catalogue record for this book
is available from the British Library

Library of Congress Cataloguing in Publication Data
Arestis, Philip, 1941–
    Re-examining monetary and fiscal policy for the 21st century / Philip Arestis, Malcolm Sawyer.
        p. cm.
    Includes bibliographical references and index.
    1. Monetary policy. 2. Fiscal policy. 3. Inflation (Finance) I. Sawyer, Malcolm C. II. Title.

HG230.3.A66 2004
339.5—dc22

2004047966

ISBN 1 84376 583 7

Typeset by Manton Typesetters, Louth, Lincolnshire, UK.
Printed and bound in Great Britain by MPG Books Ltd, Bodmin, Cornwall.

Contents

Figures

Tables

Acknowledgments

We are grateful to the journals named below and their editors for permission to draw on material which has already been published in their journals:

'Inflation targeting: a critical appraisal', *Greek Economic Review* (forthcoming 2004) (Chapter 2; Chapter 4, section 3.2).
'The Bank of England Macroeconomic Model: its Nature and Implications', from the *Journal of Post Keynesian Economics*, **24**(4) (Summer 2002), 529–45. Copyright © 2002 M.E. Sharpe, Inc., reprinted with permission (Chapter 3);
'Can monetary policy affect the real economy?', *European Review of Economics and Finance*, **3**(3), 9–32 (Chapter 4).
'Does the Stock of Money Have any Causal Significance?', *Banca Nazionale del Lavoro*, **56**(225), 113–36 (2003) (Chapter 5);
'On the effectiveness of monetary policy and of fiscal policy', *Review of Social Economy* (forthcoming 2004) (Chapter 7, sections 2 and 4);
'Reinventing Fiscal Policy', from the *Journal of Post Keynesian Economics*, **26**(1) (Fall 2003), 3–25. Copyright © 2003 M.E. Sharpe, Inc., reprinted with permission (Chapter 8);
'Macroeconomic Policies of the European Economic and Monetary Union', *International Papers in Political Economy*, 2004, **10**(1) (Chapter 10).

We are grateful to the Levy Economics Institute for the support on a project on monetary and fiscal policy from which this book developed.

We are also grateful to the Centre for Economic and Public Policy, Department of Land Economy, University of Cambridge, for their support and encouragement to complete this project.

We would also wish to thank Edward Elgar and his staff, especially Dymphna Evans, for being so supportive during the whole process of the preparation and publication of this book.

Philip Arestis
Malcolm Sawyer

1.   Introduction: debates over monetary and fiscal policy

1   OBJECTIVES OF THE BOOK

The 1960s saw the beginning of an intellectual battle between Keynesians and monetarists, exemplified by a series of papers in which the relative potency of fiscal and monetary policy were compared (Friedman and Meiselman, 1963; Ando and Modigliani, 1965). However, it was the 1970s which saw the ideas of monetarism sweep all before it and the decline of Keynesian economics. Monetarism combined a range of features, but there are two which stand out as particularly important and relevant for the discussion and analysis of this book (for a recent review, see Bernanke, 2003c). The first was the doctrine that 'inflation is always and everywhere a monetary phenomenon' (Friedman, 1960), which had a strong appeal in an era of rising inflation, with the 1960s and the early 1970s seeing perhaps the first sustained inflation not associated with war or the aftermath of war. Monetarism advanced the view that a sustained rise in the stock of money (caused by the government or its agencies) led to a rise in the price level. When the supply of money ran ahead of the demand for money, there was 'excess' money, which people spent, thereby bidding up output initially but then, and in a sustained manner, prices. The conclusion for economic policy readily followed: limit the growth of the money supply, and thereby limit the growth of prices, and the rate of inflation. Monetary policy became associated with control of the money supply, and a range of governments, particularly in the early 1980s, announced money supply targets. Monetary policy was assigned the sole role of the control of inflation, and alternative policies, such as incomes policy, for the control of inflation were dismissed.

Second, Friedman (1968) advanced the notion of the 'natural rate of unemployment', as a supply-side equilibrium at which the labour market would clear, where inflation would be constant and towards which the actual level of unemployment would tend rather quickly. The 'natural rate' doctrine ran counter to the prevailing Keynesian perspective in a number of respects. There was the implicit reinstatement of Say's Law whereby there would not be any general deficiency of demand. The supply-side equilibrium in effect ruled the roost: it determined the point towards which the economy would

1

quickly gravitate, and the time path of aggregate demand would not affect the equilibrium position. The macroeconomy was viewed as inherently stable and, left to its own devices, it would converge on this equilibrium position.

Monetarism based on those two features did not continue its dominance of economic thinking for long. Control of the money supply proved elusive, with governments and central banks who focused on the growth of the money supply generally failing to hit their targets. Indeed, the demand for money became unstable as a consequence of financial innovations. Poole (1970) had already demonstrated that, when the LM relationship (from the IS–LM approach with the equilibrium condition of demand for money equal to supply of money) was unstable essentially because of money-demand instability (as a result of financial innovation, for example), the rate of interest should be used as the target of monetary policy. The money supply target was quickly abandoned. But still the association between monetary policy and the control of inflation remained. The instrument of monetary policy became the setting of the key interest rate by the central bank. In many respects, the use of interest rates had never been abandoned, but their use was now directed at inflation rather than at achieving some target for the money supply (or indeed any other target such as the exchange rate). Another reason for the abandonment of concentration on money supply was that attempts to control the growth of the money supply had become associated with high and rising unemployment. The notion that the announcement of a money supply target would reduce inflationary expectations and lead to a relatively painless reduction in inflation with little unemployment was quickly dispelled.

The 'natural rate of unemployment' as formulated by Friedman (1968) could be associated with some notion of full employment, that is, Walrasian general equilibrium, and the clearing of the labour market. A more general notion of the non-accelerating inflation rate of unemployment (NAIRU), which does not necessarily embody any notions of full employment, has generally replaced the 'natural rate of unemployment' (in the sense of a clearing labour market involving full employment), although, confusingly, the term 'natural rate of unemployment' is widely used to mean that level of unemployment consistent with constant inflation. But the notion that there is a supply-side equilibrium (which has the desirable property of being associated with a constant rate of inflation), which is unaffected by what happens on the demand side of the economy, has remained a key feature of the 'new consensus' in macroeconomics. Further, the idea has also remained that changing this supply-side equilibrium requires changes in the structure and organization of the labour market. In general, the argument has been that making the labour market more 'flexible' (a term with a wide variety of meanings in this context) is required to reduce the (equilibrium) level of unemployment (and thereby reduce the actual level of unemployment).

The practice of monetary policy has encapsulated these ideas; monetary policy can focus on inflation without having any effect on the supply-side equilibrium. Further, monetary policy can only address inflation since it does not have (by assumption) any sustained impact on level of economic activity or on the rate of economic growth.

The idea of monetary policy focusing on inflation, and inflation alone, can be linked with the shift (starting in New Zealand in 1990) towards the introduction of an 'independent' central bank. In this context, an 'independent' central bank is taken to include the operational independence (from political or democratic involvement) of the central bank, combined with the statement by the government (or by the central bank itself) of the objective to be pursued by the central bank, which has generally been some variant on control of the rate of inflation. In many cases, what has been termed 'inflation targeting' has been adopted under which the central bank is either given a numerical value or range for the rate of inflation (for example, the Bank of Canada is given a specific value; the Bank of England was set a target of 2.5 per cent (with a margin of 1 per cent either side) in terms of the Retail Price Index, recently amended to 2 per cent in terms of the harmonised index of consumer prices (HICP)), or deciding by itself (the European Central Bank's case, for example, where the focus is on price stability defined as 'near to 2 per cent').[1] This has gone along with the view that interest rates are raised in the face of inflationary pressures and lowered in the face of deflationary pressures.

The shift to 'independence' of central banks was strongly pushed by some other considerations as well. The idea was developed that central banks with their expertise in monetary policy should be more trusted with decisions over interest rates (and more generally over macroeconomic policy) than elected politicians could be.[2] This line of argument built upon two separate notions. The first notion came from the idea that there was a trade-off between unemployment and future inflation (in the form of a Phillips curve). It was argued that elected politicians would favour the short-run stimulus of the economy to reduce unemployment, but this would be at the expense of higher future inflation. In contrast, central bankers were deemed 'more conservative' (Rogoff, 1985) and placed more weight on inflation and less on unemployment. Hence central bankers would be less prone than elected politicians to reflate the economy, since central bankers did not face re-election. Second, the central bank was deemed to be more 'credible' (in part reflecting the arguments just given). This enhanced credibility would mean that if, for example, interest rates were cut, this would be interpreted by the financial markets and others to indicate that inflationary pressures were low and the economy could safely be expanded, whereas a similar cut by government might be interpreted to signal the pursuit of low unemployment over low

inflation. Further, if the commitment of central banks to achieving low inflation was believed, along with its ability to actually achieve it, then expectations
of low inflation would be enhanced, and those very expectations would
enable the achievement of low inflation. The commitment of the central bank
to achieving low inflation could be 'locked in' through the setting of clear
objectives for the central bank in terms of an inflation target.

The rise in importance of monetary policy has been accompanied by a
downgrading of fiscal policy. The reduced importance of fiscal policy in
macroeconomic policy making has at least three dimensions. The first is the
virtual ending of the use of fiscal policy to 'fine-tune' the economy. The
second is that fiscal policy should be confined to operating as an 'automatic
stabilizer', and to do so around an average budget deficit position which was
constrained. The third, and most important, is that a high level of employment has largely disappeared as an objective of macroeconomic policy. Insofar
as the level of employment is a policy objective, it is to be addressed through
'pricing people back into work', through changes in the unemployment benefit system ('making work pay'), reform of labour laws, trade unions and
labour market regulations and so on. Fiscal policy had hitherto been seen as
one of the means by which high levels of employment would be achieved.
Now fiscal policy and high levels of employment as a macroeconomic objective have been largely off the political agenda.

As the title suggests, this book focuses on monetary and fiscal policies.
Much of our discussion of these policies begins from what has been termed
the 'new consensus' in macroeconomics (for example, McCallum, 2001;
Meyer, 2001a), along with its main policy prescription that has come to be
known as 'inflation targeting'. We elaborate on both these aspects in Chapter
2. In Chapter 3 we further elaborate on, and illustrate the nature of, the 'new
consensus' by referring to a specific macroeconomic model used for policy
purposes. This is the macroeconometric model as in Bank of England (1999,
2000). This 'new consensus' reflects a number of the features, which we have
outlined above: the emphasis on monetary policy rather than fiscal policy, the
essential stability of the market economy and the absence of generalized
deficient demand, the key role of a supply-side equilibrium position. We
evaluate critically some of the ideas embedded in this 'new consensus'. In
view of the central role which has been given to monetary policy in macroeconomic policy measures, it is necessary to enquire as to how monetary
policy (in the form of interest rate changes) affects the rate of inflation: is it
an effective policy instrument? Further, it is important to enquire as to whether
monetary policy has other effects on the economy, on the level of employment and of investment for example. This is undertaken in Chapter 3.

Monetarism was founded on the idea that the stock of money could be
treated as under the control of government ('helicopter money', to draw on

Friedman's, 1969, famous analogy). As such, the stock of money could be seen as *causing* inflation (or more generally the nominal level of economic activity). It becomes apparent in the discussion of the 'new consensus' that the stock of money makes little or no appearance: money has 'disappeared'. In Chapter 4 we consider the ways in which a number of authors have attempted to reinstate a causal role for money. We argue that none of these has been successful, and that money should be treated as credit money created within the banking system.

Chapter 5 provides further consideration of the effectiveness of monetary policy. When interest rate is used as the monetary policy instrument, then monetary policy is viewed as influencing the level of aggregate demand and, thereby, it is postulated, the rate of inflation. From this perspective, monetary policy can be compared with the alternative means of influencing aggregate demand, namely fiscal policy.

In Chapter 6 we put forward an alternative analysis of the inflationary process and the determination of the level of economic activity to that contained in the new consensus in macroeconomics (NCM). This view comprises four key elements: the level of demand relative to the size of productive capacity; the inherent conflict over the distribution of income; no presumption that the level of demand will generate full employment of labour and/or full capacity utilization; money seen as endogenous credit money created by the banking system.

Although the 'new consensus' has implicitly treated money as created within the banking system (in the jargon, treated money as endogenous), we argue that this 'new consensus' has not fully taken on board the consequences of treating money as endogenous. In Chapter 7 the nature and role of monetary policy when money is treated as endogenous is examined.

The rise of monetary policy has accompanied some demise of fiscal policy, particularly of discretionary fiscal policy. This is perhaps most evident in the convergence criteria of the Maastricht Treaty for a country's membership of the European single currency and in the conditions imposed on member countries by the Stability and Growth Pact. The latter now requires that a national government's budget position be in balance or small surplus over the course of the business cycle and that the deficit never exceeds 3 per cent of GDP. Discretionary fiscal policy is ruled out, but also any fiscal expansion, involving deficit, is regarded as unsustainable. Chapters 8 and 9 examine the case for fiscal policy. Numerous arguments have been advanced to the effect that fiscal policy is ineffective and/or has undesirable effects. We examine critically these arguments and conclude that fiscal policy should be 'reinstated'.

The policy framework for the new European single currency is firmly based on the perspective of the 'new consensus', a case that we establish in

Chapter 10. Drawing on the previous discussions in the book, it is argued in this chapter that this policy framework will be ineffectual in lowering unemployment or in controlling inflation.

2   THESIS OF THE BOOK

We believe this book has managed to put together a consistent thesis, which can be briefly summarized. It has demonstrated the main ingredients of the 'new consensus' in macroeconomics and how monetary policy, as it is currently practised, encapsulates them. The downgrading of fiscal policy has also been highlighted but the book has also argued for its reinstatement. Monetary policy as it is practised these days has been criticized. The economic and monetary union in Europe has been utilized to demonstrate the treatment of both monetary and fiscal policy. This policy framework and its implementation are found unsatisfactory.

There are many implications that can be derived from the analysis in this book. In the rest of this chapter we focus on the particularly important ones. The first implication relates to the role of money and of monetary policy. Inflation will generally cause an increase in the stock of money, but the stock of money itself does not cause inflation. Loans are created by banks within the inflationary process, and those loans create bank deposits and hence the stock of money can expand. How far it expands then depends on what is happening to the demand for money: money only remains in existence if there is someone willing to hold that money. Consequently, seeking to control the growth of the stock of money is fraught with difficulties, as witnessed by the failures of those governments, which sought to control the money supply in the 1980s. It proved particularly difficult to control the stock of money, as would be readily apparent from the realization that the creation of money is in the hands of the banks. If it is profitable for banks to create loans and for bank deposits to increase, then that is likely to happen.

The failure of seeking to control the money supply led to the use of interest rates as the key tool of monetary policy and to the setting of inflation targets to be achieved through monetary policy. The mechanism by which interest rates are meant to influence inflation is via their effects on aggregate demand, and the effect of aggregate demand on the pace of inflation. At best, monetary policy can only address demand inflation, and is unable to do anything about imported inflation or cost inflation. Further, the use of monetary policy in the form of interest rates is likely to have little effect on inflation: simple variation of interest rates has relatively little effect on demand, and demand has little effect on inflation. In Chapters 3 and 4, we summarize some evidence on the effect of interest rates on inflation (from the euro area, the UK and the

USA) and conclude that it is generally small: in this context small means a one percentage point change in interest rates having an effect of the order of 0.2 to 0.3 per cent on output and rather less on inflation. But further, insofar as interest rates do have an effect, it comes through effects on investment and on the exchange rate. Attempts to counter inflation through raising interest rates have detrimental effects on investment (and thereby on capacity formation) and may tend to raise the exchange rate, thereby harming export prospects. Consequently, our first conclusion is that monetary policy is an ineffective means of controlling inflation. Insofar as it does work, it has detrimental effects on the level of economic activity and on investment and future productive capacity.

The second set of implications arise from the NAIRU type of models, where the adjustment to aggregate demand from within the private sector comes from some form of 'real balance' effect, that is insofar as a rise in prices reduces the real level of aggregate demand. In that case both prices and wages are rising and perhaps real demand is then declining. This could arise if, for example, government expenditure is set in nominal terms. The more usual argument would be that the real balance effect operates through the given nominal money supply. This, however, would not operate in a credit money system. At most the real balance effect could be argued to operate on the narrow definition of money (cash, bank notes and banks' reserves with the central bank). In the UK, this definition is equivalent to a little over 3 per cent of gross domestic product (GDP), and hence a 10 per cent rise in prices would reduce the narrow definition of money (assuming no compensating change in it) in real terms by the equivalent of 0.3 per cent of GDP, and the effect of such a change in real wealth would be very much smaller. Recent estimates reported in OECD (2000) put the marginal propensity to consume out of wealth in the range of 0.02 to 0.05. It can be concluded that the aggregate demand adjustment from this source would be rather small.

Government policy (including fiscal and, especially, monetary policy) can be a significant agent of adjustment. For example, a monetary policy based on the adjustment of interest rates in response to the inflationary climate can have the effect of moving aggregate demand towards the NAIRU level. In a similar vein, fiscal policy may be used to adjust the level of aggregate demand. The adjustment would not be automatic and would require macroeconomic policy, which responds to changes in the rate of inflation and/or the level of unemployment relative to the NAIRU. Therefore the NAIRU is likely to be a weak attractor for the actual rate of unemployment. The NAIRU is a theoretical construct, which portrays an equilibrium position. Not only does the actual rate of unemployment differ from the NAIRU at any particular point in time but the NAIRU may be a weak (or zero) attractor for the actual rate of unemployment.

The third set of implications concern the importance of investment, capacity and its distribution. We take the view that the level of employment does not depend on the operations of the labour market, but rather on the level of aggregate demand. In effect there is unemployment not because real wages are too high or the labour market has failed to clear but because the demand for labour is too low, and in turn the demand for labour is too low because the level of aggregate demand is too low. Measures to reduce real wages or to change the workings of the labour market may be counterproductive (if they reduce aggregate demand), but will fail unless aggregate demand is increased. To this insight a further (and rather obvious) one is added, namely that an economy's ability to generate employment depends on the size and distribution of its productive capacity. There is little to reason to think that either aggregate demand or productive capacity will be sufficient to support full employment. We argue (see Chapter 6) that there is some form of an inflation barrier, such that, if the level of economic activity is higher than the barrier, there is a tendency for inflation to increase. But it is important to realize the nature of the barrier: it is perceived to arise from the interaction of the productive capacity of the economy and the claims on income shares.

The fourth set of implications (related to the preceding two) is that deflationary policies designed to reduce inflation will have detrimental effects on the pace of investment, and thereby on the capital stock. As the future productive capacity is thereby lower (than it would have otherwise been), the future inflation problem is made worse.

The fifth implication comes from the contrast between the inflation barrier arising from capacity constraints and the NAIRU as a labour market phenomenon. The latter view suggests that the NAIRU (and the natural rate of unemployment) depend on the characteristics of the labour market: notice the mentions of trade union powers, minimum wages, unemployment benefits and so on. Now it can be observed that those are typically characteristics which apply across the whole of the economy. Laws on trade unions, regulation of labour markets, unemployment benefits and minimum wages are characteristics that apply to the whole economy and do not (in general) vary from area to area. It is, we suggest, implausible to think that the variations in unemployment which are observed between the different regions of a country (or indeed between, say, urban and rural areas, or between ethnic groups), can be explained by variations in the labour market characteristics of the regions involved. It is much more plausible to view the variations in unemployment as arising from the industrial structure of a region and from variations in productive capacity and in the demand for the production of the region.

The sixth, and final, point relates to the focus on the role of the distribution of income. The inflation barrier depends on the extent of the conflict over the distribution of income. Higher claims by enterprises for profits would involve lower real wages and lower employment. Higher claims by workers would involve higher real wages but lower employment.

NOTES

1. Note, though, that although the ECB is 'independent', it does not view itself as pursuing 'inflation targeting' (see discussion in Chapter 10 below).
2. Keynes (1932) was the first to suggest that an 'independent' Bank of England was well equipped, and in a much better position, to conduct monetary policy than otherwise. For further details on Keynes's views on 'independent' central banks, see the recent contribution by Bibow (2002b).

2. The 'new consensus' in macroeconomics and monetary policy

1   INTRODUCTION

Alongside an emphasis on monetary policy, rather than fiscal policy, has gone the development of what now may be termed a 'new consensus' in macroeconomics and monetary policy. In this chapter we elaborate on the nature of this 'new consensus'. In Chapter 3 we illustrate it by reference to the macroeconometric model of the Bank of England. In subsequent chapters we will examine the implications of this 'new consensus' for both monetary and fiscal policy.

A possible, and important, policy implication of the 'new consensus' mode of thought is 'inflation targeting' (IT). Over the past decade, a number of countries have adopted IT in attempts to reduce inflation to low levels and/or to sustain inflation at a low level. IT has been praised by most studies as a superior framework of monetary policy (Bernanke, Laubach, Mishkin and Posen, 1999) and, to quote a recent study, 'The performance of inflation-targeting regimes has been quite good. Inflation-targeting countries seem to have significantly reduced both the rate of inflation and inflation expectations beyond that which would likely have occurred in the absence of inflation targets' (Mishkin, 1999, p. 595).[1] IT involves the manipulation of the central bank interest rate (the repo rate), with the specific objective of achieving the goal(s) of monetary policy. The latter is normally the inflation rate, although in a number of instances this may include the level of economic activity (the Federal Reserve monetary policy in the US is a good example of this category). It ought to be clarified, though, that this does not mean emphasis on output stabilization per se. Mishkin (2002b) makes the point when he argues that 'too great a focus on output fluctuations' (p. 2) may lead to suboptimal monetary policy (see also Orphanides, 2002). This is so because output stabilization is thought to complicate the authorities' communication strategy, weaken central bank credibility and make it harder to tackle time inconsistency (the difficulties of measuring potential output are also emphasized; see, for example, Orphanides, 2001). By contrast, flexible IT communicates the concerns of the authorities over output fluctuation, but does not exploit the short-run trade-off between output and inflation since the emphasis is on the latter rather than the former.

We begin by addressing the theoretical foundations of the new consensus in macroeconomics (hereafter NCM) and IT in the section immediately below, followed by an assessment of the theoretical foundations of the NCM and of IT.

2 'NEW CONSENSUS' IN MACROECONOMICS

NCM can be described succinctly in the following three equations (see, for example, Meyer, 2001b; McCallum, 2001):

$$Y_t^g = a_0 + a_1 Y_{t-1}^g + a_2 E_t(Y_{t+1}^g) - a_3[R_t - E_t(p_{t+1})] + s_1, \qquad (2.1)$$

$$p_t = b_1 Y_t^g + b_2 p_{t+1} + b_3 E_t(p_{t+1}) + s_2, \qquad (2.2)$$

$$R_t = (1 - c_3)[RR^* + E_t(p_{t+1}) + c_1 Y_{t-1}^g + c_1 Y_{t-1}^g + c_2(p_{t-1} - p^T)] \\ + c_3 R_{t-1}, \qquad (2.3)$$

where Y^g is the output gap, R is nominal rate of interest, p is rate of inflation, p^T is inflation rate target, RR^* is the 'equilibrium' real rate of interest, that is the rate of interest consistent with zero output gap which implies, from equation (2.2), a constant rate of inflation, s_i (with $i = 1, 2$) represents stochastic shocks, and E_t refers to expectations held at time t. Equation (2.1) is the aggregate demand equation with the current output gap determined by past and expected future output gap and the real rate of interest. Equation (2.2) is a Phillips curve with inflation based on current output gap and past and future inflation, and with $b_2 + b_3 = 1$, thereby yielding the equivalent of a vertical Phillips curve. Equation (2.3) is a monetary policy rule (defined by, for example, Svensson, 2003b, p. 448, amongst others, as a 'prescribed guide for monetary-policy conduct'). In this equation, the nominal interest rate is based on expected inflation, output gap, deviation of inflation from target (or 'inflation gap'), and the 'equilibrium' real rate of interest.[2] The lagged interest rate represents interest rate 'smoothing' undertaken by the monetary authorities, which is thought of as improving performance by introducing 'history dependence' (see, for example, Rotemberg and Woodford, 1997; Woodford, 1999). Variations on this theme could be used; for example, interest rate 'smoothing' in equation (2.3) is often ignored, as is the lagged output gap variable in equation (2.1) so that the focus is on the influence of an expected future output gap in this equation. It is also possible to add a fourth equation to (2.1) to (2.3) used here. This would relate the stock of money to 'demand for money variables' such as income, prices and the rate of interest, which would reinforce the endogenous money nature of this approach with the stock of money being demand-determined. Clearly, though, such an equation would be superfluous in that the stock of money thereby determined is akin to a residual and does not feed back to affect other variables in the model. In the set of equations (2.1) to (2.3) above, there are three equations and three unknowns: output, interest rate and inflation.

This model has a number of characteristics. Equation (2.1) resembles the traditional IS, but expenditure decisions are seen to be based on intertemporal optimization of a utility function. There are both lagged adjustment and forward-looking elements; the model allows for sticky prices (the lagged price level in the Phillips curve relationship) and full price flexibility in the long run. The term $E_t (p_{t+1})$ in equation (2.2) can be seen to reflect central bank credibility. If a central bank can credibly signal its intention to achieve and maintain low inflation, then expectations of inflation will be lowered, and this term indicates that it may possible to reduce current inflation at a significantly lower cost in terms of output than otherwise. Equation (2.3), the operating rule, implies that 'policy' becomes a systematic adjustment to economic developments rather than an exogenous process. It relates the setting of nominal interest rate to a target real rate of interest plus the rate of inflation. It also incorporates a symmetric approach to IT. Inflation above the target leads to higher interest rates to contain inflation, whereas inflation below the target requires lower interest rates to stimulate the economy and increase inflation. Equation (2.3) contains no stochastic shock, implying that monetary policy operates without random shocks. The model as a whole contains the neutrality of money property, with inflation determined by monetary policy (that is the rate of interest), and equilibrium values of real variables are independent of the money supply. The final characteristic to highlight is that money has no role in the model; it is merely a 'residual'. Thus monetary policy is discussed in the NCM without reference to the stock of money; in Chapter 5 we discuss at some length the significance of this omission of any reference to the stock of money.

We argue that the approach embedded in these three equations can be viewed as the 'new consensus' in macroeconomics through its emphasis on the supply side-determined equilibrium level of unemployment (the 'natural rate' of unemployment or the non-accelerating inflation rate of unemployment, the NAIRU), its neglect of aggregate or effective demand, and of fiscal policy, and the elevation of monetary policy at the expense of fiscal policy. Its IT policy implication entails a number of benefits in addition to the two referred to above in the quotation by Mishkin (1999). Further advantages have been mentioned: IT solves the dynamic time-inconsistency problem (along with central bank 'independence'); it reduces inflation variability and it can also stabilize output if applied 'flexibly' (Svensson, 1997); it 'locks in' expectations of low inflation which contains the inflationary impact of macro-economic shocks; and, while a number of countries have adopted the IT strategy (Fracasso *et al.*, 2003, refer to 'more than 20 countries'), there does not seem to be a country that, having adopted IT, abandoned it subsequently.[3]

3 INFLATION TARGETING

'Inflation targeting', as that term has come to be understood, involves rather more than focusing on the rate of inflation as an objective of economic policy. It is taken here to include the following: (i) the setting by government (normally) of a numerical target range for the rate of (price) inflation; (ii) the use of monetary policy as the key policy instrument to achieve the target, with monetary policy taking the form of interest rate adjustments; (iii) the operation of monetary policy is in the hands of an 'independent' central bank; (iv) monetary policy is only concerned with the rate of inflation, and the possible effects of monetary policy on other policy objectives is ignored (or assumed to be non-existent), with the exception of short-term effects.

We postulate that the economics of IT are firmly embedded in equations (2.1) to (2.3), especially equation (2.3). This third equation entails an important aspect for IT, namely the role of 'expected inflation'. The inflation target itself and 'expected inflation' in the form of central bank forecasts, which are thought of as providing a helpful steer to 'expected inflation', are made explicit to the public, thereby enhancing transparency, itself a paramount ingredient of IT. Consequently, inflation forecasting is a key feature of IT; it can actually be thought of as the intermediate target of monetary policy in this framework (Svensson, 1997). However, the emphasis on inflation forecasts entails a danger. This is due entirely to the large margins of error in forecasting inflation, thereby badly damaging the reputation and credibility of central banks. The centrality of inflation forecasts in the conduct of this type of monetary policy represents a major challenge to countries that pursue IT. Indeed, there is the question of the ability of a central bank to control inflation. Oil prices, exchange rate gyrations, wages and taxes, can have a large impact on inflation, and a central bank has no control over these factors. To the extent that the source of inflation is any of these factors, IT would have no impact whatsoever. Negative supply shocks are associated with rising inflation and falling output. An IT central bank would have to try to contain inflation, thereby deteriorating the recession. Even a central bank with both price stability (meaning low and stable inflation) and economic activity (meaning stabilizing output around potential output) objectives, would still behave in a similar fashion, simply because central banks are evaluated on their ability to meet inflation targets rather than output growth targets.

The model of the NCM outlined above has a number of characteristics which are relevant for inflation targeting. First, the stock of money has no role in the model. It is not mentioned in this model, though an equation relating the stock of money to output, interest rate and inflation could be added which would illustrate the residual nature of the stock of money. This raises the question of how to reclaim money such that the stock of money has some influence on the macro economy (an issue we return to in Chapter 5).

Second, the operating rule implies that monetary policy (and the setting of the rate of interest) becomes a systematic adjustment to economic develop-ments rather than an exogenous process. However, the model incorporates a symmetric approach to IT. Third, there are both lagged adjustment and forward-looking elements; the model allows for sticky prices (the lagged price level in the Phillips-curve relationship) and full price flexibility in the long run.

Fourth, the model contains the neutrality of money property, in that equilibrium values of real variables are independent of the money supply and that inflation is determined by monetary policy (that is, the rate of interest). Inflation is viewed as determined by monetary policy (in the form of the rate of interest), through the route of interest rate influences aggre-gate demand (equation 2.1), and aggregate demand influences the rate of inflation (equation 2.2). Fifth, in the long run when inflation is constant and expectations fulfilled, equation (2.1) would yield $R - p = a_0/a_3$, the real rate of interest, and equation (2.3) would be $R - p = RR^* + c_2(p_{t-1} - p^T)$, so that, $a_0/a_3 = RR^* + c_2(p_{t-1} - p^T)$, and the long-run rate of inflation would differ from the target inflation rate unless $RR^* = a_0/a_3$.

Sixth, the rate of interest RR^* is akin to the 'natural rate' of interest proposed by Wicksell (1898/1936) in that (if it is correctly set) it corresponds to constant inflation with the output gap at zero. It is implicitly assumed that, at this equilibrium rate of interest, aggregate demand is in line with aggregate supply. Alternatively this could be expressed as saying RR^* is viewed as the rate of interest which equates savings and investment with income at trend level (that is, output gap equals zero).

The most interesting aspect of this model for our purposes is the mecha-nism whereby inflation is the target. This is assumed to take place through equation (2.1) where interest rates, themselves determined by the operating policy rule as in equation (2.3), affect aggregate demand and, via equation (2.2), changes in the rate of inflation depend on aggregate demand. Then the strength, timing and predictability of the effects of changes in the rate of interest on aggregate demand become important questions. Higher (lower) interest rates tend to reduce (increase) aggregate demand, and lower (higher) aggregate demand is assumed to reduce (increase) the rate of inflation. The possibility that interest rates are regarded as a cost (by firms), leading to higher prices, is not mentioned. This simple model refers to a single interest rate, and the impact through the central bank interest rate on long-term interest rates is an issue. Furthermore, and as one of the former chairmen of the Board of Governors of the Federal Reserve System has recently argued, since the early 1980s this 'new' approach to monetary policy 'relies upon direct influence on the short-term interest rate and a much more fluid market situation that allows policy to be transmitted through the markets by some mysterious or maybe not so mysterious process' (Volcker, 2002, p. 9). This mysterious, and not so mysterious, process is taken up in Chapter 4.

4 MAIN FEATURES OF INFLATION TARGETING

There are certain features that form the key aspects of IT, which are embedded in equations (2.1) to (2.3) above. We discuss these features in this section. Before we embark upon this analysis, though, it is worth making the comment that inevitably different writers would emphasize different aspects of NCM and IT. We believe, however, that the features we summarize below are a set that most, if not all, of the proponents of NCM and IT would accept:

1. IT is a monetary policy framework whereby public announcement of official inflation targets, or target ranges, is undertaken along with explicit acknowledgment that price stability, meaning low and stable inflation, is monetary policy's primary long-term objective.[4] Such a monetary policy framework, improves communication between the public, business and markets on the one hand, and policy makers on the other hand, and provides discipline, accountability, transparency and flexibility in monetary policy. The focus is on price stability, along with three objectives: credibility (the framework should command trust);[5] flexibility (the framework should allow monetary policy to react optimally to unanticipated shocks); and legitimacy (the framework should attract public and parliamentary support).

2. The objectives of the IT framework are achieved through the principle of 'constrained discretion' (Bernanke and Mishkin, 1997, p. 104).[6] This principle constrains monetary policy to achieve clear long-term and sustainable goals, but discretion is allowed to respond sensibly to unanticipated shocks. In this way, IT serves as a nominal anchor for monetary policy, thereby pinning down precisely what the commitment to price stability means. As such, monetary policy imposes discipline on the central bank and the government within a flexible policy framework. For example, even if monetary policy is used to address short-run stabilization objectives, the long-run inflation objective must not be compromised, thereby imposing consistency and rationality in policy choices (thus monetary policy focuses public's expectations and provides a reference point to judge short-run

policies). Such an approach, it is argued, makes it less likely for deflation to occur. Indeed, 'targeting inflation rates of above zero, as all inflation targeters have done, makes periods of deflation less likely' (Mishkin, 2000, p. 5).

3. Monetary policy is taken as the main instrument of macroeconomic policy. The view is that it is a flexible instrument for achieving medium-term stabilization objectives, in that it can be adjusted quickly in response to macroeconomic developments. Indeed, monetary policy is the most direct determinant of inflation, so much so that in the long run the inflation rate is the only macroeconomic variable that monetary policy can affect. Monetary policy cannot affect economic activity, for example output, employment and so on, in the long run; the achievement of the long-run objective of price stability should be achieved at a minimum cost in terms of the output gap (deviation of actual from potential output) and deviations of inflation from target (HM Treasury, 2003).

4. Fiscal policy is no longer viewed as a powerful macroeconomic instrument (in any case it is hostage to the slow and uncertain legislative process). It has a passive role to play in that the budget deficit position varies over the business cycle in the well-known manner. The budget (at least on current account) can and should be balanced over the course of the business cycle. An implication of this argument is that 'restraining the fiscal authorities from engaging in excessive deficits financing thus aligns fiscal policy with monetary policy and makes it easier for the monetary authorities to keep inflation under control' (Miskin, 2000, p. 2). In this way, 'monetary policy moves first and dominates, forcing fiscal policy to align with monetary policy' (ibid., p. 4).

5. Monetary policy has, thus, been upgraded and fiscal policy has been downgraded. It is recognized that the budget position will vary over the course of the business cycle in a countercyclical manner (that is, deficit rising in downturn, surplus rising in upturn), which helps to dampen the scale of economic fluctuations (that is, acts as an 'automatic' stabilizer). But these fluctuations in the budget position take place around a balanced budget on average over the cycle. Such a strong fiscal position reinforces the credibility of the IT framework, thereby limiting the real costs to the economy of keeping inflation on target.

6. Monetary policy can be used to meet the objective of low rates of inflation (which are always desirable in this view, since low, and stable, rates of inflation are conducive to healthy growth rates). However, monetary policy should not be operated by politicians but by experts (whether banks, economists or others) in the form of an 'independent' central bank.[7] Indeed, those operating monetary policy should be more 'conservative', that is, place greater weight on low inflation and less weight

on the level of unemployment than the politicians (Rogoff, 1985). Politicians would be tempted to use monetary policy for short-term gain (lower unemployment) at the expense of long-term loss (higher inflation); this is the time inconsistency problem to which we referred earlier (see note 7). An 'independent' central bank would also have greater credibility in the financial markets and be seen to have a stronger commitment to low inflation than politicians do.

7. The level of economic activity fluctuates around a supply-side equilibrium. In the model above this equilibrium corresponds to $Y^g = 0$ (and inflation is equal to target rate, and real interest rate is equal to RR^*). This can be alternatively expressed in terms of the non-accelerating inflation rate of unemployment (the NAIRU) such that unemployment below (above) the NAIRU would lead to higher (lower) rates of inflation. The NAIRU is a supply-side phenomenon closely related to the workings of the labour market. The source of domestic inflation (relative to the expected rate of inflation) is seen to arise from unemployment falling below the NAIRU, and inflation is postulated to accelerate if unemployment is held below the NAIRU. However, in the long run, there is no trade-off between inflation and unemployment, and the economy has to operate (on average) at the NAIRU if accelerating inflation is to be avoided. In the long run, inflation is viewed as a monetary phenomenon in that the pace of inflation is aligned with the rate of interest. Inflation is, thus, in the hands of central bankers. Control of the money supply is not an issue, essentially because of the instability of the demand for money that makes the impact of changes in the money supply a highly uncertain channel of influence.

8. The essence of Say's Law holds, namely that the level of effective demand does not play an independent role in the (long-run) determination of the level of economic activity, and adjusts to underpin the supply side-determined level of economic activity (which itself corresponds to the NAIRU). Shocks to the level of demand can be met by variations in the rate of interest to ensure that inflation does not develop (if unemployment falls below the NAIRU). The implication of this analysis is that there is a serious limit on monetary policy. This is that monetary policy cannot have permanent effects on the level of economic activity; it can only have temporary effects, which are serially correlated. This implies further that a change in monetary stance would have temporary effects, which will persist for a number of periods before they completely dissipate in price adjustments.

5   AN ASSESSMENT OF THE THEORETICAL FOUNDATIONS OF NCM AND IT

The NCM portrays monetary policy (in the form of interest rates) as influencing aggregate demand, and thereby the rate of inflation: but how far interest rates can and do have an impact on the rate of inflation is debatable. Even if monetary policy can influence the rate of inflation via aggregate demand, it could well be that fiscal policy is a more potent way of influencing aggregate demand, and we take up the issue of fiscal policy in later chapters.

A related critical argument is that IT is an insufficient guide for monetary policy in view of balance sheets disorders (Palley, 2003). These imbalances are more likely to occur in the present environment of deregulated financial markets, essentially due to the ability of financial markets to innovate. The imbalances thereby created are not expected to have immediate effects on inflation, but can have significant employment and output costs. These disorders are asset price and debt bubbles, which IT cannot cure. The implication is that additional policy measures are required; IT by itself cannot achieve the objectives assigned to it. Furthermore, IT can create moral hazard in asset markets (ibid.). Monetary authorities pay little attention during the upturn, but are compelled to protect asset values during the downturn. This reinforces the argument about asset price bubbles to which we have just referred.

Another important critique is that of the practice of undertaking monetary policy within the IT framework by committees. This critique has been taken up by Blinder (1998) who argues that committees 'laboriously aggregate individual preferences ... need to be led ... tend to adopt compromise positions on difficult questions ... tend to be inertial' (p. 20). Committee inertial behaviour, in particular, may induce the awkward problem of 'inducing the central bank to maintain its policy stance too long' thereby causing central banks 'to overstay their stance' (ibid., p. 20). This problem may be alleviated whenever there is a strong and powerful chairman of the monetary policy committee, but even then 'a chairman who needs to build consensus may have to move more slowly than if he were acting alone' (ibid., p. 21).

It is evident from the model above that expectations on inflation are postulated to have a major influence on actual inflation (equation 2.2), and that interest rates will continue to be raised while inflation is above the target rate (equation 2.3). Inflation targeting (and indeed any policy towards inflation) can on this view bring down inflation more quickly (and maintain low inflation) if it can influence inflation expectations accordingly. It could be noted that the control of the money supply policies of the early 1980s was based on a similar premise. In other words, with tough money supply growth targets (below current rate of inflation), inflation expectations would come down, and actual inflation would then be tamed with little short-run effect on unemployment (and no long-run effect). On those occasions when that experiment was attempted (for example, in the UK, the US and even Germany), money supply targets were often missed, but, more relevant to the argument here, inflation did not come down rapidly. Money supply targets did not seem to have had the intended consequences. IT may have been more successful on this score (for a recent support of this view, see Mishkin, 2002a). The transparency and accountability aspects of IT, which are thought to enhance credibility, may have been helpful on this score (see, for example, Arestis *et al.*, 2002). However, the problem with this argument is that even non-IT central banks have been equally successful in taming inflation; and these central banks have not attempted conspicuously to become more transparent and accountable.

The issue of the validity of Say's Law and NAIRU, essentially a variable over time, have been repeatedly discussed and criticised in the literature (see, in particular, Sawyer, 1999, 2002). Suffice to say here that one can easily refer to periods when unemployment was below NAIRU and yet no inflation materialized. For example, in the US in the mid-1990s, advocates of NAIRU argued that unemployment below 6 per cent would have sparked inflation. Unemployment actually fell well below 6 per cent, but no increase in inflation materialized (see, for example, Galbraith, 1999). We take up this issue further in Chapter 4, where we discuss relevant empirical aspects. In the rest of this section we take up further criticisms of IT.

An important criticism is that adoption of a nominal anchor, such as an inflation target, does not leave much room for manoeuvre for output stabilization, which, as discussed above, is viewed by most, certainly not all, proponents as only possible in the short run. It is true, though, that there are supporters of IT who argue quite conspicuously that monetary policy should concentrate on both output and price fluctuations. Bernanke (2003b) follows Meyer (2001a) in drawing the distinction between a hierarchical mandate, in which all objectives are subordinate to price stability, and dual mandate, where the economic activity and price stability objectives are adhered to equally. Both Bernanke and Meyer support the dual mandate; indeed, Bernanke suggests that 'Formally, the dual mandate can be represented by a central bank loss function that includes both inflation and unemployment (or the output gap) symmetrically' (Bernanke, 2003b, p. 10).[8] Others argue that central bankers should not become 'inflation nutters' (King, 2002). Mishkin (2000) argues that 'the objectives for a central bank in the context of a long-run strategy should not only include minimizing inflation fluctuations, but should also include minimizing output fluctuations' (p. 3). This is known as 'flexible inflation targeting' (Svensson, 1999). Even when inflation is the only target, it is shown (Svensson, 1997; Rudebusch and Svensson, 1999) that it is optimal to respond to the determinants of the target variable, current inflation and the output gap, rather than to the target itself. This is so since both inflation and output gap determine future inflation. More recently, Svensson (2003b) argues for 'forecast targeting' (see, also, note 9), which is meant as 'a commitment to minimize a loss function over forecasts of the target variables' (p. 451). The loss function contains forecasts for both inflation and output gap as target variables.[9] However, price stability is the overriding goal in the view of the IT proponents. When Mishkin (2000) refers to the experience of the US Federal Reserve System, he argues, 'The lack of a clear mandate for price stability can lead to the time-inconsistency problem in which political pressure is put on the Fed to engage in expansionary policy to pursue short-run goals' (p. 8).

Ultimately, though, proponents utilize the dual mandate notion in a specific way. For example, Bernanke (2003a) states the case in the following manner: 'The essence of constrained discretion is the general role of a commitment to price stability. Not only does such a commitment enhance efficiency, employment, and economic growth in the *long run*, but – by providing an anchor for inflation expectations – it also improves the ability of central banks to stabilize the economy in the *short run* as well' (p. 10). So output stabilization is only a short-run possibility. However, Meyer (2001a) takes a different view, which denies the long-run concern with only price stability. He strongly suggests that 'this view is misleading in a couple of respects. First, monetary policy makers should be concerned about *two* long-run properties of the economy. One is price stability and the other is the variability of output around full employment. Policy has to be judged by its success in both dimensions. Second, policy is made in the short run, not the long run. The speed of return of output to its potential level is influenced by policy decisions and cannot be treated with indifference. It may just take too long and waste too many resources in the interim to rely on the self-equilibrating forces of the economy. Policy makers will therefore have to take into account, in practice, both objectives in their policy actions' (p. 8).

There is an important related issue, namely the desirability of low inflation within the context of the IT framework. It is generally assumed within the IT framework that lower inflation is more desirable than higher inflation, and that lower inflation can be achieved without any loss of output (as embedded in the framework of equations above). This should be judged against evidence provided by Ghosh and Phillips (1998), where a large panel set that covers IMF countries over the period 1960–96 is utilized, to conclude that 'there are two important nonlinearities in the inflation–growth relationship. At very low inflation rates (around 2–3 percent a year, or lower), inflation and growth are positively correlated. Otherwise, inflation and growth are negatively correlated, but the relationship is convex, so that the decline in growth associated with an increase from 10 percent to 20 percent inflation is much larger than that associated with moving from 40 per cent to 50 per cent inflation' (p. 674). However, the point at which the nonlinearity changes from positive to negative is thought to deserve a great deal more research. Another paper argues that 'Using a non-linear specification and the data from four groups of countries at various stages of development, this paper examines the possibility for a family rather than a single inverted U relation across countries at various stages of development. The estimated turning points are found to vary widely from as high as 15 percent per year for the lower-middle-income countries to 11 percent for the low-income countries, and 5 percent for the upper-middle-income countries. No statistically detectable, long-run relationship between inflation and growth is evident for the OECD countries' (Sepehri and Moshiri, 2004, p. 191; see also Sarel, 1996). The IT argument should also be judged in terms of statements like 'there is an optimal rate of inflation, greater than zero. So ruthless pursuit of price stability harms economic growth and well being. Research even questions whether targeting price stability reduces the trade-off between inflation and unemployment' (Stiglitz, 2003; see, also, Akerlof *et al.*, 1996).

6   THE SEPARATION OF REAL AND MONETARY FACTORS

The points just made about the desirability of low inflation are closely linked with the view that there is a separation of real and monetary factors in the economy with the supply side determining the level of economic activity, and monetary factors the price level. The assignment can then be made: monetary policy to the nominal side of the economy, and specifically to inflation, and supply-side policies to address the real side of the economy (and often, though not an intrinsic part of IT, labour market policies to address problems of unemployment). King (1997), now the Governor of the Bank of England, argues that 'if one believes that, in the long-run, there is no trade-off between inflation and output then there is no point in using monetary policy to target output. … [You only have to adhere to] the view that printing money cannot raise long-run productivity growth, in order to believe that inflation rather than output is the only sensible objective of monetary policy in the long-run' (p. 6).

The supply side of the economy is often represented in terms of an unchanging supply-side equilibrium. For example, the 'natural rate of unemployment' or the NAIRU is used to summarize the supply-side equilibrium, and the estimates provided of the 'natural rate' or the NAIRU are often presented as a single (and hence implicitly unchanging) number. In the three equations above, the supply-side equilibrium is represented as a zero output gap. A less extreme view would be that the supply-side equilibrium may change over time but not in response to the demand side of the economy. Changes in labour market institutions and laws, for example, would be predicted to lead to changes in the supply-side equilibrium. In the context of IT, the significant question is whether interest rates through their effect on the level of aggregate demand have any lasting impact on the supply side of the economy.

It can first be noted that the estimates of the NAIRU (or equivalent) do often vary over time. Gordon (1997) has, for example, provided estimates of a time-varying 'natural rate of unemployment' drawn from evidence on the relationship between price inflation and the rate of unemployment. The OECD produces estimates of the non-accelerating wage rate of unemployment (NAWRU) on a biannual basis (see OECD, *Economic Outlook* databank).

Table 2.1   Estimates of the non-accelerating wage rate of unemployment (NAWRU), selected years

	1980	1990	2000
Australia	5.42	6.77	6.54
Austria	1.91	4.64	5.10
Belgium	6.05	8.84	7.48
Canada	8.62	8.60	7.15
Switzerland	1.35	1.82	1.96
Germany	4.04	6.86	7.34
Denmark	5.62	6.94	5.06
Spain	6.16	13.26	11.53
Finland	4.28	5.55	8.84
France	5.82	9.30	9.40
United Kingdom	4.31	8.56	5.82
Greece	4.79	8.22	9.87
Ireland	13.43	14.24	6.95
Italy	6.72	9.32	9.45
Japan	1.75	2.36	3.84
Netherlands	4.69	7.55	4.40
Norway	2.20	4.64	3.56
New Zealand	1.60	6.49	5.45
Portugal	6.38	4.89	3.75
Sweden	2.18	3.37	5.00
United States	6.06	5.41	5.25

Source: OECD Economic Outlook Databank.

Estimates of the NAWRU for a range of countries at ten-year intervals are given in Table 2.1. This table provides evidence that the estimated NAWRU varies over time and differs substantially across countries. It does not, of course, tell us the factors which have led to these changes.[10]

The component of aggregate demand which is likely to be the most interest-sensitive is investment expenditure. This is supported by the results of the simulations of the effects of interest rate policy to which reference is made below, in which the effect of interest rate change on investment is larger than the effects on other components of demand. The IT framework is concerned with the effects of interest rate on aggregate demand, and thereby on the rate of inflation. But, it is, of course, the case that investment has an impact on the time path of the capital stock, and hence on the future supply-side position. For monetary policy to have no lasting supply-side effects, it would have to be assumed that the real rate of interest averaged out at the equilibrium rate, and that the effects of interest rates (relative to the equilibrium rate) were symmetrical. Even then there would be effects on investment, which would last for some time (perhaps 20 years, depending on the life of the capital stock). But this would imply that the reduction of inflation through deflationary monetary policy and higher interest rates would have a long-lasting effect on the capital stock.

7   THE CAUSES OF INFLATION

This 'new consensus' focuses on the role of monetary policy (in the form of interest rates) to control demand inflation, and not cost inflation, as is evident from equation (2.2). As Gordon (1997) remarked (though not in the context of this 'new consensus'), 'in the long run inflation is always and everywhere an excess nominal GDP phenomenon. Supply shocks will come and go. What remains to sustain long-run inflation is steady growth of nominal GDP in excess of the growth of natural or potential real output' (p. 17). The position taken on cost inflation is either that it should be accommodated, or that supply shocks come and go – and on average are zero and do not affect the rate of inflation (see, for example, Clarida *et al.*, 1999). The significance of the IT on this score is that it strongly suggests that inflation can be tamed through interest rate policy (using demand deflation) and that there is an equilibrium rate (or 'natural rate') of interest which can balance aggregate demand and aggregate supply and which is feasible, and can lead to a zero gap between actual and capacity output.

In the context of the working of monetary policy, this view of inflation, namely that it is caused by demand factors, raises four issues. The first is the question of how effective monetary policy is in influencing aggregate demand and thereby inflation. The evidence survey below (in Chapter 4) suggests that it is rather ineffectual. Second, if inflation is a 'demand phenomenon' and not a cost phenomenon, as reflected in the Phillips curve of equation (2.2), then the question arises as to whether monetary policy is the most effective (or least ineffective) way of influencing aggregate demand. In Chapter 7 below we conclude that it is not, and suggest that fiscal policy is a clear alternative policy instrument. Third, there is the question of whether the possibility of sustained cost-push and other non-demand-related inflation can be as lightly dismissed as the 'new consensus' appears to do. The version of the Phillips curve which appears as equation (2.2) is a (heavily) reduced form that does not explicitly consider wages, material costs and imported prices. A sustained money wage push makes no appearance in equation (2.2) and it would appear that there is no explicit representation of such pressures. An increase in, for example, wage aspirations on the part of workers or pressure for higher profit margins are not incorporated, though it could be argued that they would be reflected in the stochastic term. This might be acceptable if pressures for higher wages and profit margins varied in a stochastic fashion over time (and averaged to zero). But even a sequence of time periods in which wage or profit margin pressures were positive, reflected in positive stochastic terms in equation (2.2), would have long-lasting effects as one period's inflation feeds through to subsequent periods' inflation (through the lagged inflation term in equation (2.2)). Similarly, if expectations on inflation were to rise (for whatever reason), inflation would rise according to equation (2.2), and subsequent inflation would also be higher than otherwise. In the event of a sustained increase in inflation (due to cost pressures, as would seem to have been the case during the 1970s), this could only be met, in this framework, by raising interest rates and grinding down inflation by low demand and high unemployment.

Fourth, there is the issue as to whether a formulation such as equation (2.2) is the correct specification even for demand inflation: it postulates that it is the *level* of demand (as reflected in the deviation of output from trend) which influences the pace of inflation relative to expectations. When expectations reflect past inflation, this comes down to the change in inflation being related to the level of output. From a microeconomic perspective, it could be anticipated that firms seek to adjust prices relative to cost, and aim for a specific mark-up of price over costs where the mark-up may depend on the level of output (or related factors such as capacity utilization). This could be simply written as $P/C = f(Q)$ where P is price, C costs and Q output. Then the rate of change of price would depend on the rate of change of costs and of output; in other words, the pace of inflation (relative to cost change) depends on the rate of change of output. This would imply that, even so far as the rate of change of output is relevant for inflation, those charged with inflation targeting would need to pay attention to the speed of expansion or contraction. Further, if the rate of change of output rather than the level of output is relevant, there will be no supply-side equilibrium in terms of the level of output.

8 SUMMARY AND CONCLUSIONS

In this chapter we have discussed the essentials of the NCM and the associated policy framework that is known as IT. We have located the theoretical foundations of NCM and IT and identified a number of theoretical weaknesses and reservations with them. There is still the question of highlighting this theoretical framework in a real economy set-up, along with any empirical verification that may be available. We take up both issues in what follows in the next two chapters.

NOTES

1. Mishkin (1999, p. 595) is presumably using 'quite good' in the American sense of 'very good' rather than the British sense of 'moderately good'.
2. In the original Taylor (1993) monetary-policy rule formulation, that is, $R_t = RR^* + d_1 Y^g_t + d_2(p_t - p^*)$, where the symbols are as above, with the exception p^* which stands for the desired inflation rate, the coefficients are $d_1 = 0.5$ and $d_2 = 1.5$, p^* is 2 per cent and the average short-term real interest rate is 2 per cent; so that RR^* is 4 per cent. d_2 is required to be greater than one, the 'Taylor Principle', for unique equilibrium in sticky-price models (Taylor, 1999; Woodford, 2001). For a recent critique and further elaboration, as well as for a discussion of rules of monetary policy and a suggestion for describing IT as a 'forecast-targeting rule', or 'forecast targeting' (with the Reserve Bank of New Zealand being cited as an example of this procedure), see Svensson (2003b). This is essentially what Blinder (1998) describes as 'dynamic programming' and 'proper dynamic optimization'.
3. One can, of course, argue that since the first country to have adopted it (New Zealand) only did so in 1990. It is thus too soon to declare the strategy as 'quite good', especially so in the rather 'serene' environment, which the 1990s enjoyed.
4. 'Inflation targeting' in this policy framework is preferred to 'money supply targeting'. This is essentially due to the instability of the LM because of the unstable demand-for-money relationship (see, for example, HM Treasury, 2003). See, also, King (1997) who argues for the superiority of IT over a money supply rule, in that it results in optimal short-run response to shocks, in a way that money growth targeting does not. Svensson and Woodford (2003) demonstrate the conditions under which IT might achieve this goal.
5. Credibility is recognized as paramount in the conduct of monetary policy to avoid problems associated with time inconsistency. The time inconsistency problem may be briefly summarized. Central banks that pursue discretionary monetary policies with the specific objective of improving real economic activity (output or unemployment) in the short run may very well cause inflation without any gains in economic activity in the long run (see, for example, Barro and Gordon, 1983). It is argued that a policy which lacks credibility because of time inconsistency is neither optimal nor feasible (Kydland and Prescott, 1977; Calvo, 1978; Barro and Gordon, 1983). The only credible policy is the one that leaves the authority no freedom to react to developments in the future, and even if aggregate demand policies matter in the short run in this model, a policy of non-intervention is preferable.

6. 'Constrained discretion' is actually viewed as 'middle ground' between 'rules' and 'discretion'. It is 'an approach that allows monetary policymakers considerable leeway in responding to economic shocks, financial disturbances, and other unforeseen developments. Importantly, however, this discretion of policy makers is constrained by a strong commitment to keeping inflation low and stable' (Bernanke, 2003a, p. 2).

7. It is important to distinguish between goal independence and instrument independence (Debelle and Fischer, 1994; Fischer, 1994). The argument is usually couched by the proponents in terms of goal dependence, that is, it is more democratic for the government to set the goal of price stability, and for the central bank to pursue that goal by independently setting the instrument(s) of monetary policy (see, for example, Bernanke, Laubach, Mishkin and Pasen, 1999). Instrument independence is justified on two grounds: it resolves the problem of time inconsistency and enables the central bank to be forward looking in view of the long and variable lags in monetary policy. There are of course exceptions to this rule, as for example with Rogoff (1985) who argues for both goal and instrument independence, and for the appointment of a 'conservative' governor to run monetary policy.

8. Bernanke (2003a) has actually argued that 'In practice ... this approach has allowed central banks to achieve better outcomes in terms of *both* inflation and unemployment, confounding the traditional view that policymakers must necessarily trade off between the important social goals of price stability and high employment' (p. 2).

9. Svensson (2003b) identifies two problems with a general 'forecast targeting'. The first is the extent to which the objectives of the central bank are well specified. For example, central banks do not specify directly a weight for the output-gap target, as they should. The second problem is that such an approach may not be fully 'optimal' in a forward-looking environment, although this problem 'can potentially be solved by a commitment to a specific targeting rule' (ibid., p. 455).

10. It should also be noted that these are estimates of the NAWRU, which come from the econometric estimation of a model of the economy, and hence the estimates are reliant on the model used.

3. The macroeconometric model of the Bank of England

1 INTRODUCTION

In this chapter we elaborate on the nature of the 'new consensus' in macroeconomics and illustrate it by reference to the macroeconometric model of the Bank of England.[1] In subsequent chapters we examine the implications of this 'new consensus' for both monetary and fiscal policy. The purpose of this chapter is to examine the nature of the macroeconometric model, and we do not discuss here the monetary policy regime of the Bank of England even though this macroeconometric model is one of the elements used to forecast economic events on which the Monetary Policy Committee of the Bank of England draw when making policy decisions on interest rates. Inflation targeting is the central objective of the Bank of England's monetary policy, and that has been extensively discussed in the previous chapter.

The Bank of England macroeconometric model is, of course, much more complex than the three-equation model (which was used to describe the NCM) approach in the previous chapter. Even the simplified 'stripped down' version of the Bank of England model described below contains more than three equations. There are two features of the Bank of England model relative to the NCM model to which we draw attention. First (and perhaps inevitably), the Bank of England model is an open economy model with equations for the determination of the exchange rate, whereas the NCM model was a closed economy one. Second, whereas the NCM model had a simple Phillips curve type of relationship for price inflation, the Bank of England model involves both price change equation(s) and wage change equation(s). However, the interaction of these price and wage changes equations serves to provide (in equilibrium) a supply-side equilibrium, equivalent to the equilibrium in the NCM model where the output gap was equal to zero.

2 THE MACROECONOMETRIC MODEL OF THE BANK OF ENGLAND AS AN EXAMPLE OF 'NEW CONSENSUS'

The Bank of England (1999, 2000) has presented a report on its approach to macroeconometric modelling. The general implication of that document is that a pluralist approach is adopted where the models utilized include small-scale macroeconomic models and vector autoregression models. Here we focus on the macroeconometric model. This is undertaken as we believe that the model reveals the underlying structural equations and enables us to interpret the general mode of the Bank's analysis. In doing so, however, we are mindful that the model 'should not be viewed as having a fixed specification. Rather, it is a model that can be operated in different ways, and which can be readily adapted to reflect changes in the economic environment' (Bank of England, 1999, p. 25). The Monetary Policy Committee (hereafter MPC) in their document on the transmission mechanisms of monetary policy (Monetary Policy Committee, 1999) have drawn upon the model. It is important to consider the implications of the macroeconometric model for the formulation of monetary policy and its channels of influence throughout the economy.

We provide a verbal outline of the nature of the macroeconometric model of the Bank of England. The equations and definition of variables are given in Table 3.1. Before examining these equations there are certain key features of the macroeconomic model worth emphasizing (see Bank of England, 1999, pp. 25–6, for more details).

The first feature is that a real equilibrium consistent with a simple Cobb–Douglas production function (with constant returns to scale and diminishing marginal returns to each factor) is assumed. There are two important properties of this equilibrium. One property is nominal neutrality; that is, the price level does not affect long-run real equilibrium, which is ensured by assuming static homogeneity, implying that the real equilibrium is not affected if, for example, the level of all nominal variables is doubled; the other property is inflation neutrality; that is, the Phillips curve is vertical, which is ensured by assuming dynamic homogeneity so that the real equilibrium is not affected by the growth rates of nominal variables; consequently, there is no long-run trade-off between inflation and unemployment or between inflation and output. The long run is viewed as depending on the supply side of the economy. However, in the short run changes in business investment depend on prior changes in investment and changes in GDP, while in the long run the ratio of the capital stock to output depends on cost of capital. Thus the supply side changes as investment occurs.

The second feature is that there is a nominal equilibrium, determined by a selected anchor specified in terms of a target for a nominal variable, currently the inflation rate. A feedback rule for nominal interest rates ensures that the nominal anchor achieves its target. Monetary policy (in the form of the setting of the key interest rate) responds to the current rate of inflation relative to the target rate of inflation. A higher (lower) interest rate lowers (raises) aggregate demand which then is viewed to have an impact on the rate of inflation. In the long run it is assumed that the target for the rate of inflation can be achieved, and this would be reached through high (low) interest rates used to lower (raise) the rate of inflation.

A third feature is that the price level is related to the quantity of money so that sustained increases in prices cannot occur without an accompanying increase in the money stock. However, the stock of money adjusts to the level of prices rather than vice versa. The stock of money is endogenous but in the long run nominal equilibrium moves in line with the price level.

The fourth feature is that a sluggish adjustment of nominal and real variables is assumed. It takes time for the economy to respond to shocks that move it away from equilibrium. Real and nominal inertia, essentially in the wage–price system, are assumed to prevail where the speed of adjustment depends on inflation expectations and the exchange rate amongst other variables. A fifth feature is that the UK economy is an open economy, and consequently output and inflation are strongly influenced by developments abroad, and by exchange rate movements.

The full set of equations which describe our simplified version of the Bank of England macroeconometric model is given in Table 3.1. The first ten equations are behavioural, and the remaining eight are definitional. We now provide a brief discussion on each of the behavioural equations.

Equation 3.1 is the aggregate demand equation with consumer expenditure taken as a function of income, rate of interest, unemployment rate, taxes and real wealth; investment expenditure is made a function of capacity utilization and real cost of capital; exports is related to total foreign demand, proxied by world trade, and the real exchange rate; government consumption and investment are treated as exogenous and imports is assumed to be a function of domestic income and the exchange rate. The interest rate utilized here is that set by the Bank of England by some operating rule (see equation (3.7)), and it is implicitly assumed that other interest rates (long rate, deposit rate, mortgage rate and real cost of capital) move in sympathy with that 'repo' rate. Other interest rates are introduced into the Bank of England model but the relationship of those interest rates to the 'repo' rate does not depend on the variables which enter our formulation of the model, and hence we treat those relationships as constant. The real cost of capital depends on the real rate of interest (see equation (3.15)), with the latter via equation (3.17) being defined as the difference between the nominal rate of interest and lagged price inflation. Hence aggregate

*Table 3.1   Simplified version of the Bank of England's macroeconometric
model*

(3.1) $C[Y, R, UR, T, (WTH/P)] + I(CU, RCC) + X(WTR, RER) + G - Q(Y, RER) = Y$,

(3.2) $CU = Y - Y(L, K)$,

(3.3) $W/P = N[UR, (W/P)^T, F]$,

(3.4) $P/W = CU(CU)$,

(3.5) $ER = [ER_{t+1,}(R - R_w), RPRE]$,

(3.6) $(M/P) = (M/P)[Y, (RD - R), WTH/P]$,

(3.7) $R = R\{[(PR) - (PR)^T], CU\} + PR$,

(3.8) $PR = PR[WR(-1), (PR)_w, CU]$,

(3.9) $WR = WR[PR(-1), (W/P) - (W/P)^T, UR, F]$,

(3.10) $RPRE = RPRE(BAL)$,

(3.11) $W = W_{-1}x(1 + WR)$,

(3.12) $P = P_{-1}x(1 + PR)$,

(3.13) $UR = U/(L + U)$,

(3.14) $U = (PARR)x(POP) - L$,

(3.15) $RCC = RCC(RR)$,

(3.16) $RER = [(ER)x(P)]/(P_w)$,

(3.17) $RR = R - (PR)^e_{-1}$,

(3.18) $BAL = [Xx(P_X) - Qx(P_Q)] + BIDP + BTRF$.

Notes:
Endogenous variables: BAL = balance of payments, CU = capacity utilization, ER = nominal exchange rate, L = employment, M = stock of money, P = price level, PR = rate of price inflation, R = nominal rate of interest, RCC = real cost of capital, RER = real exchange rate, RR = real rate of interest, U = unemployment, UR = unemployment rate, W = nominal wage, W/P = real wage, WR = rate of wage inflation, Y = income.
Exogenous variables: $BIDP$ = balance of interest, dividends and profits, $BTRF$ = balance of transfers, F = labour market flexibility, G = government consumption plus investment, K = capital, $PARR$ = participation rate, POP = population, PR_w = rate of world price inflation, P_w = world prices, RD = interest rate on deposits, $RPRE$ = risk premium, R_w = world interest rate, T = tax revenue, $(W/P)^T$ = target real wage, WTH = nominal wealth, WTR = world trade.

---

demand is a function of income, nominal and real interest rates, capacity utilization, real wealth and real exchange rate.

Equation (3.2) defines capacity utilization as the difference between actual output and the level of output that would be predicted given employment and capital stock (estimated via the Cobb–Douglas production function referred to above). Presumably the idea here is that, if employment is relatively low, the capital stock will be underutilized, and output will be low relative to what would be produced with a fully utilized capital stock; hence capacity utilization on this measure would be recorded as negative. Consequently, capacity utilization depends on GDP relative to employment hours and the capital stock. It is estimated by residuals from a production function, that is (all in logs) GDP minus a constant and a weighted average of employment hours and the capital stock (presumably this works on the basis that as, say, employment hours rise, GDP rises more than indicated by the weighted average as capital stock is used more effectively, and hence measured capacity utilization rises). As employment hours rise, the recorded change in capacity utilization depends on marginal product of labour minus average product of labour.

Equation (3.3) is a real wage equation derived from the wage inflation equation for constant inflation. In this equilibrium equation, the real wage depends on the rate of unemployment (negatively), the target real wage and a measure of 'labour market flexibility'.

Equation (3.4) is similarly derived from the price setting equation, with prices marked over costs and the size of the mark-up depending on demand pressures. This provides an equation, which relates the (inverse of the) real wage to the level of capacity utilization. In effect the combination of equations (3.3) and (3.4) would solve out to give a NAIRU. The combination of equations (3.2), (3.3) and (3.4) can be seen to provide the supply-side equilibrium in terms of constant inflation rate. With equation (3.2) providing a mapping between capacity utilization and unemployment, a solution could be derived for a non-accelerating inflation rate of unemployment (NAIRU).

In equation (3.5) the nominal exchange rate is taken to depend on the exchange rate expected to prevail a period ahead (derived in a model-consistent manner), the interest rate differential (between the UK and global interest rates) and a term denoted as the risk premium (even in the long run). It is evident from equation (3.10) below that this risk premium brings in the influence of the current account deficit on the exchange rate. This equation combines an interest rate parity view of exchange rate movements with some pressure from the current account. The significant feature of this interest rate parity approach is that a divergence of domestic interest rates from world interest rates has implications for changes in the exchange rate.

Equation (3.6) determines the real stock of money. The form of the equation is that the real stock of money depends on income, wealth and interest rate differential. This can clearly be read as a demand for money equation, and interpreted as the stock of money (in real terms) being demand-determined. It is notable that the stock of money does not enter into any other equations, and is akin to being a residual item.

Equation (3.7) describes a possible reaction function for the setting of interest rates by the Bank of England. Specifically, the nominal rate depends on the deviation of inflation from its target rate and on capacity utilization, and hence is akin to a Taylor rule for the setting of the key interest rate.

Equations (3.8) and (3.9) describe the inflation process. Price inflation depends on lagged wage inflation, world prices and capacity utilization. Wage inflation is related to lagged price inflation, the gap between actual and target real wage, the unemployment rate and degree of flexibility in the labour market. Imposing the condition of constant inflation, and wage inflation equal to price inflation, would generate equations (3.3) and (3.4).

Equation (3.10) indicates that the measure of the risk premium for the exchange rate depends on the current account position, and in effect this means that a current account deficit places downward pressure on the exchange rate through the risk premium effect in equation (3.5).

The remaining equations are definitional. The model consists of 18 equations and 18 endogenous variables. Through equations (3.3) and (3.4), the level of economic activity is set on the supply side of the economy, at a level corresponding to the NAIRU. The level of aggregate demand (equation 3.1) adjusts to the supply side, mainly through interest rate and exchange rate adjustments.

3   IMPLICATIONS

There are five interrelated implications that we derive from this model. The first concerns the relationship between the growth of the stock of money and the pace of inflation. It can be noted that the stock of money is demand-determined and acts essentially as a residual item in this model. It is demand-determined in that the only equation with the stock of money as the dependent variable (and then it is for broad money, M4) is equation (3.6), and this is clearly intended to be a demand for money equation. The stock of money is a residual in the sense that it does not enter anywhere else within the model.[2] There is no 'supply of money' equation nor is there any equation for loans, credit or similar. Bank of England (1999) is clear on this issue: 'Though money does not have a causal role in this framework unless the money supply is targeted by interest rate policy, the money supply will move in line with the price level in the long-run nominal equilibrium, in the absence of persistent shifts in velocity' (p. 26).[3] The Bank of England (1999) concludes that 'sustained increases in prices cannot occur without an accompanying increase in the money stock. That does not mean that money causes inflation. When the short-term nominal interest rate is viewed as the policy instrument, both money and inflation are jointly caused by other variables' (p. 13). The crucial implication which follows is that it would indeed be the case that the growth of the stock of money and the rate of inflation will be broadly similar, and that it may appear that 'inflation is always and everywhere a monetary phenomenon', but the implied direction of causation is from prices to the stock of money.

The second implication concerns the nature of the supply-side equilibrium, which as indicated above corresponds to a form of the NAIRU. An increase in capacity (capital stock) would shift this latter relationship with a given level of employment corresponding to a lower level of capacity utilization. Hence the NAIRU would be seen to depend on the level of capacity. The NAIRU is generally viewed as a labour market phenomenon, and hence actions to change the NAIRU should focus on the labour market. However, the NAIRU is based on the interactions of price and wage determination, and the abilities of firms to employ labour and to supply output and their pricing and output decisions are also relevant. Specifically, the productive capacity of firms is relevant for their ability to offer employment and influences the real wages that they offer: we have argued this more formally in a number of papers (for example, Arestis and Biefang-Frisancho Mariscal, 2000; Sawyer, 1999, 2002) and return to this point in Chapter 6.

Two particular questions can be asked on the relevance of the NAIRU. The first is whether the NAIRU is a strong attractor for the actual level of unemployment. That is to say, are there relatively strong forces at work in the economy, which would take the economy relatively quickly to the NAIRU? If there are not, then it is possible that, over long periods of time, the economy is not operating at or near to the NAIRU. The theorizing on the NAIRU has failed to produce any convincing arguments that the NAIRU will be a strong attractor (for further discussion, see Sawyer, 1999). It should first be recalled that the models from which a NAIRU is developed would see the equilibrium as involving an equilibrium real wage along with equilibrium (un)employment. Two adjustment mechanisms from the private sector, which push the economy towards the NAIRU, could be envisaged: the adjustment of real wages and the adjustment of aggregate demand. The adjustment of real wages faces the difficulty that real wages are influenced by the movements of prices and wages, and when (for example) unemployment is low and capacity utilization high, both wages and prices would be expected to be rising, and there is no guarantee that real wages will adjust in the required manner. For aggregate demand, there is no reason to think that there will be a movement of aggregate demand towards the NAIRU level.

The second question is whether the NAIRU is aggregate demand sustainable. In other words, are there reasons to think that the appropriate level of aggregate demand will arise to underpin the NAIRU, and if it did whether it would be sustained in the sense that the incomes (wages, profits and so on) generated at the level of output corresponding to the NAIRU would lead to expenditure which would be equal to output (and also to income). If Say's Law (that supply creates its own demand) can be held to apply to all levels of supply, the problem would be solved. But this would require the assertion of a substantial extension to Say's Law. Say's Law is taken to mean that the intention of people to supply is also an intention to demand: an individual wishes to supply labour in order to buy goods and services. The sum of the intentions to supply is then taken to be equal to the sum of intentions to demand: full employment (in the sense of all those willing to work doing so) results if the intentions to supply labour come to fruition and, if they do, the full employment income will all be spent. It is generally recognized that the NAIRU does not (generally) correspond to a position of full employment. Hence the assertion here is not just that full employment income would all be spent, but that the level of income corresponding to the NAIRU would all be spent. In the Bank of England's model (and more generally) the rate of interest is varied to cause changes in the level of aggregate demand. The issue of the aggregate demand sustainability of the NAIRU can then be seen as the question whether there is an achievable interest rate at which aggregate demand equals the NAIRU supply level.

The third implication is derived from the view that the influence of interest rates on inflation runs through the impact on the level of aggregate demand, and then the impact of aggregate demand on the pace of inflation. This stands out clearly in the diagram in Monetary Policy Committee (1999), reproduced as Figure 3.1. Putting the second of those links on one side for the moment, we focus on the first one. There are two related questions here: first, how does the impact of interest rates on the level of aggregate demand compare with the alternative, that is fiscal policy; and second, how does the range within which fiscal policy can be varied compare with the range within which monetary policy (interest rates) can be varied?

The simulations reported in Bank of England (1999, p. 36) (and discussed at greater length in the next chapter) for a one percentage point shock to nominal interest rates, maintained for one year, reaches a maximum change in GDP (of opposite sign to the change in the interest rate) of around 0.3 per cent after five to six quarters:[4] 'temporarily raising rates relative to a base case by 1 percentage point for one year might be expected to lower output by something of the order of 0.2 per cent to 0.35 per cent after about a year, and to reduce inflation by around 0.2 percentage points to 0.4 percentage points a year or so after that, all relative to the base case' (Monetary Policy Committee, 1999, p. 3). The cumulative reduction in GDP is around 1.5 per cent over a four-year period. Inflation responds little for the first four quarters (in one simulation inflation rises but falls in the other over that period). In years 2 and 3 inflation is 0.2 to 0.4 percentage points lower (the simulation is not reported past year 3). It should also be noted here that the simulation which is used varies the interest rates for one year: in the nature of the model, there are limits to how far interest rates can be manipulated, and this has some reflection in reality. In the models reviewed by Church *et al.* (1997), a stimulus of £2 billion (in 1990 prices) in public expenditure (roughly 0.3 per cent of

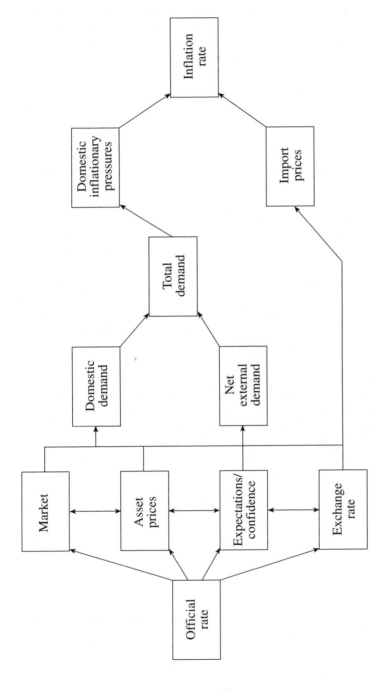

Source: Bank of England (1999).

Figure 3.1 How changes in the official interest rate affect the inflation rate

GDP) raised GDP in the first year by between 0.16 per cent and 0.44 per cent and between 0.11 per cent and 0.75 per cent in year 3.[5] Bank of England (1999) are forced to conclude that 'even for a given set of assumptions, the effects of a change in interest rates are highly uncertain, because of uncertainty about the true value of the parameters underlying the model' (p. 36).

The fourth implication is related to the previous two. It can be noted that 'the' interest rate has been treated as endogenous. We have simplified matters to talk in terms of a single nominal interest rate, in effect making the assumption that the spectrum of interest rates rests upon the central bank discount rate, but unless there are significant effects (on aggregate demand) from changes in the spectrum of interest rates, this simplifying assumption is innocuous. In the Bank of England model both the nominal rate and the real rate of interest influence aggregate demand. There is then a rate of interest which generates a level of aggregate demand consistent with the supply side-determined level of economic activity. However, the expected exchange rate has been treated as an exogenous variable in equation (3.5), and there is an implied rate of change of the exchange rate in that equation. We would expect that a constant exchange rate would require equality between domestic interest rate and world interest rates (apart from any risk premium). There is then a conflict between the (domestic) interest rate required to balance aggregate demand and aggregate supply and that required to maintain the exchange rate (whether in nominal or in real terms).

The fifth implication relates to monetary policy. The MPC has been charged with setting the central bank interest rate on a monthly basis with the objective of achieving an inflation target, which is currently set at 2.0 per cent +/– 1 per cent (of the Harmonized Index of Consumer Prices). Treasury (1999) puts it this way: 'It is important to recognize that the goal of monetary policy should be price stability' (p. 12). It is notable that in Treasury (1999) and Monetary Policy Committee (1999) there is no mention of the supply of money (in the sense of the amount of money supplied by the central bank or by the banking system) and little mention of the demand for money. The Bank of England's model incorporates a demand for money equation, which can be presumed sufficiently stable and reliable for inclusion in their model. But since the demand for money is a residual with no feedback into the rest of the model, it would be of little consequence if it were not stable. The Treasury appear to take a different view. For example, 'The development of global capital markets, financial deregulation, and changing technology led to significant and unanticipated changes in the velocity of circulation of money. As a result, there was no clear and stable relationship between money demand and inflation over this period, making it impossible to rely on fixed monetary rules to deliver price stability' (Treasury, 1999, p. 12). Gordon Brown (1999) makes a similar point and then remarks that 'fixed intermediate monetary targets assume a stable demand for money and therefore a predictable relationship between money and inflation' (p. 6) but argues that the demand for money is not stable and hence argues that intermediate monetary targets should not be used.

It could be said that monetary policy (in the form of the setting of a key interest rate) now has little to do with the stock of money. The supply of money is not mentioned, and the demand for money is either viewed as unstable (Treasury) or is treated residually (Bank of England). As noted above, in Bank of England (1999) there is an equation for M4 (but not for other monetary aggregates) which is a demand equation in real terms, and hence the stock of money relative to nominal income depends on wealth and interest rate differential (deposit minus base). Hence the stock of money is seen as determined by nominal income, wealth and interest rate differential. But the direction of causation runs from income and the other variables in the relationship to demand for money (and hence the stock of money), for, as the Monetary Policy Committee (1999) remark, 'monetary and credit aggregates must be willingly held by agents in the economy' (p. 11). Thus the stock of money is determined by nominal income and interest rates rather than the rate of change of money determining the rate of inflation.

Monetary Policy Committee (1999) argue that 'monetary policy works largely via its influence on aggregate demand in the economy. It has little direct effect on the trend path of supply capacity. Rather, in the long run, monetary policy determines the nominal or money values of goods and services – that is, the general price level' (p. 3). There is a sense in which there is no longer a monetary policy in the sense of concern over either the demand for or supply of money. It is rather that interest rate policy has become aggregate demand policy. It used to be that fiscal policy was associated with aggregate demand policy; now it is monetary policy. The view on inflation that is implicit in this appears to be as follows. Domestic inflation depends on a range of factors such as unemployment relative to the NAIRU and, insofar as those factors depend on the level of aggregate demand, they can be influenced by variations in the interest rate. It is necessary to take a broader view of the inflationary pressures than just unemployment (relative to NAIRU) or output (relative to trend), and variations in interest rates' response to the perception of those inflationary pressures. Nevertheless, the rate of interest influences aggregate demand and the exchange rate (which in turn influences aggregate demand but also the price of imports) and it is only through those routes that interest rate can have an impact on the rate of inflation.

The sixth implication relates to what may be termed a form of the classical dichotomy. In one sense it could be said that the Bank of England's model is close to being a 'real side' model of the economy. The equation for the demand for money, equation (3.6), could be removed from the model without any consequence for the properties of the model. But monetary policy in the form of interest rate policy does have an effect. A change in the rate of interest has an impact on the real cost of capital. It also has a more general impact on the level of aggregate demand and thereby on capacity utilization. The real cost of capital and capacity utilization influence investment, and thereby the evolution of the capital stock. The implication for aggregate demand and for capacity utilization, and thereby for inflation, is that they are affected.

These effects may be in some relevant sense small, but that may arise because the impact of monetary policy on aggregate demand is small: it could then be said that monetary policy is ineffectual. Even if the effect is small, it does not change the theoretical point that monetary policy can have long-lasting real effects. Monetary policy is not neutral.

These characteristics appear also in the Bank of England model and, since the Bank of England model lies within the NCM, with the absence of any significant role for money and an operating rule that makes policy responsive to economic events. However, the Bank of England model adds three features. First, in an open economy, the domestic rate of interest cannot persistently diverge from the world rate of interest without a persistent change in the exchange rate. There are significant constraints on domestic interest rates. Second, interest rates directly and indirectly influence investment, and thereby monetary policy has real effects. Third, fiscal policy influences the level of aggregate demand in that government expenditure and taxation enter equation (3.1). Fiscal policy and monetary policy then influence aggregate demand and thereby, in this model, changes in the pace of inflation. Any target rate of inflation can be achieved in this model provided that there are sufficient deflationary policies to reduce the rate of inflation cumulatively. However, deflationary policies have effects on investment, which can influence the supply-side equilibrium of the economy.

It is notable that, in the NCM model discussed in the previous chapter and in the Bank of England model (and in many others), there is no market-based mechanism by which the economy moves to the long-run supply-side equilibrium. The assumed mechanism is the operation of monetary policy according to some rule which is close to the Taylor rule; that is, the real interest rate set is based on a 'natural' real rate of interest, deviations of output from trend and difference of actual inflation with target rate of inflation. If the 'natural' rate of interest were set incorrectly (for example in the model presented in Chapter 2, if RR^* is not set equal to a_0/a_3), the inflation target would not be attained. It is also, of course, the case that the (implicit) use of other policy rules for monetary policy (for example setting the interest rate to achieve an exchange rate target) would not in general lead to the achievement of the inflation target.

4 SUMMARY AND CONCLUSIONS

This chapter has sought to analyse the basic nature of the Bank of England's macroeconometric model, in an attempt to highlight the NCM model as described in Chapter 2. It has argued that the Bank of England's model is essentially based on an endogenous money supply view, in that the stock of money is demand-determined and the stock of money itself has no causal effect on the rate of inflation or the level of economic activity. Monetary policy operates through the setting of the key interest rate, and the effects of such policy (which are seen as uncertain in magnitude) operate through channels such as effects on investment and the exchange rate. In many respects, therefore, the model belongs to that category of macroeconomic models that have the characteristics of the 'new' consensus in macroeconomics.[6]

Can it be said that 'central banks ultimately determine the inflation rate' (Meyer, 2001a, 2001b)? In the NCM model reported in Chapter 2, and that of the Bank of England, the inflation rate is determined in the long run by the target rate of inflation. The central bank is often given the objective of achieving that rate of inflation, and seeks to achieve that objective through interest rate policies. In the long term, the central bank would have to set an interest rate that is consistent with that rate of inflation. It can be seen that the real rate of interest in the NCM model (see Chapter 2) is equal to a_3/a_0, and hence depends on the effect of interest rates on output (a_3) and on a_0. Treating a_0 as including the effects of fiscal stance, overseas demand and so on would indicate that the equilibrium interest rate depends on those other factors. Further, the central bank may not be able to achieve that equilibrium real rate of interest insofar as it diverges from overseas interest rates, and any difference between domestic interest rate and foreign interest rate would have implications for changes in the exchange rate.

NOTES

1. The estimation of macroeconometric models is subject to revision and updating. Further the nature and structure of a model changes over time. The Bank of England model discussed here was the one in use *circa* 1998–2002, as described in Bank of England (1999, 2000). At the time of writing, this model was in the process of being replaced by a substantially changed version.
2. Net financial wealth is included, as part of nominal wealth, but bank deposits would not constitute net wealth, as they are liabilities of the banking system.
3. It could be claimed that equation (3.6) should be read as a price level equation, that is, P as a function of M. However, it is not estimated in that way; rather it is estimated with real money stock as the dependent variable, thus clearly implying that it is meant to be a demand for money relationship.
4. The precise figures depend on assumptions concerning the subsequent responses of the setting of interest rates in response to the evolving inflation rate.

5. The construction of the models effectively imposes a supply side-determined equilibrium. 'Each of the models ... now possess static homogeneity throughout their price and wage system. Consequently it is not possible for the government to choose a policy that changes the price level and hence the natural rate of economic activity. [With one exception] it is also impossible for the authorities to manipulate the inflation rate in order to change the natural rate' (Church *et al.*, p. 96).

6. As this book was going to press, the Bank of England announced that a new macro-economic model is being built which is not very different from the one summarized in this chapter. In the words of the Bank of England 'the new model does not represent a change in the committee's view of how the economy works or of the role of monetary policy. Rather, recent advances in economic understanding and computational power have been used to develop a macroeconomic model with a more clearly specified and coherent economic structure than in previous models used by the committee' (BEQB, 2004, p. 188).

4. Can monetary policy affect inflation or the real economy?

1 INTRODUCTION

This chapter is to investigate the extent to which monetary policy can have significant effects on inflation or on the real economy. The use of monetary policy to focus on inflation alone is clearly based on the view that monetary policy will have a significant effect on inflation, and the view that monetary policy will have no effect on the real economy (other than a short-run effect on aggregate demand, which in turn is seen to influence inflation). The objective is to examine monetary policy within the NCM. This involves the manipulation of the key central bank interest rate (often the 'repo' rate), with the specific objective of achieving the goal(s) of monetary policy.

In this chapter we examine the channels through which changes in the rate of interest may affect the ultimate goal(s) of policy. Indeed, this aspect is of considerable importance and relevance to current monetary developments. A recent conference at the Federal Bank of New York on 'Financial Innovation and Monetary Transmission'[1] readily acknowledged that this change in the conduct of monetary policy, along with financial innovation and the evolving behaviour of firms, has altered the channels through which monetary policy affects the economy.

2 THE TRANSMISSION MECHANISM AND THE CONTROL OF INFLATION

The most interesting aspect of the 'new consensus' for the purposes of this chapter is the mechanism whereby inflation and other policy objectives are the target. This is assumed to take place through equation (2.1) where interest rates, themselves determined by the operating policy rule as in equation (2.3), affect aggregate demand and, via equation (2.2), changes in the rate of inflation depend on aggregate demand. Then the strength, timing and predictability of the effects of changes in the rate of interest on aggregate demand become important questions. Higher (lower) interest rates tend to reduce (increase) aggregate demand, and lower (higher) aggregate demand is assumed to reduce (increase) the rate of inflation. The possibility that interest rates are regarded as a cost (by firms), and hence that higher interest rates may lead to higher prices, is not mentioned.

There are, to begin with, the channels traditionally identified in the literature: the interest rate channel, the wealth effect channel, the exchange rate channel (although this particular channel may not be as traditional as claimed), and what has been termed the 'monetarist channel' (but which is not the direct impact of the stock of money). Two further channels have been identified more recently: these two are essentially a credit channel normally discussed as comprising two channels: the narrow credit channel (sometimes referred to as the balance sheet channel), and the broad credit channel. Figure 4.1 portrays schematically the six channels just referred to.[2]

We now discuss the six channels briefly. The two credit channels, the narrow credit channel and the broad credit channel, are distinct but complementary ways whereby imperfections in financial markets might affect real magnitudes in the economy. They are concerned with the way changes in the financial positions of lenders and borrowers can affect aggregate demand in the economy, on the assumption of credit market frictions.[3] The narrow credit channel (also labelled the 'bank lending channel'; see Hall, 2001) concentrates on the role of banks as lenders (Roosa, 1951; Bernanke and Blinder, 1988). Banks rely heavily on demand deposits subjected to reserve requirements as an important source of funding economic activity. When there is a change in total reserves as a result of changes in monetary policy, bank reserves will be affected, thereby affecting their supply of loans to the private sector. Given that a significant number of firms and households depend on bank lending, ultimately aggregate demand and inflation will be affected. Indeed, as Hall (2001) puts it, 'This channel may be potentially significant if increases in interest rates lead to a reduction in the supply of bank loans and if these loans are imperfect substitutes for other forms of finance' (p. 4).

The broad credit channel (also labelled the 'balance sheet channel'; see Hall, 2001) describes how the financial health of borrowers can affect the supply of finance and ultimately aggregate demand (Bernanke and Gertler, 1989, 1999; Bernanke et al., 1999). This channel relies heavily on an imperfect information assumption in terms of the supply of external finance to firms. This is that lenders charge borrowers a premium to cover monitoring costs, and it is the firm's financial position that determines their external finance premium. So that low (high) gearing, that is, high (low) internal finance, implies small (large) external finance premium. Two important implications follow: the first is that there is a role for corporate cash flows. A policy-induced increase (decrease) in the rate of interest raises (lowers) the firm's gearing ratio, that is, the proportion of a given investment that must be financed from external funds, thereby

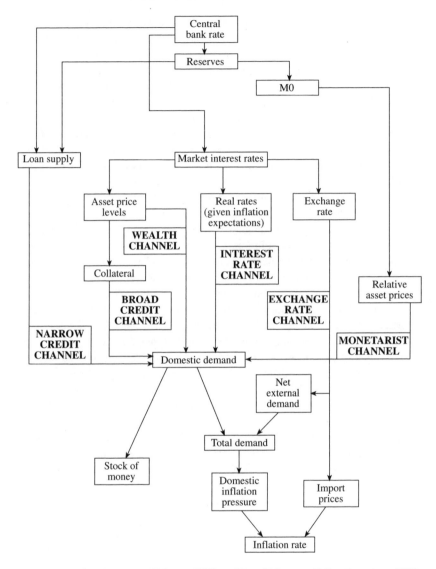

Source: Based on Kuttner and Mosser (2002, p. 16) and Monetary Policy Committee (1999, p. 1) with significant modifications.

Figure 4.1 Monetary policy transmission

increasing (decreasing) the required premium to cover monitoring costs. The second implication is that asset prices play an important role as they determine the value of collateral that bank customers (firms and consumers) can use to support loan applications. In the presence of information asymmetries, agency costs and other credit market frictions, collateral values are paramount. As the value of the collateral declines, say because of falling asset prices due to higher policy-induced interest rates, the borrower premium increases. Consequently, the impact on investment and consumption can be significant as a result of this 'financial accelerator' effect and, *mutatis mutandis*, in the case where the value of collateral increases. Changes in asset prices are important in the case of the wealth effect channel too. The mechanism in this case works via consumer expenditure where the consumption function is hypothesized to depend on consumer wealth. Policy-induced changes in interest rates affect the value of asset prices and thereby the real value of consumer wealth. This in its turn leads to changes in consumer expenditure.

We may take next the interest rate channel and the monetarist channel together. These two channels depend heavily on the assumption made about the degree of substitutability between money and other assets. If this degree is very high between money and financial assets, particularly short-term liquid assets, then changes in the money supply will have significant effects on interest rates. Given some degree of price stickiness, real interest rates and the user cost of capital would also be affected. To the extent that the components of aggregate demand are interest rate-sensitive, policy-induced changes in interest rates would have a significant impact on the level and pace of economic activity. This channel may also include 'availability' effects. Financial institutions may decide not to adjust their interest rates in response to a change in the central bank interest rate, but rather to apply some form of credit rationing (Stiglitz and Weiss, 1981). In this channel, therefore, interest rates provide more information than money supply changes. Monetary policy can be undertaken with greater certainty by acting directly to influence and control interest rates than by seeking to control the money supply. Monetary authorities have to provide however much monetary base it takes to achieve their target interest rate. If, by contrast, the degree of substitutability between money and a wide range of assets, including real assets, were high, the impact of money supply changes would crucially depend on relative price changes. This monetarist channel, therefore, works through relative asset price changes. Interest rate changes do not play a special role, other than as one of many relative price changes. Since the effect of monetary policy is on relative 'real' rates, it is pointless looking at the rate of interest to represent the thrust of monetary policy. Monetary policy should, thus, set the money supply and let interest rates become the endogenous magnitude. It is relative asset prices that can have an impact on aggregate demand.

The sixth channel of the impact of monetary policy is the exchange rate channel. It links monetary policy to inflation via two routes. The first is via total demand and works through the uncovered interest rate parity condition. The latter relates interest rate differentials to expected exchange rate movements. Policy-induced changes in domestic interest rates relative to foreign interest rates would affect the exchange rate and this would lead to balance-of-payments changes. The overall level of aggregate demand would thereby be affected, influencing the inflation rate. The second route works through import prices. Changes in the exchange rate affect import prices directly, and these influence the inflation rate. We should note, in the context of the exchange rate channel, that exchange rate movements have proved very difficult to model satisfactorily. The theory of interest rate parity indicates a close relationship between interest rate differentials and expected exchange rate movements, which would severely limit variations in interest rates. However, the model does not seem to work empirically (see Chapter 7). Exchange rate variations have proved notoriously difficult to model, regardless of the theoretical framework adopted.

In view of this analysis, it is important to examine the quantitative impact of changes in the rate of interest on both the level of economic activity and the rate of inflation, in an attempt to verify or otherwise the channels through which monetary policy works.

3 EMPIRICAL EVIDENCE

We rely on two types of evidence in assessing the impact of monetary policy. We look first at empirical evidence that is based on macroeconometric models, and then at evidence that emanates from the application of single equation techniques.

3.1 Empirical Evidence based on Macroeconometric Models

It would be useful to be able to assess quantitatively the effects of monetary policy through the six channels outlined above. This, however, is not possible, for a number of reasons. The channels of monetary transmission are not mutually exclusive, in that the overall response of the economy to changes in monetary policy incorporates the combined effects of all the channels. This concurrent operation of multiple channels entails an important challenge, namely that it becomes very difficult to assess the strength and contribution of the individual channels to the overall impact of monetary policy on the inflation rate. A further and related problem is that of isolating the change in the strength and importance of the channels of monetary transmission through time. The evolutionary nature of these changes and the fact that many of the structural changes occur concurrently, are additional problems. The most serious difficulty in this context is the fact that these changes and any of their effects on the transmission mechanism take relatively long periods to become evident. All in all, the aspects we have just discussed clearly imply that the link between monetary policy and the real economy changes over time (see Kuttner and Mosser, 2002, especially pp. 17–18). Evidence that the monetary transmission itself has changed has been provided by Boivin and Giannoni (2002a), using VARs in the case of the US for the period 1960 to 2001, and by Boivin and Giannoni (2002b) where a small-scale structural model is employed (see also Fair, 2001). An additional, and as serious a challenge, is that of simultaneity. Central banks normally relax policy in the wake of weaknesses in the economy and tighten policy when there are strengths in the economy. Put another way, 'how is it possible to isolate the effect of interest rates on economic conditions when interest rates are themselves a function of economic conditions?' (Kuttner and Mosser, 2002, p. 23). This potentially endogenous response of policy to economic conditions is another serious impediment to any attempt to identify and isolate the effects of the different monetary transmission channels. It is paramount to bear in mind these observations in the attempt to assess the quantitative effects of monetary policy.[4]

The claim that monetary policy is an effective and powerful tool for macro-economic management depends on a range of assumptions. One of the assumptions is that variations in the rate of interest have substantial effects on aggregate demand and thereby on the rate of inflation. In this section we seek to summarize the results of some recent simulations undertaken by others, based on macroeconometric models. In doing so we are able to draw on relevant work undertaken for the euro area, for the USA and for the UK.

In their work on the impact of monetary policy in the euro zone, Angeloni *et al.* (2002) argue that 'VAR and structural model analyses for the euro area confirm sizeable and plausible monetary policy effects on output and prices. In the VARs, an unexpected increase in the short-term interest rate temporarily reduces output, with the peak effects occurring after roughly one year. Prices respond more slowly, hardly moving during the first year and then falling gradually over the next few years. Again, these VAR properties are similar to those reported for the US. The structural models of the US and the euro area broadly confirm this picture' (p. 21). The estimated effect of a one standard error monetary policy shock (approximately 30 basis points) on prices is 0.00 in year 1 and –0.07 per cent in year 3 with a decline in output in year 1 of 0.15 per cent and 0.05 in year 3.[5]

In Table 4.1 we provide some results from simulations with macro-econometric models based on Angeloni *et al.*'s Table 2. These results indicate that a one percentage point increase in the rate of interest held for two years

Table 4.1   Effects of monetary policy change

| | EMM | | AWM | |
100 basis point increase for two years	year 1	year 3	year 1	year 3
Effective exchange rate	1.6	0.0	1.6	0.0
Consumer prices	–0.09	–0.31	–0.15	–0.38
GDP	–0.22	–0.31	–0.34	–0.71
Consumption	–0.12	–0.19	–0.27	–0.54
Investment	–0.34	–1.22	–0.81	–2.96

Notes: EMM (Eurosystem Macroeconometric Models of national central banks) calculations; AWM (ECB area-wide model) calculations; year 1 and year 3 refer to yearly average deviations from baseline.

Source: Angeloni *et al.* (2002, Table 2).

leads to prices lower by between 0.3 to 0.4 per cent after three years, and hence that the rate of inflation over those three years is around 0.1 per cent per annum lower than it would have been otherwise. As far as we are aware no statistics are available by which we can judge whether this should be regarded as a statistically significant reduction. In any event, we would judge these reductions as relatively small. It can also be noted that the effects on investment are larger than the effects on consumption expenditure, and one implication of this is that monetary policy can have long-lasting effects in that the size of the capital stock is affected.

These authors also provide some comparisons between the euro area and the US. They report the effects of a 50 basis points short-term interest change on a range of economic variables. The effects are reported after one year and three years (that is, variations for quarter 4 and quarter 12 relative to a baseline). They give the semi-elasticity multipliers, and these are summarized in Table 4.2 below. The general impression from this table is that the results for the US are not dissimilar from those for the euro zone, though the effects of interest rate changes on investment appear more muted in the USA.

Van Els *et al.* (2001) report results for the euro area countries, where 'The monetary policy shock was a two-year increase of the short-term policy interest rate by 1 percentage point from 2001Q1–2002Q4. From and including 2003Q1 a return to baseline values was assumed' (p. 22). A footnote adds that 'this meant that the experiment was a temporary one, as a permanent change in the nominal interest rate would force most models onto an explosive path'. Furthermore, 'the exercise on national models is conducted on the basis that the change in monetary policy has taken place simultaneously in all

Table 4.2   Impact of changes in interest rates

	Effects after one year			Effects after three years		
	Euro area EMM	Euro area AWM	US FRB-US	Euro area EMM	Euro area AWM	US FRB-US
CPI	−0.02	−0.03	−0.05	−0.15	−0.21	−0.57
GDP	−0.11	−0.24	−0.14	−0.49	−0.63	−0.52
Consumer expenditure	−0.10	−0.25	−0.17	−0.38	−0.62	−0.64
Investment expenditure	−0.59	−0.68	−0.17	−2.43	−2.07	−1.08

Note: FRB-US: Federal Reserve Board, US; CPI: consumer price index.

Source: Angeloni *et al.* (2002, Table 3).

euro area countries' (p. 8). They find that 'Two stylised facts appear to be at variance with the traditional view of the monetary transmission mechanism, namely the low elasticity of the cost-of-capital in estimated spending equations and the high degree of amplification, that is, the empirical evidence that though central bank's actions induce relatively small and transitory movements in open market interest rates, nevertheless they have large and persistent effects on the purchase of long-lived assets, such as housing or production equipment' (p. 10).

Moreover, in Figure 6.1 of Van Els *et al.* (2001), a summary is provided of the common assumptions underlying the response pattern of the euro exchange rate vis-à-vis non-euro countries along with the long-term interest rate (10-year bond). These exercises suggest that the interest rate increase implies an appreciation of the euro exchange rate, with respect to non-euro currencies, of 1.6 per cent on average in the first year and 0.6 per cent in the second. The figure shows a peak appreciation in the exchange rate of 2 per cent and a decline back to zero into the tenth quarter. The long-term rate peaks at 0.2 per cent during quarter 1, gradually declining back to no increase in quarter 9, when the short-term rate returns to a zero increase.

The authors find substantial differences between countries of the euro zone, which is relevant for the operation of a single monetary policy. They conclude that 'At one extreme there are countries, like Germany, Benelux and Finland, where a policy tightening is effective in curbing inflationary pressures at mild costs in terms of output losses, while there are other EMU countries, in particular Greece and Portugal, where the increase in interest rates engenders a marked contraction in economic activity and only a modest restraint on price developments. The remaining countries are located in-between, though somewhat closer to the core region' (p. 48). Further, 'the distribution of the national responses of investment is very wide, with maxima ranging between –0.3 per cent for Germany and France and –3.6 per cent for Italy and Ireland' (p. 39). Although it is generally implicit, this paper also indicates the role of unemployment in dampening down inflation: 'The impact of the monetary policy shock on unemployment is a crucial element in the process of monetary policy transmission on prices in the medium and long term' (p. 39).

The overall conclusions that Van Els *et al.* (2001) draw from these results are on the following lines: 'In terms of the impact of monetary policy on output, a 1 percentage point rise in short-term interest rates is found to have a maximum aggregate effect in NCBs [National Central Bank] models of –0.4 per cent after 2 years. The maximum aggregate effect on prices is also –0.4 per cent but in this case it occurs 2 years later, reflecting the fact that in most of the models prices react more slowly and largely in response to changes in economic activity. The dominant channel of transmission in the first two years – both in terms of its impact on output and on prices – is the exchange rate channel. However, in terms of the impact on output, from the third year of the simulation onwards the user cost of capital channel becomes dominant' (p. 52).

The tables in the Annex of the Van Els *et al.* paper give results by country and for prices, GDP, consumption, investment and unemployment. A summary of these results is given in Table 4.3.

The rather small effect of the interest rate change on the rate of inflation is again apparent, with a substantial effect on the level of investment. The way the results are presented suggests that output rises back to its benchmark level a few years after the interest rate policy is switched off. But this means that, for a two-year increase in interest rates of one percentage point, there is a loss of output which is never recovered and the cumulative loss of output is equivalent to 1.1 per cent of annual output (summing the GDP row in the first part of Table 4.3). For unemployment, the created total of unemployment is equivalent to 0.6 per cent of a workforce year. In the case of the price level, there is, within the forecast period, a reduction in the price level; in the aggregate model this amounts to around 0.4 per cent. But the rate of inflation is not permanently affected in the aggregate model; by year 5, inflation is back to the benchmark level. Much of the effect on inflation comes through the exchange rate. Presumably, when the interest rate policy is reversed, the exchange rate effect is also reversed, leaving no permanent effect on inflation from that channel.

Table 4.3   Effects of a one percentage point increase in interest rate sustained for two years

	2001	2002	2003	2004	2005
Aggregate (based on national models)					
GDP deflator	–0.04	–0.20	–0.35	–0.43	–0.41
Inflation*	–0.04	–0.16	–0.15	–0.08	+0.02
GDP	–0.22	–0.38	–0.31	–0.14	–0.02
Private consumption	–0.12	–0.23	–0.19	–0.06	0.01
Investment	–0.34	–1.04	–1.22	–0.80	–0.39
Unemployment	0.04	0.11	0.17	0.17	0.11
Area-wide model (AWM)					
GDP deflator	–0.10	–0.31	–0.44	–0.57	–0.76
Inflation*	–0.10	–0.21	–0.13	–0.13	–0.19
GDP	–0.34	–0.71	–0.71	–0.63	–0.57
Private consumption	–0.27	–0.58	–0.54	–0.43	–0.37
Investment	–0.81	–2.37	–2.96	–2.63	–2.42
Unemployment	0.10	0.39	0.58	0.62	0.58

Note: * Percentage point change in inflation: not calculated in original paper, own calculations from preceding line.

Source: Van Els *et al.* (2001, Annex).

The results of simulations undertaken by the Bank of England for the UK were reported in the following way.

> To illustrate the point that the simulation responses of inflation and output will depend on the specific assumptions made, we show three different simulations: First, the coefficients in the Taylor rule on the deviations of inflation from target and output from base are set at 0.5. Second, the coefficient in the Taylor rule on the deviation of inflation from target is increased to 1.0, suggesting that the monetary authority responds more strongly to inflation deviations from target. Third, the coefficient on the deviation of inflation from target in the Taylor rule is increased further to 1.5, suggesting that the monetary authority will respond even more strongly to inflation deviations from target. (Bank of England, 2000, pp. 16–17)[6]

The results of these exercises for inflation and GDP are documented as follows:

The maximum effect of the temporary interest rate increase on real activity occurs after about one year, and the maximum effect on inflation occurs after about two years. For the benchmark simulation, where the Taylor rule with a weight of 0.5 on the deviation of inflation from target is adopted, the level of GDP falls by about 0.3 per cent at the end of the first year, recovering to base after three years. Inflation remains broadly unchanged during the first year, reflecting the degree of nominal inertia in the economy, but by the beginning of the third year has fallen by just over 0.3 percentage points. Thereafter, it returns slowly to base. (Ibid., pp. 16–17)

The simulations reported in Bank of England (1999, p. 36) for a one percent-age point shock to nominal interest rates, maintained for one year, reaches a maximum change in GDP (of opposite sign to the change in the interest rate) of around 0.3 per cent after five to six quarters.[7] They are described in this manner: 'temporarily raising rates relative to a base case by 1 percentage point for one year might be expected to lower output by something of the order of 0.2 per cent to 0.35 per cent after about a year, and to reduce inflation by around 0.2 percentage points to 0.4 percentage points a year or so after that, all relative to the base case' (Monetary Policy Committee, 1999, p. 3). The cumulative reduction in GDP is around 1.5 per cent over a four-year period. Inflation responds little for the first four quarters (in one simulation inflation rises but falls in the other over that period). In years 2 and 3 inflation is 0.2 to 0.4 percentage points lower (the simulation is not reported past year 3). It should also be noted here that the simulation which is used varies interest rates for one year. It is in the nature of the model that there are limits to how far interest rates can be manipulated, and this has some reflection in reality.

The conclusions we draw from this brief survey of some empirical evidence are along the following lines. First (at least within the context of the macroeconometric models), there are constraints to a permanent change in the rate of interest. We would see the effect of interest rate on the exchange rate (when interest rate parity is assumed) as being a significant element in this (in that an interest differential between the domestic interest rate and foreign interest rate leads to a continual change in the exchange rate). However, we remain sceptical of the empirical validity of that link (see further discussion in Chapter 7).

Second, and this is clear in the case of the euro area models, when interest rates have an effect on aggregate demand this comes through from substantial changes in the rate of investment (see Table 4.2). This means that interest rate variations can have long-lasting effects, in that the effects on investment will lead to changes in the size of the capital stock. Third, the effects of interest rate changes on the rate of inflation are rather modest (for example, see the second row of figures in Table 4.3). A one percentage point change in interest rates is predicted to lead to a cumulative fall in the price level of 0.41 per cent in one case and 0.76 per cent in the other, after five years. The rate of inflation declines by a maximum of 0.21 percentage points.

A recent ECB (2002e) publication confirms our general conclusion that the effects of monetary policy are small.[8] A one percentage point increase in interest rate for two years reduces output by between 0.31 per cent and 0.71 per cent after three years. The reduction in the price level is estimated at between 0.19 per cent and 0.38 per cent after three years. However, the ECB study concludes that 'the impact of monetary policy is neutral in the long run, that is, a permanent change in the money supply (associated here with a temporary change, in the opposite direction, in the central bank instrument, the policy-controlled interest rate) has no significant long-run effect on real GDP, but does lead to a permanent change in the price level' (p. 45). The ECB (ibid.) recognizes, however, that 'all these estimates are surrounded by a significant degree of uncertainty. This is partly due to the fact that the analysis is, by necessity, based predominantly on data from the period before the introduction of the euro. Hence the results may be subject to change as a consequence of the introduction of the new currency and the related change in the "monetary policy regime"' (p. 44). The same study also concludes that monetary policy has temporary effects on output. Both sets of results are consistent with money neutrality and nominal and real rigidities in the goods and labour markets, characteristics that are consistent with those of the 'new consensus' in macroeconomics.

We find the ECB (2002e) conclusions somewhat misleading, though, in the following ways: (i) the change in the money supply in most econometric models arises as a consequence of a change in the demand for money (from a change in prices, output and interest rates), and the money supply does not have a causal impact on the price level; (ii) the interest rate change is held for two years and then reversed, and hence there cannot be a permanent change in the level of aggregate demand in these simulations. If the level of aggregate demand does not change, the level of output does not change; (iii) any effects of interest rate changes on investment and thereby on future productive capacity appear to be ignored; and (iv) it is unclear as to whether monetary policy of the form used here (a temporary increase in the rate of interest) has any effect on the rate of inflation. The price level is reported as being lower, but no results are given for the rate of inflation. Calculations from Table 4.1 (the difference between columns of the results for consumer prices, as in ECB, 2002e, p. 45) suggest that the reduction in inflation in year 3 is small (−0.08, −0.10 and 0.09 per cent in the three estimates).[9] At some point, the price level following the temporary interest rate increase stabilizes at its new lower level as compared with the base case. This could be taken to imply that inflation after the interest rate increase will return to the base case level, that is, no reduction in inflation results from the interest rate increase.

3.2 Empirical Evidence based on Single Equation Techniques

A number of studies have reviewed the empirical work undertaken on the impact of monetary policy within the 'inflation targeting' (IT) framework. This work uses single equation econometric techniques normally. The studies reviewed ask a number of questions with the most pertinent being the following: whether IT improves inflation performance and policy credibility, and whether the sacrifice ratio, that is, the cost of lowering inflation, does not increase significantly over the period of IT implementation. In the mid-1990s, Leiderman and Svensson (1995) reviewed the early experience with IT, with, however, a rather limited number of observations. Later studies (Bernanke *et al.*, 1999; Corbo *et al.*, 2001, 2002; Clifton *et al.*, 2001; Arestis *et al.*, 2002; Johnson, 2002; Neumann and von Hagen, 2002) inevitably afforded longer periods and more data. A reasonably comprehensive review of the empirical literature on IT (Neumann and von Hagen, 2002) concludes in the same manner as the other studies before it had done, and just cited. These conclusions can be summarized quite briefly. This evidence supports the contention that IT matters. Those countries which adopted IT managed to reduce inflation to low levels and to curb inflation and interest rate volatility. Indeed, 'of all IT countries it is the United Kingdom that has performed best even though its target rate of inflation is higher than the inflation targets of most other countries' (ibid., p. 144).[10]

The evidence, however, is marred by three weaknesses (Neumann and von Hagen, 2002): the first is that the empirical studies reviewed fail to produce *convincing* evidence that IT improves inflation performance and policy credibility, and lowers the so-called 'sacrifice ratio' (ratio of change in unemployment relative to change in inflation). After all, the environment of the 1990s was in general terms a stable economic environment, 'a period friendly to price stability' (ibid., p. 129), so that IT may have had little impact over what any sensible strategy could have achieved; indeed, non-IT countries also went through the same experience as IT countries (Cecchetti and Ehrmann, 2000). The second weakness is that, despite the problem just raised of lack of convincing evidence, the proponents argue very strongly that non-adoption of IT puts at high risk the ability of a central bank to provide price stability (for example, Bernanke *et al.*, 1999, 'submit a plea' for the Fed to adopt it; also Alesina *et al.*, 2001, make the bold statement that the European Central Bank could improve its monetary policy by adopting IT; neither study provides any supporting evidence, though. And yet both the Fed and the European Central Bank remain highly sceptical

(Gramlich, 2000, and Duisenberg, 2003a, do not actually regard IT as appropriate for the USA and the euro area, respectively). The third weakness refers to the argument that in a number of countries (for example, New Zealand, Canada and the UK) inflation had been 'tamed' well before introducing IT (Mishkin and Posen, 1997), an argument that implies that the role of IT might simply be to 'lock in' the gains from 'taming' inflation, rather than actually being able to produce these gains. Bernanke *et al.* (1999) admit as much when they argue that 'one of the main benefits of inflation targets is that they may help to "lock in" earlier disinflationary gains particularly in the face of one-time inflationary shocks. We saw this effect, for example, following the exit of the United Kingdom and Sweden from the European Exchange Rate Mechanism and after Canada's 1991 imposition of the Goods and Services Tax. In each case, the re-igniting of inflation seems to have been avoided by the announcement of inflation targets that helped to anchor the public's inflation expectations and to give an explicit plan for and direction to monetary policy' (p. 288).

Neumann and von Hagen (2002) produce further evidence which enables them to conclude that IT has proved an effective 'strategy' in the fight against inflation. This is based on the argument that, whenever IT was adopted, countries experienced low inflation rates, along with reduced volatility of inflation and interest rates. However, the evidence produced by the same study cannot support the contention that IT is superior to money supply targeting (for example, the Bundesbank monetary targeting between 1974 and 1998) or to the Fed's monetary policy in the 1980s and 1990s, which pursues neither a monetary nor an inflation targeting policy. A further finding of Neumann and von Hagen's paper is that Taylor rules suggest that central banks focus more on the control of inflation after adopting inflation targeting, thereby implying that price stability will be achieved, a result supported by the VAR evidence, which indicates that the relative importance of inflation shocks as a source of the variance of interest rates rises after adoption of inflation targeting.

Mishkin (2002a) in discussing Neumann and von Hagen (2002), however, points out that, since both short-term and long-term coefficients on inflation in the Taylor rules estimated relationships are less than one, the inflation process is highly unstable, the implication here being that, when inflation rates rise, the central bank increases the rate of interest by a smaller amount, thereby reducing the real rate of interest. This is of course an inflationary move by the central bank when the opposite was intended. This is also true for the non-IT countries, like the USA, a result that is again contrary to Taylor's (1993) finding, which argues that for the USA it is greater than one in the post-1979 period when allegedly monetary policy performance improved relative to the pre-1979 period.

Mishkin (2002a) identifies another interesting problem, which relates directly to the VAR approach. This is that, since this approach does not contain any structural model of dynamics, the interpretation that inflation shocks contribute to the variance of interest rates need not imply necessarily increased focus on the control of inflation. This is so since, if inflation shocks contribute to interest rate variability in an IT era, inflation expectations will prevent inflation from deviating much from the inflation target; this would imply that the central bank is less focused on inflation, not more. Consequently, this would clearly suggest 'that the VAR evidence in the paper, tells us little about the impact of inflation targeting on the conduct of monetary policy' (ibid., p. 150).

Ball and Sheridan (2003) measure the effects of IT on macroeconomic performance in the case of 20 OECD countries, seven of which adopted IT in the 1990s. They conclude that they are unable to find any evidence that IT improves economic performance as measured by the behaviour of inflation, output and interest rates. Note that better performance was not evident for the IT countries. Clearly, inflation fell in these countries and became more stable; and output growth stabilized during the IT period as compared to the pre-IT period. But then the same experience was evident for countries that did not adopt IT. Consequently, better performance must have been due to something other than IT. When performance is compared, the fall in inflation is larger for IT countries than for non-IT countries, a result that is similar in many ways to that of Neumann and von Hagen (2002); the latter see it as a further benefit of IT.[11] Ball and Sheridan (2003), however, suggest that the evidence they produce, and by implication that of Neumann and von Hagen (2002), does not support even this modest claim of IT benefit. This is explained by resorting to further evidence of countries with unusually high and unstable inflation rates where this problem disappears irrespective of their adoption of IT. Indeed, controlling for this effect, the apparent benefit disappears altogether. The apparent success of IT countries is merely due to their having 'high initial inflation and large decreases, but the decrease for a given initial level looks similar for targeters and non-targeters' (Ball and Sheridan, 2003, p. 16). The same result prevails in the case of inflation variability and inflation persistence. As to whether IT affects output behaviour and interest rates, Ball and Sheridan conclude in the same vein that IT does not affect output growth or output variability, nor does it affect interest rates and their variability.

A recent study by Bodkin and Neder (2003), examines IT in the case of Canada for the periods 1980–89 and 1990–99 (the IT period). Their results, based on graphical analysis, clearly indicate that inflation over the IT period did fall, but at a significant cost to unemployment and output, a result which leads the authors to the conclusion that a great deal of doubt is cast 'on the theoretical notion of the supposed long-run neutrality of money', an important, if not the most important, ingredient of the theoretical IT framework. They also suggest that the 'deleterious real effects (higher unemployment and ... lower growth) during the decade under study suggests that some small amount of inflation (say in the range of 3 to 5 percent) may well be beneficial for a modern economy' (p. 355).

4   SUMMARY AND CONCLUSIONS

This chapter has been concerned with the impact of monetary policy on the real economy, within the NCM and IT. Within this approach, monetary policy becomes identified with interest rate policy, with little or no reference to the stock of money (on any measure of money).[12] It has generally been the case that setting an inflation target is the main (and often the only) objective of monetary policy. Indeed, monetary policy can be seen as aggregate demand policy in that the interest rate set by the central bank is seen to influence aggregate demand, which in turn is thought to influence the rate of inflation. Monetary policy has become the only policy instrument for the control of inflation, but it can at best only address demand inflation.

One of the key issues of this approach is the recognition of the many channels through which monetary policy is seen to operate. This means that the chain from a change in the central bank discount rate to the final target of the rate of inflation is a long and uncertain one. In light of the relationship between the exchange rate and the interest rate expressed in the interest rate parity approach, there are constraints on the degree to which the domestic interest rate can be set to address the domestic levels of aggregate demand and inflation. In view of the central place given to monetary policy in macro-economic policies and the length of the chain from central bank interest rate to rate of inflation, it is important to consider the empirical estimates of the effects of monetary policy. We have summarized results drawn from the euro zone, the USA and the UK, and have suggested that these empirical results point to a relatively weak effect of interest rate changes on inflation. We have also suggested that on the basis of the evidence adduced in this chapter, monetary policy can have long-run effects on real magnitudes. This particular result does not sit comfortably with the theoretical basis of the NCM and IT monetary policy.

The empirical work undertaken on IT has also been critically assessed. It would appear that Mishkin's (1999) premature statement that the reduction of inflation in IT countries 'beyond that which would likely have occurred in the absence of inflation targets' (p. 595), is not supported by any theoretical reasoning or empirical evidence. We would therefore conclude overall, along with Ball and Sheridan (2003), that the recent 'low-inflation' era is not different for IT and non-IT countries. Consequently, IT has been a great deal of fuss about really very little.

NOTES

1. The proceedings of the conference have been published in the Federal Reserve Bank of New York *Economic Review*, **8**(1), 2002 issue.
2. The construction of Figure 4.1 has been strongly influenced by comparable figures in Monetary Policy Committee (1999, p. 1) and in Kuttner and Mosser (2002, p. 16).
3. The assumption of credit market frictions is important in that it is normally hypothesized that lending and borrowing are indifferent amongst internal funds, bank borrowing and equity finance. This assumption relies on a frictionless world, where lenders and borrowers have the same information about risks and returns, costlessly monitor the use and repayment of borrowed funds in the case of lenders, and are not faced with search and transaction costs. In addition to these agency costs, lenders and borrowers have no concerns about corporate controls, and there is no tax discrimination of sources of finance. In the real world of credit markets, frictions are abundant, so that the heroic assumptions of frictionless credit markets do not generally hold.
4. See Federal Reserve Bank of New York (2002) for more details on the problems and issues discussed in the text.
5. The VAR estimates are taken from Peersman and Smets (2001). Their Graph 1 indicates that the upper 90 per cent confidence interval on prices is at or above zero (compared with the base case); that is, prices may not decline at all.
6. It would also be possible to vary other aspects of the simulation, for example by altering the assumptions about how expectations are formed. However, it should be emphasized that, even for a given set of assumptions, the effects of a change in interest rates are highly uncertain, because of uncertainty about the value of the parameters underlying the model and about the specification of the model itself.
7. The precise figures depend on assumptions concerning the subsequent reactions of the setting of interest rates in response to the evolving inflation rate.
8. The same macroeconometric models are utilized in the ECB (2002e) study as ours, namely, EMM and AWM, with the difference that the ECB study also incorporates the multi-country model of the National Institute of Economic and Social Research (NIGEM). The inclusion of results from the latter does not change in any way the general thrust of the argument.
9. The three estimates being those of AWM, EMM and NIGEM (see note 18).
10. Anecdotal evidence has also been propounded to make the IT case. Bernanke (2003b) suggests that 'central banks that have switched to inflation targeting have generally been pleased with the results they have obtained. The strongest evidence on that score is that, thus far at least, none of the several dozen adopters of inflation targeting has abandoned this approach' (p. 1).
11. It is actually viewed by Neumann and von Hagen (2002) as evidence of 'convergence', in that, on average, IT countries converge to the inflation rates of the non-IT countries in the targeting period.
12. It could also be added that there is no attempt to control other variables such as credit availability.

5.   Does the stock of money have any causal significance?

1   INTRODUCTION

In the 'new consensus macroeconomics' discussed in earlier chapters, it was evident that the stock of money is seen to operate as a mere residual in the economic process. Others have commented on the absence of the stock of money in many current debates over monetary policy. For example, Laidler (1999) states that 'the Quarterly Projection Model which nowadays provides the analytic background against which Bank [of Canada] policies are designed, includes no variable to represent this crucial aggregate [stock of money]' (p. 1). King (2002) makes the case in even stronger language; he argues that, 'as price stability has become recognised as the central objective of central banks, the attention actually paid to money stock by central banks has declined'. Surprisingly perhaps, 'as central banks became more and more focused on achieving price stability, less and less attention was paid to movements in money. Indeed, the decline of interest in money appeared to go hand in hand with success in maintaining low and stable inflation' (p. 162). This has prompted a number of contributions that, wittingly or perhaps unwittingly, have attempted to 'reinstate' a more substantial role for money.

In this chapter we argue that these attempts to 'reinstate' money in current macroeconomic thinking entails two important implications. The first is that they contradict an important theoretical property of the 'new consensus' macroeconomic model, namely that of dichotomy between the monetary and the real sector. The second is that some of these attempts either fail in terms of their objective or merely reintroduce the problem rather than solving it. We include in the first category the class of models that rely on 'frictions' in credit markets (for example, Bernanke and Gertler, 1999), and in the second category the contributions by Meyer (2001b), McCallum (2001) and Laidler (1999).

We proceed by rehearsing the argument of missing money, along with a number of attempts to 'reinstate' money, and then assess these four attempts to 'reinstate' money (see also Arestis and Sawyer, 2003a).

2 THE OMISSION OF MONEY

In Chapter 2 we summarized the NCM and elaborated on its main features, and argued that an important feature of NCM is the absence of any role for the stock of money. The case was revisited in Chapter 3 in connection with discussion of the Bank of England model, which was viewed as belonging to the NCM theoretical framework. In both instances it was argued that money in this world is merely a residual. An equation relating the stock of money to output, interest rate and inflation could be added which would illustrate the residual nature of the stock of money determined by the demand for money (as is illustrated in the next section). Even so the model contains the neutrality of money property, in that equilibrium values of real variables are independent of the money supply and that inflation is determined by monetary policy (that is, the rate of interest). This is not a surprising result since the money stock is not embedded in the model. But even if the money stock were introduced in terms of a fourth equation representing the demand for money, it would still be the case that money is both a residual and neutral. Inflation is viewed as determined by monetary policy (in the form of the rate of interest) through the route of aggregate demand, namely interest rate changes influence aggregate demand (see equation (2.1)) and aggregate demand influences the rate of inflation (see equation (2.2)).

In the next section we concentrate on the characteristic of the 'new consensus' model that relates to the lack of any causal role for the stock of money. This does not, however, mean that this model rejects all the propositions associated with monetarism (though it appears to involve rejection of any causal role of the stock of money on the rate of inflation). Two of its most important propositions are clearly embedded in the model. The first is that monetary policy determines inflation in that inflation converges to the rate set as the objective of monetary policy. The second is that the level and the growth rate of potential output are not affected by monetary policy. It is still the case that control of inflation is viewed as being in the hands of central banks; we can, thus, 'clearly see the influence of monetarism in the consensus model. Monetarism focused attention on the role of central bank in determining inflation by emphasizing the relation between money and inflation. The consensus model may bypass money, but it has retained the key conclusion that central banks ultimately determine the inflation rate' (Meyer, 2001b, p. 3).

3   FOUR WAYS TO 'REINSTATE' MONEY

3.1   LM and Stable Demand for Money

Meyer (2001b) proposes that, since the new 'consensus' model is underpinned by the relation among money, output and inflation, money can be
'reinstated' by adding a fourth relationship to the set of equations (2.1) to
(2.3) as in Chapter 2 above; this would be the 'old' LM equation. In this way
a fourth variable would be introduced explicitly, the stock of money:[1]

$$M_t = d_0 + d_1 R_1 + d_2 Y_t^g + d_3 E_t(p_{t+1}) + s_3, \qquad (5.1)$$

where M is the stock of money and s_3 represents stochastic shocks.

The author recognizes, however, that adding equation (5.1) to the system
of equations (2.1) to (2.3) of our Chapter 2 does not solve the problem, in that
the 'LM curve ... is not part of the simultaneous structure of the expanded
model' (Meyer, 2001b, p. 3). This simply solves for the stock of money
consistent with the values of output, prices and the interest rate as these are
simultaneously determined by the solution of equations (2.1) to (2.3). In this
scenario, therefore, the role of the LM is merely to identify the stock of
money that the central bank would have to provide given the policy rule and
the shocks to the economy.[2] Under these circumstances, Meyer (2001b) suggests that the 'money supply has become a less interesting, minor endogenous
variable in the story' (p. 4). Concern about the stock of money, though, has
helped to create a consensus that central banks should be responsible for
preventing sustained inflation, but this has not been extended to embrace the
proposition that money has an important causative role in macroeconomic
models or monetary policy.

However, in the same paper, Meyer (2001b) argues that appending an LM
equation such as equation (5.1) to the system of equations (2.1) to (2.3), is
still valid and produces a meaningful way of 'reinstating' money in the new
'consensus' macroeconomic model. It is suggested that, 'if the money demand equation (underlying the LM curve) is stable, there will be a stable
relationship between money and inflation in the long run' (p. 4). Consequently, so long as the demand-for-money equation is stable, a long-run
relationship between money and prices is implicit in the new 'consensus'
model. Under these conditions, 'monitoring money growth has value, even
for central banks that follow a disciplined strategy of adjusting their policy
rate to ongoing economic developments. The value may be particularly important at the extremes: during periods of very high inflation, as in the late
1970s and early 1980s in the United States, and when the policy rate is driven
to zero in deflationary episodes, as in the case of Japan today' (ibid., p. 14).

However, Meyer gives no reason to think that monitoring money growth has value: the amount of money in existence would be determined by demand, and the demand for money depends on current and past values of prices, income and so on. It would then seem that the stock of money does not even have any 'predictive' power, unless it is argued that the demand for money depends on expected future prices and income, in which case the stock of money could be said to contain some information on those expectations (in that those expectations influence the demand for money which in turn determines the stock of money). Even in this case, the stock of money would have no causal effect on future prices and income.

It is clearly the case that, if the demand for money is stable in terms of output, prices and the rate of interest, the growth of stock of money will be closely linked with the growth of prices (inflation); this is derived by differentiating the demand for money equation with respect to time. However, using the demand for money equation would suggest that changes in the stock of money are coincident with or lag behind changes in prices. If, though, expected changes in prices were relevant for the demand for money, a scenario could be envisaged in which actual changes in price lagged changes in demand for money. Nonetheless, the stock of money may be seen as a forward indicator of nominal expenditure when it is recognized that loans are taken out to finance nominal expenditure, and that increases in loans lead to increases in bank deposits and the stock of money.

3.2 A Four-equation Model

McCallum (2001, p. 146) begins by adding equation (5.1) to the system of equations (2.1) to (2.3) but argues that this would be superfluous since the stock of money would not affect the behaviour of Y^g, p and R. It would merely stipulate the amount of money that is needed to implement the policy rule (2.3). There would be no need to specify equation (5.1) in terms of determining Y^g, p and R. However, McCallum argues, it would be wrong to view equations (2.1) to (2.3) without any monetary aggregate. This is so since 'the central bank's control over the one-period nominal interest rate ultimately stems from its ability to control the quantity of base money in existence' (ibid.). In the same contribution, McCallum argues that this could be seen from equations (2.1) to (2.3). Taking the case where $Y^g = 0$, and assuming the absence of smoothing, so that $c_3 = 0$, we would have from equation (5.1) that $[R_t - E_t(p_{t+1})] = a_0/a_3$, so that, from equation (2.3), we may derive (2.3'):

$$a_0/a_3 = r^e + c_2(p_t - p^T). \tag{2.3'}$$

Consequently, if the central bank sets the equilibrium real rate of interest, r^e, at a_0/a_3, then actual inflation will be equal to the central bank's target value p^T. The upshot is that the rate of inflation is determined by central bank behaviour: specifically the target rate of inflation is achieved through the setting of the real rate of interest at the equilibrium rate (this assumes, of course, that the central bank does not misestimate the equilibrium real rate of interest, thereby setting the interest rate inappropriately with resulting rising or falling inflation). The Phillips curve parameters are of no consequence for the underlying rate of inflation, so that inflation appears as a monetary-policy phenomenon rather than a non-monetary phenomenon governed by the Phillips curve, or, indeed, a stock (or quantity) of money phenomenon. The model reflects current practice in macroeconomic policy. Monetary policy is seen to influence inflation via aggregate demand. An alternative policy regime could be one where fiscal policy was used to influence aggregate demand, and thereby the rate of inflation. Equation (2.3), reflecting monetary policy, would be replaced by an equation in which fiscal policy is adjusted according to deviation of inflation from target and output from trend level. In such a case, inflation would be a fiscal policy phenomenon.

In view of these characteristics, McCallum (2001) proposes a four-equation system with the addition of a demand for money equation and the inclusion of the stock of money. His precise model differs in a few respects from the model presented above (for example, he includes a term involving government expenditure minus expected government expenditure in equation (2.1), and does not include interest rate smoothing in equation (2.3); that is, he treats c_3 as zero). However, we can represent his amendment in the following way:

$$Y_t^g = a_0 + a_1(Y_{t-1}^g) + a_2 E(Y_{t+1}^g) - a_3[R_t - E_t(p_{t+1})] \\ + a_4[m_t - E_t(m_{t+1})] + s_1, \tag{2.1'}$$

$$p_t = b_1 Y_t^g + b_2(p_{t-1}) + b_3 E_t(p_{t+1}) + s_2, \tag{2.2}$$

$$R_t = RR^* + E_t(p_{t+1}) + c_1 Y_{t-1}^g + c_2(p_t - p^T) + c_3 R_{t-1}, \tag{2.3}$$

$$m_t = m_0 - m_1 \rho_t + m_2 y_t + s_3, \tag{5.1'}$$

where m is the logarithm of M (real value of stock of money), ρ is the logarithm of R, y is the logarithm of actual output, and interest rate smoothing is assumed so that now c_3 is different from zero. Equation (5.1') is the result of an optimization procedure, where the elasticity of the demand for money with respect to ρ is constant, and is equal to 1 with respect to spending, proxied here by output. McCallum (2001), then, asks the question whether the inclusion of $[m_t - E(m_{t+1})]$ in equation (5.1') provides vital information which would otherwise be missing, thereby biasing the results. The theoretical justification is based on the proposition that the size of money holdings has an impact on transaction costs. An unexpected increase (decrease) in money balances lowers (increases) transaction costs, thereby affecting expenditure. This would lead to a positive sign for the coefficient a_4.[3] Calibration analysis is utilized which demonstrates that 'although it is theoretically incorrect to specify a model without money, the magnitude of the error thereby introduced is extremely small' (ibid., pp. 149–50). This is a finding that is consistent with those of Ireland (2001), whose econometric estimates of a parameter similar to a_3 are statistically insignificant. These results support the widely held view that a term like $[m_t - E(m_{t+1})]$ in an aggregate expenditure relationship performs poorly at the empirical and theoretical level (see, for example, King, 2002).

McCallum's (2001) overall conclusion is that 'policy analysis in models without money, based on interest rate policy rules, is not fundamentally misguided'. However, the author is adamant that these policy rules are not necessarily 'preferable to ones based on a controllable monetary aggregate, such as total reserves or the monetary base' (p. 157).

3.3 Passive Money and Active Money Views

The third view comes from Laidler (1999), where a distinction is drawn between a passive money view and an active money view of endogenous money. In both views money is endogenous but with an important difference.[4] It is only the passive money view that is consistent with the theoretical framework described by equations (2.1) to (2.3). In the passive money view, money supply is treated as having no role to play in the determination of output and inflation. This corresponds to the horizontal LM case within the IS/LM framework. It may be noted in passing, though, that the LM is horizontal here not because of the operation of any liquidity trap (which is associated with the demand for money) but rather through the central bank maintaining a given rate of interest, and providing whatever reserves are demanded at that rate of interest. Under these circumstances the rate of interest, rather than the money supply, is the policy variable under the control of the monetary authority. The LM becomes horizontal at the rate of interest set by the monetary authority, and with given IS aggregate demand is determined. The supply of money passively adjusts to accommodate the demand for money. Inflationary targeting requirements and an expectations-augmented Phillips curve complete the story; hence equations (2.1) to (2.3). Open economy considerations require the authorities to opt for a flexible exchange rate regime, although it must be said that the 'new consensus' assumes away the complexities of the open economy model. It is essentially a closed economy model. Clearly, in this framework, money has no active, causal, role.

The active money view retains the traditional causative significance of money supply with respect to output and inflation. Money, it is argued, still has a powerful causal effect on output and inflation. This view begins by recognizing that the transmission mechanism of the passive money view as expressed in equations (2.1) to (2.3) is incomplete in that it ignores the role of credit. A change in the rate of interest produces a change in the borrowing needs of the non-bank public. This change affects the money holdings required to finance purchases of goods, services and assets. Economic agents are thus off their demand for money: in the passive money view, economic agents move along their demand for money, they are never off it. A qualification may be added to the argument at this juncture. Individuals should be seen as 'forced' off their demand for money schedule only if the amount of money they hold goes outside the range that they had set for the buffer stock. Hence a relatively small increase in the stock of money would not 'force' individuals off their demand curve.

This is the *buffer stock* idea of money demand, the idea that money holdings constitute a target of an inventory. The level of buffer stock is subjected to fluctuations around the target, as income and expenditure are influenced by shocks of all types.[5] A relevant shock is a change in the aggregate money supply, not initially matched by a change in the target money holdings. To the extent that this is a *permanent* change, economic agents would hold stocks of real money balances whose implicit service yield is different from that on other assets. A significant change in the size of the buffer stock will thus ensue. This requires a change in one or more of the variables in the demand for money (rates of return, including own rate, opportunity cost of holding money, output and the price level), change to bring the quantity of money demanded into equilibrium with the new money supply. Consequently, 'the quantity of money is an endogenous variable in the economic system, but it clearly plays an active role in the transmission mechanism' (Laidler, 1999, p. 10). The ultimate outcome of this process is very difficult to gauge. Indeed, Laidler suggests 'there seems virtually no limit to the possibilities, a sure sign of some deficiency in our theoretical understanding of the matters under discussion' (ibid., p. 11).

The usual analysis runs in terms of the effects of an increase in the requirement for loans to finance new investment, but once the investment has occurred, savings and profits are generated and some or all of the loans are paid off. Laidler considers a different case where there is a permanent increase in the demand for loans: it could be said for loans to fund investment rather than for loans to finance investment. As Laidler indicates, an increase in loans requires a corresponding increase in bank deposits. A new equilibrium will be reached when banks are willing to meet the increased demand for loans, when the public is willing to hold the increased bank deposits and the banks are willing to allow the public to hold increased deposits. Tracing the effects of the increased demand for loans is complex in that it requires some assumption as to why there is an increased demand for loans (what are people going to do with those loans which have a cost?) and how relative interest rates (on loans, bank deposits and other financial assets) adjust to bring equality between demand and supply of loans and demand and supply of bank deposits. When there is a disequilibrium and there is not an equality between the amount of bank deposits in existence and the public's willingness to hold bank deposits, it could be said that bank deposits (money) are playing an active role, in that steps are being taken to adjust holding of money to that which is desired. However, the underlying cause in this story is the change in the demand for loans: without that change, the stock of money would not change.

The empirical evidence on these views of money is also deficient. Vector error-correction modelling (VECM) using Canadian data has been utilized to disentangle the theoretical intricacies discussed in this subsection (Hendry, 1995). Two relevant conclusions are pertinent: money plays an active role in the transmission mechanism but there is also a 'non-trivial passive element to money's role in that mechanism' (Laidler, 1999, p. 14).

3.4 Credit Market 'Frictions'

The approach labelled here 'credit market frictions' is developed within a rather different perspective, namely from a focus on the operation of banks, the creation of loans and thereby the creation of bank deposits. This approach has been developed in connection with the relationship between asset prices and the real economy (Bernanke and Gertler, 1999). The relationship is made operational through the 'balance sheet channel'. It relies on two major assumptions. The first is that the ratios of capital to assets and debt to assets are important. The second is that credit markets are characterized by 'frictions', such as 'problems of information, incentives, and enforcement in credit relationships' (ibid., p. 87). An important implication of these credit market imperfections is that borrowers with strong financial backing can obtain credit more readily and at lower cost than otherwise. Credit market 'frictions' imply that cash flows and balance-sheet positions are key determinants of agents' ability to borrow and lend.

The existence of credit market 'frictions' implies that firms and households use some of their assets as collateral in the borrowing activities in order to ameliorate the 'frictions' referred to above. Consequently, these 'frictions' create an environment where external finance is more expensive than internal finance when the former is not covered by collateral. This defines what is labelled as the 'external finance premium', namely the difference between the cost of funds raised externally and the opportunity cost of funds internal to the firm. This premium affects the overall cost of capital, thereby affecting invest- ment decisions and aggregate demand; and as Bernanke *et al.* (1999) put it, 'In short, when credit markets are characterised by asymmetric information and agency problems, the Modigliani–Miller irrelevance theorem no longer applies' (p. 4). Under such circumstances a change in asset values can potentially have substantial effects. For example, a decline in asset values reduces available collateral which impedes potential borrowers' access to credit. At the same time, lenders' ratio of capital to assets is reduced, thereby decreasing potential lending and/or discriminating against certain bank-dependent sectors such as small business. The inevitable impact of deteriorating balance sheets and re- duced credit flows is primarily on spending and, thus, on aggregate demand in the short run. In the long run, aggregate supply may very well be affected since capital formation is adversely influenced, along with working capital. These are also accompanied by significant multiplier effects, referred to as the 'financial accelerator' that affects output dynamics (Bernanke and Gertler, 1989; see, also, Bernanke *et al.*, 1996, 1999). 'Financial accelerator' also includes feed- back effects on asset prices, emanating from declining spending and income along with forced asset sales, thereby producing 'debt deflation'.

Generally speaking, the 'financial accelerator' mechanism relies on endog- enous developments in credit markets that work to propagate and amplify shocks to the macro economy. The mechanism in this context relies heavily on the link between the 'external finance premium' and the net worth of potential borrowers, defined as 'the borrowers' liquid assets, plus collateral value of illiquid assets less outstanding obligations' (Bernanke *et al.*, 1999, p. 4). In the presence of credit market 'frictions', the 'external finance pre- mium' is inversely related to the net worth of borrowers. The lower the net worth of borrowers and thus the weaker their ability to provide collateral, the higher the required agency costs, so that lenders must be compensated for higher agency costs, implying a higher 'external finance premium'. The whole process, however, is highly non-linear, in that 'if balance sheets are initially strong, with low leverage and strong cash flows, then even rather large declines in asset prices are unlikely to push households and firms into the region of financial distress, in which normal access to credit is jeopard- ised, or to lead to severe capital problems for banks. Put another way, the extent to which an asset-price contraction weakens private sector balance sheets depends on the degree and sectoral distribution of initial risk exposure' (Bernanke and Gertler, 1999, p. 84).

The quantitative aspects of this approach are revealing. Bernanke *et al.* (1999) undertake calibration exercises of the model that includes credit mar- ket 'frictions' and the 'financial accelerator' effect of an unanticipated 25-basis point decline in the nominal interest rate strongly supports the model's key contentions. More concretely, the output response is about 50 per cent greater, and the investment response nearly twice as great, in the model with the credit market factors than in the baseline model that excludes them. The persistence of these effects is also substantially greater, with 'output and investment in the model with credit-market imperfections after four quarters are about where they are in the baseline model after only two quarters' (ibid., p. 35). A further important result of the same study is 'the tendency for policy effects to linger even after interest rates have returned to normal' (p. 36).

The relevant question in this context is the extent to which this model is amenable to embedding the stock of money within it in such a way that the stock of money has a causal role. To begin with, the credit market 'frictions' model does not explicitly discuss the stock of money. The model includes bank deposits only and households hold these, which are matched by loans held by businesses. At the aggregate level, bank deposits equal bank loans so that the net worth of the private sector is unchanged by changes in bank deposits. Now, as has been seen earlier, the role of net worth relative to capital stock is particularly stressed in this model. It is the case then that households hold the base money, which is created by the central bank, and consequently that does not affect the net worth of firms. In Bernanke *et al.* (1999), households hold 'base' money (issued by the government), but the government funds its budget deficit such that sufficient 'base' money is supplied to satisfy the demand for money (which is related to consumer expenditure and the nominal rate of interest). Hence the stock of 'base' money can be viewed as endogenously determined by the demand for money. The stock of money can still be seen as relevant in this context when money is seen as one of many assets, and as such it is part of the 'collateral', and both households and firms need to hold the asset labelled 'money', although the implication is that the stock of anything that can serve as 'collateral' could be relevant. It ought to be noted, however, that if money here is base money, then the model would need changing to explain why banks would hold base money (a barren asset) other than for transactions demand purposes. If money is bank deposits, for collateral purposes it would need to be netted out against loans, and since it is assumed that households hold deposits and not loans (or at least households hold more deposits than loans), firms have negative net worth vis-à-vis the banks, and an increase in the stock of money would reduce their wealth, which would tend to deflate demand. There is, further, the question of why firms would use money as a collateral, rather than use the money to finance whatever expenditure they wished to undertake. It would have to be assumed that banks were willing to lend firms a multiple of their holdings of money, but for the banks that would be close to unsecured lending.

4   MODEL ASSESSMENT

The aim of this section is to ascertain whether the treatment of money undertaken succeeds in 'reinstating' it in the sense of having a causal role in the respective models. We also examine the implications for the main theoretical aspects of the 'new consensus' model as discussed in Chapter 2.

We begin with the Meyer (2001b), 'LM and Stable Demand for Money', contribution. The thrust of the argument in this approach falls squarely on the stability of the demand for money. But even if the demand for money is stable, it would still be the case in this approach that the stock of money is demand-determined, and the demand for money depends on current and past values of prices, income and so on. However, the whole point of the 'new consensus' on monetary policy is that the demand for money relationship has been shown to be sufficiently unstable to render monetary policy in the form of monetary targeting uncertain. It is also the case that the degree of this uncertainty is made even worse by the fact that the channels through which monetary targeting works its potential impact through the economy is by far more indirect than that of the monetary policy operating rule of equation (2.3). It is thus the case that Meyer (2001b) does not offer a satisfactory solution to the problem in hand; it merely restates it. Furthermore, Clarida *et al.* (1999) demonstrate that 'Large unobservable shocks to money demand produce high volatility of interest rates when a monetary aggregate is used as the policy instrument. It is largely for this reason that an interest rate instrument may be preferable' (p. 1687). This is particularly the case when narrow monetary aggregates are used, though broad monetary aggregates are also of little use. Their relationship with aggregate economic activity variables is too unstable to be of any usefulness. It is for this very reason that most, if not all, of major central banks' models do not even include a monetary aggregate of any form.[6] Not only are the shocks just referred to the cause of high interest rate volatility, but they occur quite frequently. The global monetary history of the last 30 to 40 years clearly testifies to this statement. It thus becomes difficult to sustain the argument that the demand-for-money relationship can be reasonably stable for a sufficient period of time to make it possible, and sensible, to rely on monetary aggregates. We are back to the original question of how to 'reinstate' money in a macroeconomic model.

McCallum's (2001) contribution is an attempt to introduce the stock of money directly into equation (2.1), which then requires a fourth equation to explain that stock. The key assumption in McCallum's framework is that of a tight relationship between the stock of money and the size of transaction costs. For example, a higher volume of the stock of money lowers transaction costs and enhances consumption expenditure. The trouble with the propositions of this approach, however, is that they 'do not appear to be empirically significant nor do they correspond to the main channels of policy as seen by earlier generations of economists' (King, 2002, p. 171).

It should be noted that McCallum (2001) treats the stock of money as created by the central bank, and assumes that the central bank may either set the interest rate or determine the stock of money. His utility maximization framework is set up in terms of an exogenously determined stock of money. The link between the rate of interest and the stock of money is said to come (p. 148, equation 18) from the Fisher identity between nominal interest rate, real rate and the (expected) rate of inflation. This enables McCallum to say that the roles of nominal interest rate and stock of money can be reversed, and the stock of money treated as endogenous and the (nominal) rate of interest as exogenous. But the stock of money is here only endogenous in the sense that its rate of growth, assumed to be equal to the expected rate of inflation, is linked with (equal to) the difference between the nominal rate of interest and the (equilibrium) real rate of interest. There is no discussion of which definition of money is appropriate here – monetary base (relevant to the central bank), narrow money (such as M1, relevant for transactions purposes) or broad money – but the implication of endogeneity is clear.

In Laidler's (1999) contribution it is stated that the monetarist case 'calls for the authorities to set a course for *a supply of money determined independently of the demand for it*, it treats money as an *active* variable in the transmission mechanism of monetary policy' (p. 3). When money is bank money created through the granting of loans, there is a stage at which the supply of money (stock of money) is independent of the demand for it. There is then some adjustment process through which the supply (stock) and the demand are reconciled. If by assumption (that the demand for loans has permanently increased) the stock of money (bank deposits) increases and cannot be diminished, adjustments will follow which could be said to involve the stock of money. However, it has to be remembered that the stock of money will not remain higher unless the demand for loans remains higher. Money is created through the loan creation process, and that money will be spent (that being the purpose of securing the loan) and will be accepted (money being a generally accepted medium of exchange). In general, those receiving the money will not wish to retain it (money being a barren asset) but will wish to dispose of it in some way, whether through spending, repayment of loans or purchase of financial assets. Only in that limited sense can money play an active role.

Turning to the fourth approach considered above, King (2002) seeks to use the idea that money can alleviate frictions in the financial markets to restore the causal role of money. That money can alleviate 'frictions' in financial markets emanates crucially from its ability to provide liquidity to the financial system in general and financial markets in particular. King argues that

'Money enables individuals, both households and firms, to avoid borrowing should they hit a cash-flow constraint. Since the probability of experiencing such a constraint falls as the stock of money rises, changes in money could affect relative asset returns' (ibid., p. 172). Money is one of many assets, and changes in its quantity can have an important effect via its impact on borrowers' balance sheets. However, one person's bank deposit is another person's loan, and the possession of a loan raises the probability of having to borrow. A further qualification to King's (2002) argument is that it does not state how the change in the money stock occurs. It seems to resort to an exogenous money argument for, in an endogenous context, some change in 'tastes' will lead to changes in prices (rates of return) and in quantities.

However, when 'credit market frictions' are considered, it would seem that monetary policy can have effects on real activity in both the short run and the long run. Quite simply, credit rationing affects the firms' (and others') ability to carry through expenditure decisions, including those on investment. Thereby investment expenditure is influenced by monetary policy, and hence the future level and structure of productive capacity. Evidence has been produced that shows that the monetary policy in the form of interest rate changes may have effects on real activity (Bernanke et al., 1997). We have indicated above, in Chapter 4, that monetary policy in the form of interest rate changes has a stronger impact on investment than on other types of expenditure. There is, however, dispute as to the precise amount and the extent of its impact: are there short-term effects only (Clarida et al., 1999) or long-run effects as well (as we argued above)?

The last conclusion is actually supported by the 'new consensus' approach. For example, Bernanke and Gertler (1999) are very clear when they argue that 'Deteriorating balance sheets and reduced credit flows operate primarily on spending and aggregate demand in the short run, although in the longer run they may also affect aggregate supply by inhibiting capital formation and reducing working capital. There are also likely to be significant feedback and magnification effects' (pp. 82–3). These conclusions are significant for the purposes of this chapter. Recall that two propositions, that monetary policy determines inflation only, and that the level and growth rate of potential output are not affected by monetary policy, are at the heart of the 'new consensus'. The analysis we have just conducted clearly suggests that monetary policy influences not just inflation but also long-run output through effects on investment. Indeed, the level of and growth of potential output can be affected by the analysis afforded by the credit market 'frictions' as elaborated above. The theoretical dimension of the 'new consensus', therefore, may have to be recouched and reformulated to account for these theoretical implications. Clearly, though, the credit market 'frictions' argument would also have to be revised to account for the changes suggested above if money is to be firmly reinstated within the confines of this model.

The argument could be put forward that Laidler's (1999) notion of active money would fit in with the approach of Bernanke and Gertler (1999) in the following sense. What Laidler (1999) would identify as active money, Bernanke and Gertler (1999) would think of as liquidity that removes credit constraints. It also seems to be the case that in both approaches it is entirely ignored that there are two sides to the balance sheet, so that, when the stock of money is high, the stock of loans outstanding is also high, in that at least collectively people have taken out loans that would enable them to spend. It might also mean that, when the stock of money is high, there are credit limits (as the stock of loans is high). It might also mean that, when the stock of money is high, the stock of loans is also high, but still credit limits prevail.

5 SUMMARY AND CONCLUSIONS

In this chapter we have examined a number of attempts to reinstate money essentially in this macroeconomic model. These attempts have been found either to fail in their objective or to be accompanied by serious theoretical implications. It has been argued that the latter approach is promising, especially in terms of its implications, namely that the impact of monetary policy can have both real and nominal effects.

We may conclude with a brief comment on the nature and role of money in the economy. When money is viewed as exogenous money, the supply of money is a macroeconomic phenomenon, in that there is one agency (usually government or central bank) that determines the level of the stock of money for the whole economy. The supply of money cannot be disaggregated into the supply of money by individual economic agents. Individuals have a demand for money, and the developments in the economy depend on how the sum of the individuals' demand for money compares with the given stock of money.

In an endogenous money approach, money is bank credit money, which is created during the loan expansion process.[7] The creation of money depends on the willingness of banks to grant loans and of the public to take out loans: the continuing existence of money depends on banks' willingness to accept bank deposits and the willingness of the public to hold bank deposits. In the endogenous money approach, there is a 'supply of money' by individual banks (which is more accurately a willingness to allow deposits to be held) that can be summed to give an overall supply of money. Further, the stock of money changes as a consequence of other changes that are taking place, the clearest example being that, when the stock of loans changes, there will be changes in the stock of bank deposits. The recent developments on monetary policy, some of which have been summarized in this study, deal with money as if it were endogenous, but without labelling it as such and, more seriously, without providing relevant theoretical arguments for the endogeneity of money.

We would suggest that a fruitful way forward is to develop theoretical arguments on the premise of endogenous money, and to study the process of credit creation (and thereby the creation of bank deposits) rather than just model the stock of money as a residual. This would also have to analyse the credit system, and explain how the demand for loans is (or is not) satisfied by the banks. Such an approach would be more fruitful and would, indeed, provide a more promising attempt to deal with monetary phenomena.

NOTES

1. We prefer to use the term 'stock of money', rather than 'money supply', here in that the term supply of money implies that the amount of money is determined by the suppliers of money. In this context, the argument is that equation (5.1) is based on a demand for money approach, with the added assumption that the stock of money is determined by the demand for money.
2. If stock of money is interpreted as M1 (or a broader definition of money), then this should be interpreted as the amount of money which the central bank would have to ensure that the banks provide.
3. There are other theoretical arguments for the inclusion of $[m_t - E(m_{t+1})]$ in equation (2.1′), in addition to transaction costs emphasized in McCallum (2001). These arguments are summarized in Leahy (2001, pp. 161–2), and include non-separable utility, utility constraints, cash-in-advance constraints, segmentation of the goods and assets markets, and the lending view.
4. There is a sharp distinction between endogeneity and exogeneity on the one hand and passive and active views on money on the other hand. The passive and active views on money are actually based on the proposition that money is endogenous in any case. Laidler (1999, section 3) is very explicit on the importance and precise distinction of these notions.
5. These shocks range from economy-wide to localized shocks, foreseen and unforeseen, as well as transitory and permanent. The analysis in the text assumes permanent shocks; transitory shocks are unlikely to have any significant effects in that, by their very nature, it is expected that they are quickly reversed. Brunner and Meltzer (1993) argue for the relative importance of the transitory versus permanent shocks distinction, in relation to that between economy-wide and localized shocks.
6. This is certainly the case for the models of the Bank of England, the European Central Bank and the Federal Reserve System.
7. For discussion of endogenous money approach see Cottrell (1994) and Howells (1995); for the implications for monetary policy see Chapter 7 below.

6.   The inflationary process

1   INTRODUCTION

It can be readily seen from our previous discussion of the NCM (especially Chapter 2) that the view of inflation within the NCM is one of 'demand pull' only. The simple model used in Chapter 2 drew heavily on the reduced form of the Phillips curve in which price inflation was linked to output (relative to trend) and expected inflation, and hence with demand. In this chapter we outline what we see as a more suitable framework for the analysis of the 'inflationary process'. In our perspective on inflation, demand and changes in demand have a role to play, but there are other important ingredients, notably the role of cost and distributional pressures, imported inflation, the size of productive capacity and endogenous money. These other ingredients are of equal, if not of greater, importance in our understanding of the 'inflationary process'.

Another important ingredient of the NCM approach is the assertion of a supply-side equilibrium level of output (or, equivalently, employment) which is unaffected by the path of the economy. This may be seen by reference to equation (2.2) in Chapter 2, where a zero output gap corresponds to this supply-side equilibrium. This generates the significant conclusion that deflationary policies (whether designed to reduce inflation or used for other purposes) do not have any long-lasting impact on the level (or growth) of output.

The nature of the supply-side equilibrium is also of considerable relevance for economic performance and economic policy. The question may be posed as to what are the factors which determine the supply-side equilibrium, and specifically what factors determine the volume of employment associated with that supply-side equilibrium. It is not readily apparent in the 'stripped down' version of the NCM approach presented in Chapter 2 that the labour market is seen as playing the key role in the determination of the supply-side equilibrium. A relationship such as equation (2.2) (see Chapter 2) is often referred to as the Phillips curve, and the origin of the Phillips curve was a 'trade-off' between wage changes and unemployment. The rate of unemployment at which real wages would be constant (and hence wage inflation equal to expected price inflation) has often, following Friedman (1968), been labelled the 'natural rate of unemployment'. In Friedman's original paper, and in much subsequent work, the determinants of the 'natural rate of unemployment' are seen to relate to the labour market. These have been given a number of meanings, ranging from the form and extent of trade union power and influence, to the setting of minimum wages, and to the operation of unemployment benefits and so on. Thus the view has been formed that the supply-side equilibrium depends on the labour market, and that measures to make the labour market more 'flexible', and thus less 'regulated', will lower the 'equilibrium' rate of unemployment.

In this chapter we present a rather different analysis of the macro economy; it is one that we utilize in the chapters that follow. The significant implications which we draw out of our analysis are the following:

- the pace of inflation cannot be associated with a single factor (such as demand) but rather arises from interactions between a range of factors: in our analysis this range of factors includes the level of productive capacity, the struggle over income shares, the level and rate of change of output and the international inflationary environment;
- what may be viewed as a supply-side equilibrium position, that is one consistent with a constant rate of inflation, depends on the scale of the capital stock (and therefore productive capacity) and hence is constantly changing as investment occurs, changing the capital stock;
- there are no strong market forces which push the economy towards that 'equilibrium position'.

We begin this chapter by elaborating on the key elements of this structuralist view of inflation, supplemented by an investment relationship that completes the picture. An attempt to draw out the implications of the structuralist analysis to the inflationary process is then provided. This is followed by a discussion of a number of empirical questions, before we conclude this chapter.

2   SOME KEY ELEMENTS OF A STRUCTURALIST VIEW

There are three key aspects of the structuralist view of inflation, namely the role of endogenous money, the determination of prices and the determination of wages, and these are now discussed in turn.

Endogenous Money

Inflation cannot be fully discussed without some reference to money. The view of inflation and money advanced here (and indeed, though not generally recognized, in the NCM model) is that inflation (and notably changes in the rate of inflation) arises from what may be termed 'real factors' and that the stock of money expands alongside the rise in prices. As we have seen above, and discuss further below, in Chapter 7, money is endogenous credit money created by the banking system, and comes into existence through the loan process, and the extent of money creation depends on the demand for loans and the willingness of banks to satisfy that demand. Rising prices will require firms and others to seek loans to cover the rising cost of inputs and so on, and higher prices raise the demand for money. The stock of money and prices rise broadly in line and at the same rate, but the causation is seen to run from prices, or nominal income more generally, to money.

In the exogenous money story, it is the rate of increase of the money supply which drives the inflationary process, and the precise mechanisms of price and wage determination may not be particularly significant in the inflationary process. In effect price and wage determination may be the conduit of inflation, but inflation is seen to arise from 'excessive' monetary growth. But when money is treated as endogenous, and the changes in the stock of money arise from the inflationary process itself, it is necessary to give attention to the price and wage determination processes.

The endogeneity of money is an important element in the analysis of the inflationary process since it leads to the notion that inflation is not caused by expansion of money, though the expansion of money will occur alongside inflation. Further, the endogeneity of money is also important for the rest of the analysis conducted in this book. Consequently, money is given prominence not merely in this chapter but in the rest of the book. It is for this reason that the coverage of this key aspect is rather short in this chapter.

Pricing

There are many ways in which firms set their prices: the ways may vary according to the nature of the industry and markets in which they operate, to their own objectives and organization and so on. (Sawyer, 1983; Lee, 1998). However, there is a broad similarity amongst these various theories of pricing, in that there is the general view that price is set by reference to the level of average costs, which can be summarized as price is set as a mark-up over average costs. If we write this general view as

$$p = [1 + m(cu)] \cdot (lc + mc), \tag{6.1}$$

where p is price, m is a mark-up which depends on capacity utilization (the presumption being that, at high levels of capacity utilization, firms will be able to set a higher mark-up), lc is unit labour costs, and mc unit material costs.

It has often been assumed that enterprises operate subject to (approximately) constant average direct costs and with significant excess capacity so that further expansion can be undertaken without costs (and presumably prices) rising. This 'stylized fact' has often been invoked to explain some degree of price constancy with respect to the level of demand, and evidence (for example Sawyer, 1983) supports the view that price changes are little related with the level of (or changes in) demand. However, the view that average direct costs are broadly constant would add up to the point of full capacity, after which average costs may rise rapidly.

The pace of price increases would then be seen to depend on a combination of the pace of cost increases (actual and anticipated) and the rate of change of capacity utilization. At the level of the individual firm, at least, price inflation arises from cost inflation. It should be further noted that the level of capacity utilization (which would reflect, inter alia, the level of demand) is viewed as influencing the level of prices, and hence the rate of change of prices would be influenced by the rate of change of capacity utilization (and hence rate of change of aggregate demand). This, of course, stands in contrast to the view of the Phillips curve, which stresses the effects of the level of demand (as reflected in, for example, the level of unemployment) on the rate of inflation.

The general view of price inflation, which follows from equation (6.1), is that the rate of price change depends on the rate of change of costs and of capacity utilization. One further element could be added, namely a catch-up effect. Equation (6.1) can be read to indicate the price that a firm desires to charge if it had full information. But price is typically set ahead to transactions as the price at which the firm wishes to trade, and then the firm sells whatever is demanded at the price, which it has set. Mistakes can, of course, be made: the firm may misestimate cost changes, make mistakes in forecasting demand and so on. In any decision period, then, the firm's pricing decision depends on estimates of cost and demand change, and some catch-up (or catch-down) of price. This can be written as

$$\dot{p} = a_0\dot{w} + a_1\dot{f} + a_2c\dot{u} + a_3\{p(-1)/[lc(-1) + mc(-1)] - R\}, \qquad (6.2)$$

where $R = 1 + m(cu)$ is the desired mark-up of the firm (in light of the demand conditions which it faces), and a dot over a variable indicates proportionate rate of change of the variables concerned.

Both equation (6.1) and equation (6.2) can now be further utilized. Equation (6.1) can be expanded and rearranged to give an equation for the real product wage (at the level of the firm). This is

$$\frac{w}{p} = \frac{1}{1+m(cu)}\frac{1}{l}mc \cdot \frac{1}{l}, \qquad (6.3)$$

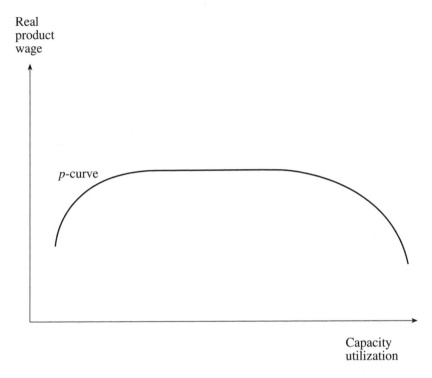

Real
product
wage

p-curve

Capacity
utilization

Figure 6.1   The p-curve

where *l* is amount of labour per unit of output. This is portrayed in Figure 6.1. Using equation (6.2) we can also envisage that, for points above the line, prices will tend to rise faster than wages (as indicated) and conversely for points below the line.

Each point on the curve labelled '*p*-curve' in Figure 6.1 (which would be a point on the line of equation (6.3)) corresponds to a particular level of demand facing the firm. As a result of that level of demand, the firm selects a price (which best serves its interests), and the level of capacity utilization is a result of that level of demand. The relationship in equation (6.3) is between real product wage and capacity utilization. For a given capital stock this can be translated into a relationship between real product wage and output (or employment).

Figure 6.2 portrays an aggregate relationship between employment and real wage. To derive the aggregate level relationship we can proceed as follows. For a given level of demand, there would be a specific point on the *p*-curve of each individual firm, indicating a specific real product wage and level of capacity utilization and of output. Form the weighted average of the real product wage

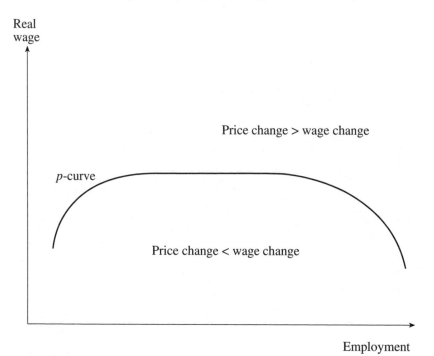

Figure 6.2   The p-*curve: wage and price pressures*

of each firm to form the overall real wage. Add together the level of output of each firm to give the aggregate level of output. Repeat the exercise for a different level of demand to map out the aggregate relationship.

Three points stand out regarding the aggregate relationship as portrayed in Figure 6.2. The first is that the position of the *p*-curve depends on the capital stock of the economy. The relationship between price and wage depends on capacity utilization but, the greater is overall capacity, the greater can output be. An increase in the number of firms (and hence in capacity) in the economy would shift the *p*-curve to the right: more individual *p*-curves are being added together to generate the aggregate relationship.

The second point is that the pace of price inflation depends on a variety of factors. These include cost pressures, whether from wages or from materials, which would include the effects of exchange rate and world prices on imported prices, the rate of change of capacity utilization and attempts by firms to restore profit margins.

The third is that the 'height' of the *p*-curve depends on the mark-up which firms can extract and that may be summarized as reflecting the degree of market power of firms. The more market power they possess, the higher would be the mark-up, and the lower the real product wage (and hence the lower would be the *p*-curve).

In Figure 6.2 we have also indicated the presumed price dynamics.

Wage Determination

There are numerous views as to how wages are determined (and also numerous wages in which wages are actually determined). Our approach differs substantially from those that view wages as set in a competitive labour market. At least in terms of the algebraic representation of the equilibrium relationship between real wages and employment, many of the approaches that are compatible with ours lead to similar outcomes; for example, trade union bargaining models, efficiency wage models (for more details see Sawyer, 2002, and Layard *et al.*, 1991, especially chs 8 and 9).

The approach to wage determination adopted here comes from suggesting that the rate of change of money wages depends on three sets of factors. The first is the general level of price inflation, such that the faster is the anticipated rate of price inflation (which may be much influenced by the recent experience of inflation) the higher will be the claims for money wage increases. This may happen in a one-for-one manner: that is, with each 1 per cent increase in the anticipated rate of inflation leading to a 1 per cent increase in rate of increase of wages.

The second set is the desire by workers to move the current real wage towards some target real wage. The larger is the gap between the target real wage and the current real wage, the greater will be the push by trade unions and others to close the gap. The target real wage can be viewed in terms of the aspirations and expectations of the workers and trade unions, which in turn depend on factors such as real wage resistance, notions of fair wages and so on. A somewhat different perspective on the target real wage would be to view it as the underlying outcome from bargaining between unions and employers.

The third set is the relative power of employees and employers and hence the ability of workers to secure wage increases. The relative power can depend on many factors, including the general political climate, the nature of industrial relations and labour laws and so on. But the macroeconomic factors which stand out in this regard are those related to unemployment, including the rate of unemployment and the rate of change of unemployment.

This target real wage hypothesis (Sargan, 1964; for detailed elaboration, see Sawyer, 1982a, 1982b; Arestis, 1986) is based on a collective bargaining view of wage determination, which can be set out as

$$\dot{w} = a_1 + a_2 \dot{p}_{-1} + a_3 U + a_4 (w_{-1} - p_{-1} - T), \tag{6.4}$$

where dots over variables again indicate rate of change, w is the log of money wages, p is the log of prices, U is rate of unemployment and T is the log of target real wages. The coefficient a_2 may be close to unity, and a_3 and a_4 are signed as negative. The rate of nominal wage increase depends on the rate of inflation, unemployment (reflecting bargaining power) and the difference between actual real wages and target real wages.

The equilibrium relationship when the rate of wage change equals the rate of (lagged) price change is given in the following equation:

$$a_1 + a_3 U + a_4 (w - p - T) = 0, \tag{6.5}$$

assuming for convenience that $a_2 = 1$. Defining unemployment as $U = (L_f - L)/L_f$, where L_f is full employment (assumed given) and L is actual employment, yields

$$\frac{L}{L_f} = \frac{a_1}{a_3} + 1 + \frac{a_4}{a_3}(w - p - T), \tag{6.6}$$

which gives a positive relationship between real wage and employment and is drawn as the w-curve (which reflects the wage determination process) in Figure 6.3. The inflationary dynamics (from equation (6.4)) are such that for points below the w-curve, wages rise faster than prices, and for points above wages rise less rapidly than prices. In terms of Figure 6.3, the position of the w-curve depends on the coefficients a_1, a_4 and the target real wage. In representational terms, any factor which could be viewed as changing one (or more) of those parameters would lead to a shift in the w-curve, and thereby in the inflation barrier.

3   INVESTMENT

The approach to investment is Kaleckian in spirit (cf. Kalecki, 1943), with factors such as profitability and capacity utilisation impacting on investment. The significant aspect of investment is that it is sensitive to the level of aggregate demand, and that there is not an optimal capital stock, which is solely determined by relative prices.

The rate of investment relative to the capital stock K is a positive function of the rate of profit (Π), and capacity utilization (cu):

$$I/K = b_0 + b_1 \Pi + b_2 cu. \tag{6.7}$$

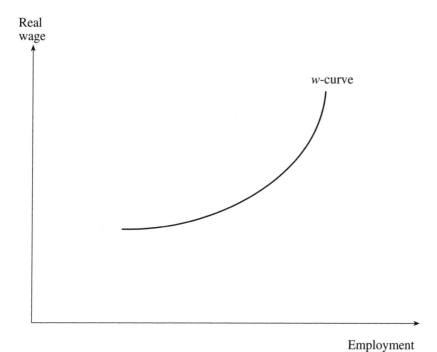

Real
wage

w-curve

Employment

Figure 6.3   The w*-curve*

This can be mapped into a function of real wages and employment to give

$$I/K = b_0 + b_1[1 - (W/P)(L/Y)][Y(L,K)/K] + b_2 Y(L,K)/K, \qquad (6.8)$$

since the share of profits is given by the expression $[1 - (W/P) \cdot (L/Y)]$ and K is a measure of capital stock. In the context of a net investment function and a no-growth economy (or treating all appropriate variables as normalized on the underlying rate of growth), the condition of a constant capital stock gives

$$b_0 + b_1[1 - (W/P)(L/Y)] \cdot [Y(L)/K] + b_2 Y(L)/K = 0, \qquad (6.9)$$

from which a zero (net) investment locus can be obtained which involves a positive relationship between the real wage and employment. Two possible positions of the zero investment locus are drawn in Figure 6.4: *IA* when 'animal spirits' are high and *IB* when they are low (investment is more often positive for *IA* than for *IB*). When aggregate demand is relatively high, the economy would be operating to the right of the zero investment locus: net

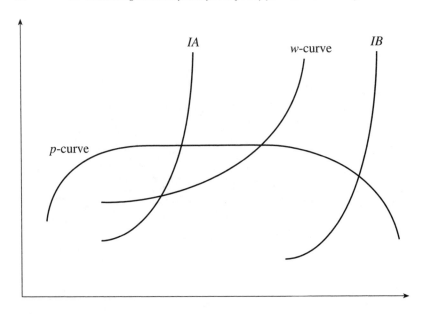

Figure 6.4   The p-*curve and the* w-*curve brought together*

investment is positive, the capital stock is rising and the *p*-curve would be shifting upwards.

It is important that Figure 6.4 is not interpreted in isolation, with some idea that the inflation barrier is a supply-side equilibrium towards which the economy tends. We repeat the point above that there are no automatic forces pushing the economy towards the point where the *p*- and *w*-curves meet each other. Further the course of the economy cannot be understood without reference to the level of aggregate demand. In this context, aggregate demand is important not only in that it determines the level of economic activity (which may have some effect on the rate of inflation), but also through its influence on the rate of investment. The evolution of the capital stock would ensure that the stock of productive capacity changes, and that would be reflected in terms of a shift of the *p*-curve in Figure 6.4. It is also necessary to recall that money is viewed as endogenous, and hence, as inflation proceeds, the stock of money will expand, but there is little point in attempting to control inflation through monetary policy (particularly through control of the money supply); inflation is not a monetary phenomenon.

The level of aggregate demand in this framework can be derived (taking the case of a closed private economy for reasons of simplicity) by equating savings and investment; that is, with a differential savings propensity out of wages and profits, this is

$$b_0 + b_1\left(1 - \left(\frac{W}{P}\right)\left(\frac{L}{Y}\right)\cdot\left(\frac{Y(L)}{K}\right)\right) + b_2\frac{Y(L)}{K} = s_0 + s_1\left(\frac{W}{P}\right)\left(\frac{L}{Y}\right)\left(\frac{Y(L)}{K}\right)$$

$$+ s_2\left(1 - \left(\frac{W}{P}\right)\left(\frac{L}{Y}\right)\left(\frac{Y(L)}{K}\right)\right)$$ (6.10)

This can be rearranged to give

$$(b_0 - s_0)K + (b_1 + b_2 - s_2)\left(\frac{Y}{L}\right) = (s_1 - s_2 + b_1)\frac{W}{P}.$$ (6.11)

The sign of this relationship may be positive or negative: in the terms of the Bhadhuri and Marglin (1990) analysis, it will be positive if there is a stagnationist regime and negative if there is an exhilarationist regime. If the Keynesian stability condition applies, then $b_1 + b_2 - s_2$ will be negative, and hence the sign of the relationship depends on $s_1 - s_2 + b_1$. In Figure 6.5, the *AD* curve represents equation (6.11) under a stagnationist regime: the posi-

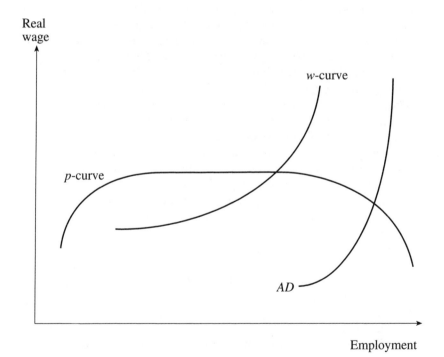

Figure 6.5   The interaction of p- *and* w-*curves*

tion and slope of the *AD* is arbitrary. It illustrates that demand differs from the inflation barrier, and the position of the *AD* curve will influence, in conjunction with the prevailing real wage, the level of economic activity and the pace of inflation.

4   IMPLICATIONS OF STRUCTURALIST ANALYSIS FOR THE INFLATIONARY PROCESS

The general implication of this is that inflationary problems arise when demand runs ahead of capacity, even when there is unemployment of labour, for there may simply be inadequate capacity to support the full employment of labour (or the capacity may be distributed across regions in a way which does not match the distribution of potential workers). When enterprises operate with high levels of capacity, they are faced with rising unit costs: prices rise relative to wages in these circumstances, and hence real wages fall, but money wages cannot catch up with prices to restore the initial real wage. Consequently, in this approach, inflation rises when the level and composition of demand increase past the point where production can increase at around constant costs, and into the range where unit costs are rising (and bottlenecks appearing). Measures such as 'reform of the labour market', are then irrelevant for the level of unemployment and of inflation. It is rather the level, composition and distribution of the capital stock which is relevant for unemployment and inflation.

The second, and related, set of inflationary pressures comes from the inherent conflict over the distribution of income. The ability of the economy to reconcile the conflict depends, inter alia, on the productive capacity of the economy (the 'size of the cake'). The determination of the level of economic activity which corresponds to constant inflation, what we term the 'inflation barrier' (also in the literature on the NAIRU and on the 'natural rate of unemployment'), involves the notion that wages and prices rise together. The difference in the rate of increase of wages and that of prices is equal to the rate of labour productivity growth. In other words, the distribution of income between wages and profits will remain constant. This serves as a reminder that there are basic conflicts over the distribution of income. If all groups and classes in society were in effect content with the existing distribution of income, it could be expected that there would not be a problem of inflation: at a minimum it would mean that the rate of inflation was constant. An increase in inflation can be viewed as arising from some combination of intention of some groups to increase their share of income and enhanced opportunity to do so. A higher level of demand for labour may, for example, be seen as enhanced opportunity for workers to increase their share. But a related higher level of demand for output would allow firms to increase their profits. The 'conflict theory' of inflation can be seen as based on this insight.

The intersection of the *p*-curve and *w*-curve in Figure 6.4 may be thought of as an inflation barrier. This implies that, if the level of aggregate demand pushes the level of economic activity much above the 'inflation barrier' (and particularly if the rise in economic activity is rapid), inflation will tend to rise, *mutatis mutandis*, if the level of aggregate demand pushes the level of economic activity much below the 'inflation barrier'. This does not imply that the economy will operate at or even tend towards the inflation barrier. The level of economic activity will be set by the level of aggregate demand with no market forces tending to move the level of aggregate demand towards the inflation barrier. There may be policy forces, which might be able to do so. For example, to the extent that monetary policy can influence aggregate demand, the latter can be geared towards the inflation barrier. But then the inflation barrier would be constantly changing as investment takes place. There is an in-built form of hysteresis in this approach. This relates to the time path of aggregate demand, which influences investment and the latter in its turn causes changes to the capital stock.

This 'inflation barrier' has some similarities with the non-accelerating inflation rate of unemployment (NAIRU), but there are some important differences, at least of interpretation. The first difference is that the NAIRU approach is generally embedded in a view that the level of demand will adjust to the NAIRU, usually through the operation of some form of the real balance effect.[1] In the approach developed here, since money is treated as endogenous, in which case there is no real balance effect, there appears to be a lack of any market-based forces which lead to aggregate demand adjusting to a level consistent with the inflation barrier. Actions on aggregate demand taken by governments (in the present climate specifically changes in interest rate) may be a mechanism by which aggregate demand moves towards a level consistent with the inflation barrier.

Second, in the NAIRU approach there is a form of separation between the supply side and the demand side of the economy. In contrast here we stress that aggregate demand influences (and is influenced by) the rate of investment, which changes the capital stock, thereby having supply-side effects on productive capacity. This would also imply that the inflation barrier is continuously changing as investment occurs, and there is no implication that the inflation barrier remains unchanged over time. Third, the NAIRU approach has become associated with the idea that the structure of the labour market (notably the degree of rigidity or flexibility, however those terms may be defined) is the major determinant of the size of the NAIRU (and thereby of the level of unemployment). Whilst, as will be indicated below, the conditions of the labour market may have some impact on the inflation barrier, it is not seen as a major determinant.

The level of aggregate demand governs the level of economic activity. As demand fluctuates, so does the level of economic activity. The general experience of unemployment in market economies, along with the observation of substantial disparities in unemployment across economic regions, suggests that aggregate demand is often inadequate to support full employment and/or that there is a lack of productive capacity to employ all those wishing (or having) to work. The level of economic activity thus depends on the level of aggregate demand, and there is no presumption that the level of demand will generate full employment of labour and/or full capacity utilization. Investment has a crucial dual role to play in our model. The first is through its impact on aggregate demand. The second is through its enhancing impact on capital stock. Further, there is no automatic mechanism which takes the level of aggregate demand to any supply-side equilibrium. The mechanisms which feature in other approaches to economics, such as adjustment of real wages to clear the labour market, or the operation of the real balance effect, are explicitly rejected.

The *p*-curve and the *w*-curve may have substantial ranges over which they are near to horizontal and, if that is so, any precise identification of the inflation barrier will be difficult and indeed the inflation barrier will be more like a plateau than a point. Further, since investment is always taking place, the *p*-curve will be continually shifting (even if that leads to rather small changes in the inflation barrier). It will also mean that inflation will be slow to rise (fall), as unemployment is lower (higher) than the point of intersection of the two curves in Figure 6.4.

We conclude from our analysis that the position of the 'inflation barrier' (akin to a NAIRU) depends on the size and composition of the capital stock. A larger capital stock per firm and a greater number of firms (often but not always) lead to the 'inflation barrier' being at a higher level of employment with a higher real wage. A larger capital stock will permit a higher level of aggregate demand (and higher level of employment and lower rate of unemployment) without inflation tending to rise. Investment depends on factors such as capacity utilization and profitability, which in turn are related to the level of aggregate demand. Hence the evolution of the capital stock depends on the time path of the level of aggregate demand. Higher levels of aggregate demand lead to more investment and, over time, a larger capital stock.

Changes in labour market 'flexibility' in terms of variations in wage differentials and changes in 'hiring and firing' practices, would be seen to have little effect on the inflation barrier. Where some effect may be present is when changes in, for example, trade union power, which is reflected either in the ambitions of workers in terms of the target real wage or in their ability to secure higher wages (reflected in the a_1 coefficient), shift the w-curve. For example, a reduction in worker power shifts the w-curve downwards, thereby leading to an inflation barrier that involves higher employment. It would also be the case that changes in the power and/or profit ambitions of enterprises would have an impact on the inflation barrier. Greater market power, shifting the p-curve downwards, would tend to reduce real wages and employment.

In the rest of this chapter we discuss relevant empirical features which provide support for the analytical framework postulated so far.

5   EMPIRICAL CONSIDERATIONS

The approach to inflation which has been sketched in the previous two sections suggests a significant role for productive capacity and investment. The view is taken that there is no presumption that productive capacity is always sufficient to fully employ the workforce, and that the level and composition of investment over time influences the evolution of the capital stock. There is then no presumption that there is some predetermined equilibrium capital stock such that the actual capital stock converges on that equilibrium stock. Since net investment is rarely zero (and generally positive), the capital stock is always changing, and hence the precise position of the inflation barrier is always changing. In what may be termed 'normal' times, changes in the capital stock will be rather small with little by way of change in the inflation barrier. But times of major recession or of war reduce the capital stock substantially (at least relative to trend). In the other direction a prolonged investment boom increases the capital stock (relative to trend) substantially.

Dow (1998) argues that

> in a major recession underemployment results in the deterioration and premature scrapping of physical equipment, and that disbandment or underemployment of a firm's workforce similarly results in the partial destruction of working practices and working relations. The latter constitute the intangible capital of a firm, the value of which is an important fraction of its market value as a going concern. The capital stock, physical and intangible, takes time to build up, and its destruction cannot be made good rapidly; in effect, therefore, the destruction is quasi-permanent. In this way demand shocks impact on supply. A major recession causes a downward displacement of the growth path of productivity (or potential or capacity output); after the recession, the 'stable growth' mechanism described by the first mechanism will in the absence of further shocks start to operate again; that is, normal growth will be resumed from the low point of the recession. (Dow, 1998, p. 369)

He produces estimates of the impact of five major recessions in the UK, which are summarized in Table 6.1.

Table 6.1   Estimates of depth of recession or scale of fast growth as
compared with trend in the UK* in terms of GDP growth

	Start	End	Method A	Method B
Recession				
1	1920	1921	−6.3	−6.3
2	1929	1932	−11.9	−11.9
3	1973	1975	−7.8	−8.3
4	1979	1982	−6.0	−6.0
5	1989	1993	−11.6	−6.4
Fast-growth phases				
1	1922	1925	4.7	4.7
2	1933	1937	9.5	8.5
3	1972	1973	4.1	4.3
4	1985	1988	7.4	6.4

Notes: * Percentage change in output from start to end of recession or fast-growth phase *less*
(years × annual trend percentage growth rate); method A 'assumes changes in percentage of
labour unemployment during a major recession measure the degree to which overall economic
capacity is unemployed'; method B 'makes use of the short-term relationship between output
and employment'.

Source and quotations: Dow (1998).

The significance of this is that it implies that substantial (negative) changes
in capacity can occur as the result of recession, which have long-lasting
effects, and this is quite consistent with the views we have outlined above.
Below we consider the falls in unemployment in the UK, USA and Canada
during the 1990s, which occurred without an upswing in inflation, and
argue that the major investment boom of the 1990s underpinned the falls in
unemployment. In this section we attempt to throw some light on a number
of relevant issues raised so far in this chapter, especially in the last two
sections. We begin by looking at the relationship between capital stock and
unemployment. Two further issues, one concerning the determinants of
investment, and another 'labour market flexibility', also spring from our
analysis above. Brief sections on regional unemployment and on declining
unemployment and low inflation in the 1990s, render support to our thesis
on 'labour market flexibility'.

5.1 Capital Stock and Unemployment

The increases in the level of unemployment experienced in the 1980s and into the 1990s as compared with, say, the 1960s (especially in Europe) were substantial. The oil price shock of the mid-1970s could be seen as effectively reducing capacity, as heavy energy-using plant and equipment became unprofitable. High levels of unemployment and excess capacity can be expected to have led to a substantial reduction in the capital stock below what it would have been if there had been sustained full employment. Indeed, on the basis of the argument developed above, the corresponding increase in the inflation barrier must have been substantial. In some respects, this says little more than that enterprises will adjust the capital stock to the prevailing demand for output (and level of employment), but it suggests a clear mechanism through which the level of (un)employment experienced will be reflected in the estimated NAIRU.

There is evidence to support this view, though the empirical work to which we refer has been undertaken within analytical frameworks which have some similarities to the one outlined here, albeit with some differences as well. Arestis and Biefang-Frisancho Mariscal (1997) conclude from their empirical work for the UK (1966 to 1994) that 'unemployment is significantly determined by capital shortages. Capacity is not fixed and investment depends on expected profitability and the expected long-term rate of interest' (p. 191). In a subsequent paper, they find that 'the NAIRU is determined by long-term unemployment, worker militancy and the capital stock' (Arestis and Biefang-Frisancho Mariscal, 1998, p. 202). In work on Germany and the UK these authors in another paper (Arestis and Biefang-Frisancho Mariscal, 2000) conclude that 'adverse demand shocks affect employment and investment. When shocks reverse, unemployment may not fall to previous levels due to insufficient capital' (p. 487). Miaouli (2001) utilizes annual data from the manufacturing sector of five European countries and concludes that 'the empirical analysis verifies that in all countries, accumulated investment in the private sector influences employment in a positive way' (p. 23). Rowthorn (1995) finds that, 'when manufacturing and services are combined, capital stock has a large, statistically significant impact on employment' (p. 33) in equations estimated for a cross-section of OECD countries. Rowthorn therefore concludes, 'The problem of unemployment is ultimately one of investment' (p. 38).

Stockhammer (2004) aims 'to contrast and test the NAIRU hypothesis and a Keynesian explanation of unemployment in a time series context. For the NAIRU explanation, wage push variables are key to explain the rise of unemployment in Europe, for Keynesians the slowdown in capital accumulation is' (p. 19) the key. This proposition is tested using data from the mid-1960s to the mid-1990s for Germany, France, Italy, the UK and the US. He concludes that 'the NAIRU specification performed poorly, with only the tax wedge having a positive effect on unemployment as predicted. As to the Keynesian approach, the role of capital accumulation was confirmed. Whereas capital accumulation is robust to the specification and can be pooled across countries, the tax wedge is not. In the Keynesian specification the tax wedge has the incorrect sign, however replacement ratios are significant with the predicted sign' (p. 19). Further support comes from Alexiou and Pitelis (2003), where a panel-based study is undertaken for the period 1961 to 1998 for a number of European countries. The authors conclude that their 'analysis and empirical findings suggest that one of the potential factors behind the high and persistent European unemployment is insufficient growth of capital stock and inadequate aggregate demand' (p. 628).

5.2 Investment

The role of investment in this approach is central, and we now briefly investigate the empirical validity of the position taken on investment in this chapter. In a general sense, when studying the behaviour of investment, we may refer to economic activity variables (such as capacity utilization), essentially based on the accelerator investment model, interest rate/cost of capital variables and quantity of finance variables. The distinction between cost of finance and quantity of finance effects relies heavily on the assumption of imperfect capital markets. The imperfection of capital markets is explained by resorting to a number of factors, but asymmetric information between lenders and borrowers, which might lead to credit rationing, is the most predominant one (Stiglitz and Weiss, 1981; Bernanke and Gertler, 1989). Financial variables and constraints are explicitly included in investment models through the usage of cash flow variables in the menu of explanatory variables for investment (see, for example, Minsky, 1975; Fazzari, 1993; Fazzari and Peterson, 1993; Fazzari et al., 1988).

Financial factors as crucial determinants of investment have attracted a great deal of interest. External funds are no longer thought to be perfect substitutes for internal funds, in view of the recognition that capital markets are imperfect. The quantity of finance variables can be internal finance variables (such as corporate profits viewed as a critical variable in terms of internal finance; high corporate profits indicate greater capacity of the corporate sector to generate internal funds) and external finance variables (such as the ratio of debt to investment, an external cash flow component, on the assumption that a high debt environment is less likely to provide a stable financial base necessary for investment to materialize). Internal funds and net worth variables are thought to be particularly significant variables in the study by Hubbard (1998), where the relationship between capital market imperfections and investment is reviewed. The conclusions reached are: '(1) all else being equal, investment is significantly correlated with proxies for changes in net worth or internal funds; and (2) that correlation is most important for firms likely to face information-related capital-market imperfections' (p. 193). The importance of the external funds and cash flow variables are also emphasized in studies by Bernanke and Blinder (1988), Bernanke and Gertler (1989, 1999) and, more recently, by Greenspan (2002). The latter argues that 'capital investment will be most dependent on the outlook of profits and the resolution of the uncertainties surrounding the business outlook and the geopolitical situation. These considerations at present impose a rather formidable barrier to new investment ... A more rigorous and broad-based pickup in capital spending will almost surely require further gains in corporate profits and cash flows' (p. 7). Furthermore, empirical evidence, summarized by Chirinko (1993), supports the contention that 'output (or sales) is clearly the dominant determinant of investment spending with the user cost having a modest effect' (p. 1881). Baddeley (2003), in a comprehensive study of investment also confirms the results of 'previous analyses that capacity utilization and output have the strongest effects on aggregate investment activity' (p. 214).

5.3 Labour Market Flexibility

The case for labour market flexibility has been recently reiterated by the proponents of the European Economic and Monetary Union (EMU) model. Issing (2003a) puts it in the following strong language in testimony before the Committee on Economic and Monetary Affairs of the European Parliament:

> The lack of determination to overcome structural inefficiencies is particularly evident in the labour markets of several EU countries. Impediments to employment creation continue to exist. Measures are needed that will encourage firms to hire additional staff. These measures need to aim at reducing firms' labour costs, among other things, through reforms of social security systems that will reduce social security contributions and through reforms of the tax and benefit systems that will lower the wages at which workers are willing to supply labour. Improving employees' education and training and facilitating labour mobility could help the workforce to better react to adverse economic shocks. In such an environment – of enhanced labour market flexibility – policies fostering labour force participation can be very effective.

Rigidities in the labour markets are actually widely held to play a key role in the explanation of high unemployment rates, especially in Europe in the 1980s and 1990s (OECD, 1994a, 1994b, 1994c; Layard *et al.*, 1994; Siebert, 1997; Elsmeskov and Scarpetta, 1998).

Baker *et al.* (2002), utilizing standardized unemployment rates for 20 OECD countries for the period 1980–99, produce empirical results that are less robust and uniform across countries than what the studies to which we have just referred show. These studies stress the 'direct links' between labour market institutions and unemployment.[2] More concretely, Baker *et al.* (2002) demonstrate that the cross-country evidence of these studies provides 'no evidence' for union density, and only 'mixed evidence' for the effects of unemployment benefits (both replacement ratio, the level of benefits relative to income and duration of benefits), 'active labour market' policies and employment protection laws. As for structural reforms (or labour market deregulation), the authors argue that the usage of 'the degree to which a country complied with their policy descriptions' is inappropriate. When the 'volume' of reforms is used instead, there is no significant impact of structural reforms on NAIRU.

The Baker *et al.* (2002) study poses the question of 'reverse causality' in the studies they discuss, to conclude that, 'While clearly not universal, this evidence of reverse causation provides serious grounds for viewing test results showing a correlation between high unemployment and long benefit duration' (p. 28). Similarly, these studies play down the empirical support of the beneficial role of collective-bargaining coordination and active labour market policies. As Baker *et al.* suggest in their assessment of this literature, 'While the literature is widely viewed to provide strong evidence for the labour market rigidity view, a close reading of the leading papers suggests that the evidence is actually quite mixed, as several of the studies explicitly acknowledge' (p. 43).

The study by Baker *et al.* (2002) also provides its own empirical evidence for 20 OECD countries spanning 40 years, 1960–1999.[3] Different time periods are utilized, and different combinations of variables. The most comprehensive measure of institutions and policies utilized can only account for a minor part of the differences in the evolution of unemployment. The evidence in this chapter provides little or no support for the labour market rigidity explanation. An index of the extent of labour market deregulation in the 1990s is constructed, but this variable, too, showed no meaningful relationship between labour market deregulation and shifts in the NAIRU.

Palley (2000) examines the OECD job strategy (1994a, 1994b, 1994c), which had emphasized the role of labour market reforms and flexibility in reducing unemployment. He concludes (on the basis of regression analysis of changes in unemployment in the mid-1990s) that 'actions taken to reform labor markets do not explain any of the reduction in the rate of unemployment. There is some evidence that reforms of the educational system may have lowered total employment growth, which could be the result of young people staying in school longer. There is also stronger evidence that business sector reforms have lowered total employment growth, and reduced the quality of employment by slowing the growth of full-time employment' (p. 9). As Palley suggests, this is indirect support for the view that the cause of high European unemployment is macroeconomic in nature. In a later study, Palley (2001) presents further empirical evidence that supports this conclusion. By accounting for microeconomic and macroeconomic factors, and also for cross-country economic spillovers, he concludes that unemployment in Europe emanates from 'self-inflicted dysfunctional macroeconomic policy' (p. 3).

An OECD (1999) study is more damning to the 'labour-market-flexibility' thesis. It covers the period late 1980s to late 1990s and utilizes new and improved data on employment legislation in 27 OECD countries. It uses multiple regression analysis and techniques, so that it is able 'to control for other factors that can influence unemployment' (p. 88). The study demonstrates that employment protection legislation (a measure of labour market flexibility) has little or no impact at all on total unemployment.[4] Consequently, dismantling employment protection would not solve the current unemployment malice in the 27 countries considered in the study.

Further support to our thesis can be gauged by looking into regional disparities of unemployment. Such an exercise renders further support to the argument that labour market flexibility is based on weak foundations. This is taken up in the subsection that follows.

5.4 Regional Disparities of Unemployment

There are generally considerable variations in the rate of unemployment across the regions of an industrialized market economy: there are, of course, other important variations in the rate of unemployment, for example between ethnic groups. For convenience, we will refer here to regional variations.

The labour market interpretation of the NAIRU stresses the role of labour market institutions, laws and regulations, minimum wages and unemployment benefits in the determination of the NAIRU. Now it can be observed that these are typically characteristics which apply across the whole of the economy. Laws on trade unions, regulation of labour markets, unemployment benefits and minimum wages are characteristics which apply to the whole economy and do not (in general) vary from area to area.[5] It is, we suggest, implausible to think that the variations in unemployment which are observed between the different regions of a country (or indeed between, say, urban and rural areas, or between ethnic groups) can be explained by variations in the labour market characteristics of the regions involved. It is much more plausible to view the variations in unemployment as arising from the industrial structure of a region and from variations in productive capacity as well as in aggregate demand of the region.

In contrast, the inflation barrier approach, which we have outlined above, readily explains the differences in unemployment across regions in terms of differences in capacity and differences in the demand for the products of a region. Further, if differences in the position of the p-curve across regions (through differences in productive capacity) were substantial, there would be the observation that, across regions, there is a positive relationship between real wage and employment as the w-curve is mapped out. This would be consistent with the findings of a wage curve with such a positive relationship (see, for example, Blanchflower and Oswald, 1994).

Further support for our approach within the regional disparities of unemployment emanates from the argument that current unemployment, for example in the US, may be due to 'structural changes'. This is a real possibility when capacity is distributed across regions in a way that does not match the distribution of potential workers. This can happen when permanent relocation of workers from regions of declining industries to regions with expanding industry takes place. However, there may be a time lag involved here, where the relocation is delayed if expanding industries are faced with, for example, uncertainty or financial market weaknesses, as the case may be with the US economy currently. A recent study by Groshen and Potter (2003), which utilizes layoff trends and industry job gains and losses in the USA for the period 2001–3, is able to confirm this thesis. This evidence supports our contention that, beyond regional disparities in unemployment, investment is low owing to uncertain future demand levels and uncertain financial markets. Capacity is thereby affected, an important ingredient of our analysis.

5.5   Declining Unemployment and Low Inflation in the 1990s

After 1992, Canada, the USA and the UK experienced declining unemployment and generally declining inflation. France and Germany also experienced generally declining inflation but alongside rising unemployment in the case of Germany, and rising then falling around a high level in France. These experiences during the 1990s are well illustrated in Figures 6.6 and 6.7. The combination of falling unemployment and declining inflation in Canada, the UK and the USA is notable. At the beginning of the 1990s, most estimates of the NAIRU for the USA were in the range of 5.5 to 6.5 per cent,[6] while for the UK NAIRU estimates ranged from 6 to 8 per cent.[7] The estimates of OECD (2000) for the five countries considered here are given in Table 6.2. As is generally the case, estimates of the NAIRU tend to track the path of observed unemployment.

We suggest here that the relative experience of these five countries is consistent with the arguments advanced above. From 1992 onwards, Canada, the UK and the USA experienced high rates of growth of investment, whereas

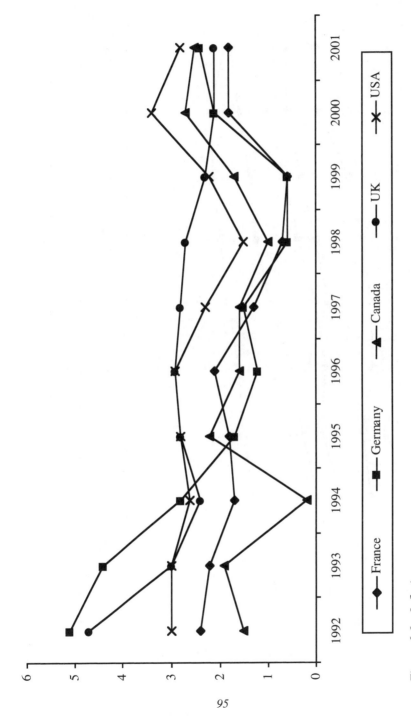

Figure 6.6 Inflation

95

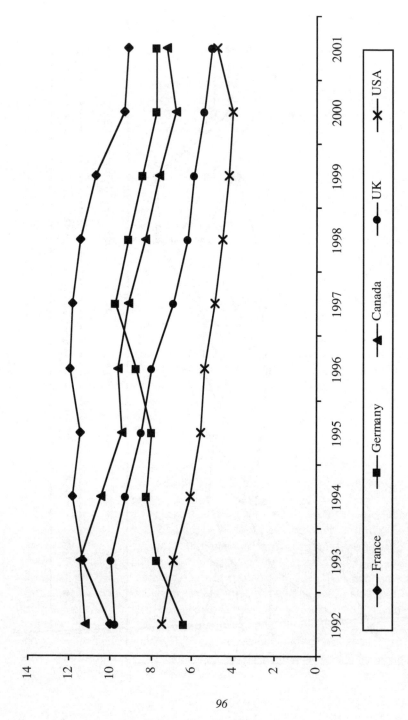

Figure 6.7 Unemployment

Table 6.2   *Estimates of NAIRU and actual unemployment (percentage of labour force)*

	Estimates of NAIRU		Actual unemployment		Change, 1990–99	
	1990	1999	1990	1999	NAIRU	Actual
France	9.3	9.5	8.6	11.1	0.2	2.5
Germany	5.3	6.9	4.8	8.3	1.6	3.5
Canada	9.0	7.7	8.1	7.6	−1.3	−0.5
UK	8.6	7.0	6.9	6.0	−1.6	−0.9
US	5.4	5.2	5.6	4.2	−0.2	1.4

Note: Unemployment rates (actual and NAIRU) are measured on commonly used national definitions.

Source: OECD (2000), Table V.1, Annex Table 21.

France and Germany did not. This is illustrated in Figure 6.8. Between 1992 and 1999, private sector non-residential investment grew by 95 per cent in the US, 64 per cent in Canada and 58 per cent in the UK, whereas it grew by 3.5 per cent in Germany and 16 per cent in France. On OECD estimates, all five countries had a substantial negative output gap in 1993. However, the growth of investment and of the capital stock meant that the decline in unemployment in Canada, the UK and the USA went alongside only modest rises in the gap between actual output and capacity output.

6   SUMMARY AND CONCLUSIONS

A model of the inflationary process has been put forward which may be characterized as the structuralist view of inflation.[8] This view of inflation focuses on the balance between demand and capacity, as well as pricing behaviour, and does not presume that there is adequate capacity to sustain full employment. This is in contrast to the prevailing NAIRU view, which pays little, if any, attention to capacity and pricing behaviour. We have argued that the essentials of this model are validated by existing empirical evidence.

In terms of policy implications, appropriate demand policies are required to stimulate investment and underpin full employment. Policies that attempt to tame inflation through higher levels of unemployment can cause the inflation barrier to fall, thereby sustaining higher levels of unemployment. Our

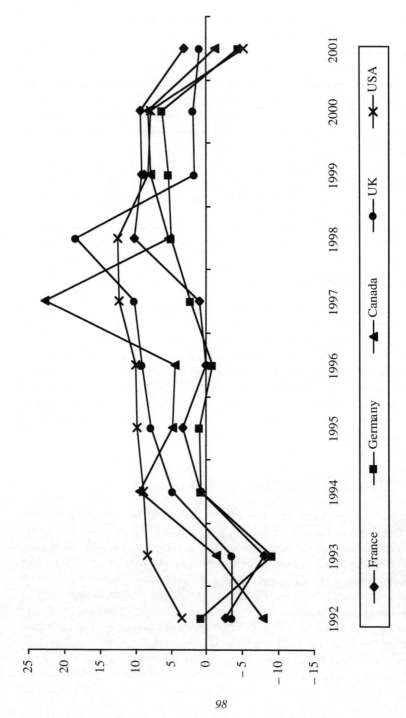

Figure 6.8   Growth of investment

approach is in sharp contrast to the one that places monetary policy and 'reform' of the labour market at the centre of anti-inflationary policy. This view of inflation views monetary policy as ineffectual (and even damaging), and views investment as central. High levels of demand are required to stimulate investment, and thereby create the future productive capacity which facilitates lower unemployment and lower inflation.

NOTES

1. For example, in their influential book, Layard *et al.* (1991) portray aggregate demand as

    $$y_d = \sigma_{11}x + \sigma_{12}r^* + \sigma_{13}(m - p) + \sigma_{14}Dpe + \sigma_{15}c^*,$$

    where *x* includes fiscal stance, world economic activity and world relative price of imports; the foreign real rate of interest is $r^* = I^* - Dp^*e$ (nominal rate of interest minus expected foreign inflation), $m - p$ is (log) real money supply, *Dpe* expected inflation and c^* expected long-run competitiveness. It can be readily seen that, if the level of demand (y_d) is to adjust to the level of output as set on the supply side, one or more of the variables on the right-hand side of the equation have to adjust. In this formulation, this would involve some combination of the fiscal stance, the real money supply and the expected rate of inflation.
2. Labour market institutions are institutions (like union density) and policies (like employment protection laws).
3. It is important to note that this data series covers the late 1990s, when unemployment rates fell sharply in the 20 countries included in the study's sample.
4. The employment protection legislation is defined broadly and covers all types of employment protection measures resulting from legislation, court rulings, collective bargaining or customary practices. The OECD (1999) study considered a set of 22 indicators, summarized in an overall indicator on the basis of a four-step procedure (pp. 115–18).
5. There are exceptions to this: for example, the minimum wage may differ across regions reflecting perceived differences in the cost of living. In a federal system, such as the US, there can be variations in the employment laws.
6. 'Tightness in the labor market is measured by the excess of CBO's estimate of the non-accelerating inflation rate of unemployment (NAIRU) over the actual unemployment rate. It is an indicator of future wage inflation' (Congressional Budget Office, 1994, p. 4). The Congressional Budget Office uses an estimate of 6 per cent for the NAIRU.
7. 'The sustainable rate of unemployment, or NAIRU, is believed to have risen in the UK during the 1970s and 1980s, but there is broad agreement that this increase has been partly reversed since the late 1980s. Although the magnitude of any fall is very difficult to estimate, most estimates of the current level of the NAIRU lie in the range of 6 to 8 per cent on the Labour Force Statistics (LFS) measure of unemployment. However, considerably lower levels should be achievable in the long run through re-integrating the long-term unemployed back into the labour market, upgrading skills, and reforming the tax and benefit systems to promote work incentives' (Treasury, 1997, p. 82).
8. For a more formal model, see Arestis and Sawyer (2003f).

7. The nature and role of monetary and fiscal policy when money is endogenous

1 INTRODUCTION

The concept of endogenous (bank) money is a particularly important one for macroeconomic analysis, especially within Keynesian economics. Bank money provides a more realistic approach to money in comparison with the exogenous, controllable money approach (in the sense that it is widely recognized that most money in an industrialized economy is bank money). Further, the concept of endogenous money fits well with the current approach to monetary policy based on the setting (or 'targeting') of a key interest rate by the central bank. In the case of endogenous money, the causal relationship between the stock of money and prices is reversed as compared with the exogenous money case. Endogenous money plays an important role in the causal relationship between investment and savings: put simply, the availability of loans permits the expansion of investment, which leads to a corresponding expansion of savings and to an (at least temporary) expansion of bank deposits.

There are currently two schools of thought that view money as endogenous. One is the 'new consensus' macroeconomics (NCM) discussed throughout this book, but at length in Chapter 2, and the other is the Keynesian endogenous (bank) money. There are significant differences in the two approaches: the most important, for the purposes of this chapter, is in the way endogeneity of money is viewed. We discuss the view of money in the NCM approach in the next section, and then the Keynesian approach in the following section. We also discuss the nature and role of monetary policy within these two approaches, before we deal with the effectiveness of both monetary and fiscal policy (see also Arestis and Sawyer, 2003c). The latter issue prepares the ground for a more thorough investigation of the effectiveness of fiscal policy in Chapters 8 and 9.

2   NCM AND ENDOGENOUS MONEY

The 'new consensus' treats money as endogenously created, though the terminology of endogeneity is not generally used. It actually sees money as a 'residual' in the setting of the central bank rate of interest.[1] Indeed, money is treated as endogenous in the sense that the stock of money has no causal significance within the approach (for example changes in stock of money do not cause inflation) and the rate of interest is treated as set by the central bank and is not market determined.[2]

The 'new consensus' model, as represented in Chapter 2 in terms of three equations, is relevant to the discussion of this chapter. Equation (2.3), though, is of particular significance here. It clearly endogenizes the setting of interest rate by the central bank and does so along the lines of the 'Taylor rule'. The significance of the use of the 'Taylor rule' is twofold. First, it treats the setting of interest rates as a domestic matter without reference to international considerations such as the exchange rate and interest rates elsewhere in the world. This is not just an attribute of using Taylor rule in the context of the closed economy model outline above, but is a more general feature of that rule.

Second, the interest rate is adjusted in response to the output gap (and to the rate of inflation which in turn is modelled to depend on the output gap). A zero output gap is consistent with constant inflation, as can be seen from equation (2.2). Equation (2.3) then implies a nominal rate of interest which translates into a real rate equal to the 'equilibrium' rate RR^*, which is consistent with zero output gap and constant inflation. From equation (2.1), the value of RR^* would need to be a_0/a_3. Provided that the central bank has an accurate estimate of RR^*, it appears that the economy can be guided to an equilibrium of the form of a zero output gap and constant inflation (at an inflation rate equal to the pre-set target). In this case, equation (2.1) indicates that aggregate demand is at a level that is consistent with a zero output gap. In a private sector economy, this would imply that the real interest rate RR^* brings equality between (ex ante) savings and investment. The equilibrium rate of interest corresponds to the Wicksellian 'natural rate' of interest, which equates savings and investment at a supply-side equilibrium level of income.

The *pre*-Keynesian view of the relationship between savings and investment could be summarized in terms of the variation of the rate of interest to equate savings and investment. Indeed Keynes (1930) himself drew on this notion after his discussion of his 'fundamental equations', the first of which was

$$P = E/O + (I' - S)/R, \tag{7.1}$$

where P is price level of consumption goods, E is money income, O is total output of goods, I' is cost of production of investment, S is savings and R is consumption goods purchased. The particular significance of his fundamental equations (of which we need to report only one here) for our current purpose concerns the link between the rate of interest and the price level. Keynes (1930) makes the point well when he argues that.

> Following Wicksell, it will be convenient to call the rate of interest which would cause the second term of our fundamental equation to be zero the *natural rate* of interest, and the rate which actually prevails the *market rate* of interest. Thus the natural rate of interest is the rate at which saving and the value of investment are exactly balanced, so that the price level of output as a whole ... exactly corresponds to the money rate of the efficiency earnings of the factors of production. Every departure of the market rate from the natural rate tends, on the other hand, to set up a disturbance of the price level by causing the second term of the second fundamental equation to depart from zero. We have, therefore, something with which the ordinary quantity equation does not furnish us, namely, a simple and direct explanation why a rise in the bank rate tends, insofar as it modifies the effective rates of interest, to depress price levels. (Keynes, 1930, p. 139)

The 'new consensus' has not explicitly discussed the relationship between savings and investment or the 'natural rate' of interest, but it is immediately apparent from the three equations (2.1) to (2.3), as presented in Chapter 2, that there is discussion of the equivalent relationship between output and demand, and that an 'equilibrium rate' similar in nature to the 'natural rate' has been introduced. It should be noted, though, that Keynes (1936) explicitly rejects the idea of a unique 'natural rate' of interest, and in effect argues that there is a 'natural rate' of interest corresponding to each level of effective demand, which would bring savings and investment into balance. Keynes (1936) argues that, in Keynes (1930),

> I defined what purported to be a unique rate of interest, which I called the *natural rate* of interest – namely, the rate of interest which, in the terminology of my *Treatise*, preserved equality between the rate of saving (as there defined) and the rate of investment. ... I had, however, overlooked the fact that in any given society there is, on this definition, a *different* natural rate of interest for each hypothetical level of employment. And, similarly, for every rate of interest there is a level of employment for which the rate is the 'natural' rate, in the sense that the system will be in equilibrium with that rate of interest and that level of employment. Thus it was a mistake to speak of *the* natural rate of interest or to suggest that the above definition would yield a unique value for the rate of interest irrespective of the level of employment. I had not then understood that, in certain conditions, the system could be in equilibrium with less than full employment. (Keynes, 1936, pp. 242–3)

In terms of equation (2.1), changes in either a_0 or a_3 would generate changes in the 'equilibrium' rate of interest. The autonomous component of consumption, expectations and 'animal spirits' governing investment, foreign demand and fiscal stance would all be captured by the a_0 coefficient. Shifts in any of those elements would be expected to change a_0 and thereby the 'equilibrium rate' of interest. In particular, the 'equilibrium rate' of interest can be seen to depend on the fiscal stance. It should be seen to leave open the issue whether fiscal policy or monetary policy is the more effective (however that is perceived). It could still be the case that the policy response to a downturn in 'animal spirits' reducing the level of investment should be a fiscal stimulus rather than an interest rate cut. The 'new consensus' says little on the strength of the impact of fiscal and monetary policy or on the lags and uncertainties surrounding the effects of these policies.

The 'equilibrium rate' of interest is deemed to be consistent with a zero output gap and constant inflation. The output gap clearly relates actual output to some notion of capacity output. This leaves unresolved the issue of the size of capacity output, and hence the relationship between employment of labour which would correspond to capacity output and full employment. There is no strong reason to think that a zero output gap would necessarily correspond to full employment.

There are (at least) six factors that may prevent the interest rate being set by the central bank to secure equality between savings and investment at full employment.[3] The first is that the 'equilibrium' real rate of interest is either negative or positive but so low as to be unattainable. This discussion is in terms of the central bank rate. It is assumed that the rate of interest on loans is above that central bank rate, and that it is the rate of interest on loans which is relevant for investment decisions. Given the risks for banks involved in extending loans, it can be assumed that there is a minimum level below which banks would not go in terms of the loan rate. In some respects this has overtones of the 'liquidity trap', but the mechanisms are different. In the case of the 'liquidity trap', it was presumed that the rate of interest on bonds was so low (and the price of bonds so high) that few would be willing to buy bonds in light of the likelihood of capital losses in doing so.

The lower limit for the nominal rate of interest may be seen as zero (or a little above), on the simple basis that the holding of cash will yield a zero rate of interest, and hence banks would not be willing to provide loans for a rate of interest below zero, and individuals and firms would not be willing to hold bank deposits at a rate of interest below zero. In this case, the lower limit on the real rate of interest depends on the rate of inflation: in the context of inflation targeting, the lower limit would be around minus the target rate of inflation. The point here is that the equation for the equality between savings and investment of the $I(r, Y_n) = S(r, Y_n)$ may not have an economically meaningful solution, where Y_n is income level for which the output gap is zero.

Second, and not unrelated to the previous point, interest rates may have very little effect on the levels of investment and savings and hence variations in the rate of interest would be ineffectual in reconciling intended savings and investment. The theoretical and empirical arguments on the ambiguity of the sign of the relationship between savings and the rate of interest are well known. However, it is notable in this respect that Kalecki's approach made just this assumption: interest rates are not mentioned in respect of savings, and investment did not depend on the rate of interest as the long-term rate of interest (deemed relevant for the level of investment) varied little and the differential between the rate of profit and the rate of interest (also seen as relevant) also varied little (Sawyer, 1985). The empirical literature on investment has often cast doubt on the impact of interest rates on investment and stressed the roles of profitability and capacity utilization. 'In the investment literature, despite some recent rehabilitation of a role for neoclassical cost-of-capital effects ... there remains considerable evidence for the view that cash flow, leverage, and other balance-sheet factors also have a major influence on spending [Fazzari *et al.* (1988), Hoshi *et al.* (1991), Whited (1992), Gross (1994), Gilchrist and Himmelberg (1995), Hubbard *et al.* (1995)]' (Bernanke *et al.*, 1999, p. 1344). These authors further note in a footnote that 'contemporary macroeconometric forecasting models, such as the MPS model used by the Federal Reserve, typically do incorporate factors such as borrowing constraints and cash-flow effects' (p. 344, n.2; see also Baddeley, 2003).

Third, the linkage from the key discount rate set by the central bank to the interest rates which influence economic decisions may be rather loose and uncertain. For example, the long-term rate of interest may be viewed as relevant for long-term investment decisions, and the response of the long-term rate of interest to changes in the key discount rate may be relatively modest and may vary over time. The banks could respond to a change in the discount rate by using a combination of changes in the interest rate on loans and changes in the credit standards which they set. Hence the impact of a change in the discount rate on interest-sensitive spending decisions depends on the decisions of banks and other financial institutions. As Keynes (1930) argued, 'the dilemma of modern banking is satisfactorily to combine the two functions. As a purveyor of representative money, it is the duty of the banking system to preserve the prescribed objective standard of money. As a purveyor of loans on terms and conditions of a particular type, it is the duty of the system to adjust, to the best of its ability, to supply this type of lending to the demand for it at the equilibrium rate of interest, that is, at the natural rate' (p. 192).

Fourth, the 'equilibrium' rate of interest has been determined in light of domestic considerations only, and may not be compatible with interest rates in the rest of the world. The central bank sets the key discount rate. Other interest rates may be more relevant for foreign exchange transactions, and indeed returns such as expected change in stock market prices might also be seen as relevant. The implicit assumption here is that the interest rates of relevance to movements across the foreign exchanges are linked to the key discount rate. The clearest case of possible incompatibility would arise if the interest rate parity theory held such that the interest rate differential between currencies is equal to the expected rate of change of the exchange rate between the currencies. A relatively high (low) real domestic interest rate would then be associated with a depreciating (appreciating) currency. But a relatively high (low) domestic interest rate is often associated with a high (low) value of the domestic currency. Those two propositions may be reconcilable if the initial imposition of a high (low) domestic interest rate is accompanied by a sharp rise (fall) in the exchange rate, followed by a steady decline (rise) in its value. However, a continuing high (low) domestic interest rate would be accompanied (according to the interest rate parity theory) by a continuing decline (rise) in the exchange rate. It is difficult to see that such a decline (rise) could continue for any substantial period of time, and hence that a relatively high (low) domestic interest rate could be sustained for any substantial period of time.

Insofar as interest rate parity holds, the difference between the domestic interest rate and the foreign interest rate will be equal to the (expected) rate of change of the exchange rate. The interest rate parity result appears not to hold empirically in the sense of the interest rate differential and exchange rate movements being closely linked. Lavoie (2000) makes the point that 'Despite dozens of studies showing that uncovered interest parity is without empirical support, neoclassical authors still rely on it, because, they would say, a more attractive relationship has yet to be found' (p. 175). This can provide the monetary authorities with some ability to vary the domestic interest rate without major effects on the exchange rate. The question then arises as to the extent to which monetary authorities have this ability and how far it is constrained by these exchange rate considerations. It was noted above that the Taylor rule neglects these exchange rate effects.

Fifth, the central bank cannot calculate and attain the real 'equilibrium rate' of interest through reasons of lack of information, it being a moving target, incompetence or, indeed, for reasons which have to do with policy mistakes in the estimation of the 'equilibrium' real rate of interest by the central bank. It can be seen in the equations given in Chapter 2 (2.1 to 2.3) that the 'equilibrium rate' depends on a_0/a_3 and these are parameters, which can and do vary over time, and they can be erroneously estimated. Shifts in the propensity to save, in the propensity to invest, in the demand for exports and in the fiscal stance could all be expected to lead to a shift in the equivalent of a_0/a_3. Information on the 'equilibrium rate' is not exactly readily available, and indeed at best can only be estimated with some lag and over a period when it can be reasonably assumed the underlying parameters are stable. The central bank has imperfect information on the equilibrium real rate of interest RR^* (assuming that such a rate does actually exist), and may aim for a real rate of interest which is not equal to a_0/a_3. It could also be noted that it has been implicitly assumed in equation (2.3) that there are no stochastic errors in decision making with accurate knowledge on the lagged output gap and inflation rate. These assumptions need to be sustained in the real world; in fact, it is almost certain that they would not. Any shift in fiscal policy, in investors' confidence or in world trade conditions would be reflected in a change in a_0, leading thereby to a change in the equilibrium real rate of interest. This would, of course, exacerbate the problems of securing information on the equilibrium rate and exacerbate the chances of policy mistakes.

Sixth, the central bank (or the government) may not wish to attain the 'equilibrium rate' of interest as defined above. In other words, the central bank does not pursue a policy rule akin to the Taylor rule. The central bank may use its interest rate for objectives other than a target rate of inflation and/ or zero output gap: these objectives could include the rate of growth of stock of money or a target level of the exchange rate. Weller (2002), for example, argues that, for the Federal Reserve over the period 1980 to 2000, 'the unemployment rate appears consistently to be a significant factor determining monetary policy. Moreover, the relative importance of the unemployment rate is greater than that of other determinants, suggesting that the Fed prioritizes stable unemployment over other goals. However, there is no indication that the Fed has a set target level of the unemployment rate. ... Also, real output and the real rate of return to the stock market appear to be significant factors during some periods between 1980 and 1990' (p. 413).

This 'new consensus' focuses on the role of monetary policy (in the form of interest rates) to control demand inflation, and not cost inflation, as is evident from equation (2.3). The position taken on cost inflation is that it should be accommodated (see, for example, Clarida *et al.*, 1999). The significance of the 'new consensus' is that it strongly suggests that inflation can be tamed through interest rate policy (using demand deflation) and that there is an equilibrium rate (or 'natural rate') of interest which can balance aggregate demand and aggregate supply and which is feasible, and lead to a zero gap between actual and capacity output. In the context of monetary policy, this raises three issues. First, how effective is monetary policy at influencing aggregate demand and thereby inflation? The evidence surveyed in Chapter 4 suggests that it is rather ineffectual. Second, if inflation is a 'demand phenomenon', the question arises whether monetary policy is the most effective (or least ineffective) way of influencing aggregate demand (and in Chapter 4 we conclude that it is not). Third, it is pertinent to ask the extent to which cost-push and similar forms of inflation can be as lightly and simply dismissed as the 'new consensus' appears to do. We would suggest that this is simply wrong, and refer the reader to the very long time that it took the oil shocks of the 1970s to work their effects through the economy.

A further aspect of the 'new consensus' is that it is recognized that there are many channels through which monetary policy operates. In Chapter 4 we reviewed the literature which identified six channels, which have been seen to play a role: the narrow credit channel, the broad credit channel, the interest rate channel, the monetarist channel, the wealth effect channel and the exchange rate channel. The significance of identifying and discussing these various channels is firstly that it gives the impression that the transmission of monetary policy depends on the expectations, behaviour and so on of a wide variety of agents, and the strength and predictability of the effects of a change in monetary policy may be rather 'loose'. It also indicates that monetary policy may have effects on a range of economic variables, which are of interest in their own right: for example, credit availability (and thereby investment expenditure), asset prices and the exchange rate. It also raises the question whether (or to what extent) interest rate policy should be concerned with economic variables other than the rate of inflation.

3 THE KEYNESIAN VIEW OF ENDOGENOUS MONEY

The concept of endogenous (bank) money has become an important one for macroeconomic analysis, especially within Keynesian economics. There is, however, an important difference between the current approach to monetary policy and the more Keynesian notion of endogenous money. The current approach sees the stock of money as a residual with no further role for it within the economy. The Keynesian notion of endogenous money entails a fully articulated theory with clear policy implications where money and credit have important roles to play in their interaction with real variables (see, for example, Fontana and Palacio-Vera, 2002, especially p. 559; Fontana and Venturino, 2003).

In the case of exogenous money (that is, where the stock of money is given causal significance) changes in the stock of money are seen to have a causal impact on variables such as the price level. In contrast, in the case of endogenous money, the causal relationship runs from nominal income to the demand for money to the stock of money. Endogenous money plays an important role in the causal relationships between investment and savings: put simply, the expansion of investment expenditure requires the availability of loans, which leads to a corresponding expansion of savings and to an (at least temporary) expansion of bank deposits.

The Keynesian view provides a theory of endogenous, essentially bank, money. The central bank sets the rate of interest and accommodates reserves as necessary. Commercial banks provide loans at a rate of interest that is a mark-up over the central bank rate of interest (the mark-up determined by the liquidity preference of banks, their market power and their attitude to risk). Unlike the 'new consensus', the Keynesian view of endogenous money pays a great deal of attention to the process by which loans and deposits are created and destroyed. The causal links between investment expenditure and loan creation and between inflation and the creation of money feature strongly in the Keynesian endogenous money literature; they are overlooked in the 'new consensus'. Although monetary policy, essentially interest rate policy, appears to be the same in both schools of thought, there are distinct differences.

A simple representation of the Keynesian endogenous money approach treats the central bank rate of interest as given, with the central bank providing bank reserves which are required (at a price which it sets). Banks provide loans at a rate of interest that is a mark-up over the central bank rate, and meets all credit demanded (subject to credit-standard requirements). The mark-up may vary as banks' liquidity preference and position, market power and attitude to risk vary. The loans are created in response to the demand for loans, and bank deposits are thereby created. The repayment of loans destroys money, and the amount of money that remains in existence depends on the demand to hold money. Money is generated within the inflationary process, and the rate of inflation influences the rate of increase of the stock of money, but money itself does not in any sense *cause* inflation.

The central bank rate can be viewed as the key rate on which all other interest rates are based, often explicitly so, as in the case of the interest rates charged by banks on loans and paid by banks on deposits. However, while that may be a useful way to proceed in the short run (which here would be that period over which the central bank holds its interest rate constant), it clearly leaves open the question of the forces that influence or determine the central bank interest rate in the longer term. This should be seen as a key issue in the analysis of endogenous money, yet it has been generally neglected. The discussion has usually pointed to the discretion possessed by the central bank and exchange rate considerations. Moore (1989) summarizes the case aptly, 'A central bank's key decision variable throughout the business cycle, and its central control instrument of monetary policy, is the nominal supply price at which it provides additional reserves. Over a wide range the central bank can determine exogenously the supply price at which it provides liquidity to the financial system. The upper and lower limits of this range are set by the size and openness of the economy and by the exchange rate regime in force' (p. 27).

However, in this Keynesian endogenous money supply literature, there has been little discussion on the underlying determinants of the discount rate set by the central bank. The Keynesian endogenous money approach recognizes the significance of the central bank rate of interest for the general level of interest rates. Indeed, it takes a strong stance on this in the sense that the central bank determines the key discount rate and can enforce that rate. This does not mean that there is some one-for-one correspondence between the central bank rate and some other specified rate of interest (and in particular the long-term rate of interest on bonds may vary only to a minor extent when the central bank rate changes). The relationship between any particular rate of interest and the central bank rate is likely to be influenced by a variety of factors, including the degree of market power of the banking system and what may be termed liquidity preference.

The causal link that runs from investment expenditure to savings requires the availability of finance to enable the investment to occur, in effect ahead of the generation of savings. Savings are available ex post to fund investment, but are not available ex ante. The level of income is perceived to adjust following an increase in investment expenditure. The notion of endogenous (bank) money with which banks are able to make loans for the financing of investment is key to an explanation of the process by which investment expands, leading to savings and income expansions. Yet the rate of interest on loans is closely linked with the rate of interest set by the central bank. The factors that influence the setting and changing of the interest rate by the central bank become crucial to the relationship between savings and investment. To take an extreme view, if the central bank could vary the rate of interest to ensure that savings and investment were continuously equated at levels that corresponded to a supply-side equilibrium (perhaps full employment), then there would be no deficient demand problem. In the previous chapter we discussed the ways in which the conclusion that interest rate policy can guide the economy to equilibrium with demand and supply in balance and inflation on target can be upset.

4   WHAT IS THE ROLE OF MONETARY POLICY WITHIN THE KEYNESIAN ENDOGENOUS MONEY ANALYSIS?

It is difficult to conceive that, when money is commodity money, a rate of interest could be paid on it. When money is bank money, the payment of interest becomes technically possible, and payment of interest and its level depend on decisions made by the banking system. The resulting rate of interest on bank deposits may be small and close to zero, but it will not be identically equal to zero, and could be expected to depend on the central bank discount rate.

Liquidity preference in a general sense refers, as the name suggests, to the degree of preference for liquidity. Financial (and other) assets vary in their degree of liquidity in terms of the volatility of their prices and of the ease of selling. Money is the liquid asset par excellence, in that its price is fixed in nominal terms and by assumption it is a readily accepted medium of exchange. But bank deposits are not fully liquid insofar as they are not a medium of exchange (though they can usually be quickly converted into a medium of exchange) and banks may themselves become illiquid and unable to repay a bank deposit immediately.

Liquidity preference can be viewed as influencing the allocation of wealth between different assets (here focusing on financial assets). A shift in liquidity preference, say, towards more liquid assets and away from less liquid assets changes the demands for those assets, which leads to changes in relative prices (price of more liquid assets rising and of less liquid assets falling) and thereby to changes in the relative rates of return on those assets. There is an exception to this in that, clearly, the price of financial assets with a fixed nominal price (for example bank deposits) cannot change, but the interest rate may be adjusted (for example the banks faced with an increased demand to hold deposits may lower the rate of interest on deposits).

In Keynes's (1936) *General Theory*, with two composite assets of money (yielding a zero rate of interest) and bonds, this leads to a rise in interest rate on bonds, and by assumption a rise in the cost of finance for investment. But that rested on the rate of interest on money being zero, such that a change in the relative rates of return on money and on bonds translates into a change in the absolute rate of return on bonds. The argument here is that, when the rate of interest on money is not tied to zero, liquidity preference can influence the relative rates of return on financial assets, but does not change the general level of the absolute rates of return in any predictable way. But it is the absolute rate of interest (in real terms) that is relevant for investment and other expenditure decisions.

Liquidity preference considerations can have an impact on the operation of monetary policy insofar as it influences relative interest rates, and relative interest rates influence aggregate demand. The 'new consensus' was described above in terms of a relative simple model with a single rate of interest. However, the elaboration of the channels through which monetary policy is transmitted points to the role of credit rationing and to changes in the structure of interest rates. Credit rationing could be said to be ever present, and the question is whether a change in the central bank discount rate will lead to a change in the extent and form of credit rationing. A higher rate of interest on loans increases the risk of default on the loan. This comes for two reasons. First, the interest payments would be higher, increasing the chances that a firm taking out a loan would be unable to meet those interest payments. Second, the structure of the portfolio of loans may shift away from lending to projects with low risk but low expected return, towards those with high risk but high expected return ones. As the rate of interest on loans rises, some of the projects with low expected returns would find that those expected returns now fall below the rate of interest on loans. The portfolio of loans shifts from low-risk to high-risk ones. Banks may then respond to a rise in the discount rate by moving towards more credit rationing rather than raising the loan rate by the full extent of the rise in the discount rate. These arguments suggest that the effects of a change in the central bank discount rate will be much less predictable than was suggested by the simple model presented above. There are changes in credit rationing and in relative interest rates to consider.

This analysis suggests a monetary policy which is rather different from that implied by the 'new consensus' analysis. Since the impact of interest rate manipulation is uncertain and unpredictable, as well as ineffective, this would suggest that interest rates should be kept as low as possible to avoid undesirable distributional effects (see, for example, Arestis and Howells, 1991). Furthermore, our earlier discussion of the channels of monetary policy in Chapter 4 does make it clear that monetary policy operates through a variety of credit channels. At present, these credit channels are only indirectly affected by monetary policy, in that, when interest rates, say, rise, there may be some impact on the willingness of banks to grant credit; in other words the extent of credit rationing changes. Under these circumstances, monetary policy is in a better position to have real effects by seeking to influence the degree of credit granted directly. The analysis of the Keynesian endogenous money clearly suggests, then, that low interest rates should be the aim of monetary policy, but use direct credit controls to affect real magnitudes and inflation in the economy.

5 THE EFFECTIVENESS OF MONETARY AND FISCAL POLICIES

A major alternative to monetary policy as a form of macroeconomic demand management policy is fiscal policy. In the NCM approach it was seen that inflation was viewed as demand-pull inflation. Even when viewed from that perspective, monetary and fiscal policies appear as alternative modes for the control of inflation. The question then arises as to the relative effectiveness of the two types of policy instruments. The effectiveness of monetary and fiscal policy can be approached along a number of routes, and we go down three here.

The first can be discussed in terms of the model outlined in Chapter 2. There are shocks to the model (s_i, with $i = 1, 2$), and these lead to changes in output and inflation, and to which monetary policy in the form of interest rate changes is seen to respond. In those terms two questions are of interest. First, how effective is an interest rate change in offsetting the shocks? That is, in effect, what are the sizes of the coefficients a_3 and b_1 (see equations (2.1) and (2.2)). These coefficients cannot be directly estimated, but we can draw on simulations of macroeconometric models to judge the effects of a change in the rate of interest on output and inflation. It was argued in Chapter 4 that, in effect, these coefficients are in some sense relatively small. It was suggested there that there are (at least within the context of the macroeconometric models utilized for the purposes of Chapter 4) constraints to a permanent change in the rate of interest. We would see the effect of interest rate on the exchange rate (when interest rate parity is assumed) as being a significant element in this, in that an interest differential between the domestic interest rate and foreign interest rate leads to a continual change in the exchange rate.

Second, when interest rates have an effect on aggregate demand this comes mainly through changes in the rate of investment. This means that interest rate variations can have long-lasting effects, in that the effects on investment will lead to changes in the size of the capital stock.

Third, the effects of interest rate changes on the rate of inflation are rather modest. A one percentage point change in interest rates is predicted to lead to a cumulative fall in the price level of 0.41 per cent in one case and 0.76 per cent in the other, after five years. The rate of inflation declines by a maximum of 0.21 percentage points. The effects of interest rate changes on output were also found to be rather small.

This perspective on monetary policy is a rather narrow one in the sense that it starts from the viewpoint that the economy is essentially stable though subject to shocks. These shocks are presumably relatively small and are not serially correlated. In the event that shocks are relatively large and are highly serially correlated, it may be better to approach monetary and fiscal policy in terms of shifts in the parameters of the model. If, for example, there is a major shock which reduces demand, and that reduction continues for a number of years, an analysis based on the downward shift of demand may be more insightful. This leads us to the second line of enquiry, namely how effective monetary policy would be in combating a fall in autonomous demand.

In order to introduce explicitly fiscal policy into the discussion, the equations used in Chapter 2 above are expanded, particularly equation (2.1). The government sector is explicitly included, though retaining the closed economy nature of the model, and the capacity level of output which is labelled Y^*. With a simple consumption function of the form

$$C_t = d_1 + d_2(1-t)Y_{t-1} - \alpha[R_t - E_t(p_{t+1})], \tag{7.2}$$

where C is consumer demand and t is the tax rate. The investment function is of the form:

$$I_t = d_3 + d_4 E_t(Y_{t+1}) - \beta[R_t - E_t(p_{t+1})], \tag{7.3}$$

where I is investment demand and government expenditure is labelled G. This leads to

$$Y_t = (d_1 + d_3) + G + d_2(1-t)Y_{t-1} - \alpha[R_t - E_t(p_{t+1})] + d_4 E_t(Y_{t+1}) \\ - \beta[R_t - E_t(p_{t+1})]. \tag{7.4}$$

With the output gap incorporated, this can be written as

$$(Y_t - Y^*) = (d_1 + d_3) + G + [d_2(1-t) + (d_4 - 1)]Y^* + [d_2(1-t)](Y_{t-1} - Y^*) \\ + d_4 E_t(Y_{t+1}) - Y^* - (\alpha + \beta)[R_t - E_t(p_{t+1})]. \tag{2.1''}$$

It is now evident that the 'equilibrium' rate of interest (for a zero output gap) is given by

$$[R_t - E_t(p_{t+1})] = (d_1 + d_3)/(\alpha + \beta) + G/(\alpha + \beta) \\ + [d_2(1-t) + (d_4 - 1)]/[(\alpha + \beta)]Y^*. \tag{7.5}$$

It is then clear that the 'equilibrium' rate of interest depends on government expenditure, and that there is not a unique 'natural rate' of interest.[4] It is, of course, possible to take the balanced budget case, and then the 'equilibrium rate' of interest would be given by

$$[R_t - E_t(p_{t+1})] = (d_1 + d_3)/(\alpha + \beta) + [(d_2 + d_4 - 1)/(\alpha + \beta)]Y^*. \tag{7.6}$$

It is also evident that the 'equilibrium rate' of interest depends on the parameters of the consumption and investment functions. The evidence from the USA and the UK (for example) during the 1990s suggests that those parameters can undergo substantial changes in the form of quoted rises in the propensity to consume (driving the household savings rate close to or below zero) and in the propensity to invest.

The empirical investigation of the effectiveness of fiscal policy is generally undertaken in the context of an econometric model that could be viewed as an elaboration of the 'new consensus' model. The econometric model is, of course, much larger and involves many leads and lags which do not appear in the 'new consensus' model, as presented in Chapter 2 above, but the econometric models generally impose the existence of a supply-side equilibrium (say the NAIRU) which is equivalent to the zero output gap for which inflation is constant.[5] With a policy regime that pushes the economy towards the supply-side equilibrium (reflected in the Taylor rule for the determination of the rate of interest) there is little room for output to diverge substantially from the supply-side equilibrium. Hence any fiscal stimulus is soon dissipated in the context of the model, leading to the empirical conclusion that fiscal policy is ineffective. In view of the constraints imposed by the nature of macroeconometric models (for example the existence of a supply side-determined equilibrium in the form of the NAIRU), it may be surprising that any positive effects of fiscal policy have been observed. The effects generally found for fiscal policy may be explicable in terms of the starting point for the simulations (say in terms of unemployment) relative to the supply-side equilibrium. Clearly, if unemployment is initially higher than the NAIRU, there is scope for a fiscal stimulus, which would (in the context of the model) push unemployment down towards the NAIRU. But it could be expected that any conclusions drawn on the effects of fiscal policy would be sensitive to the starting point used.

The NCM (or equivalent) provides little role for fiscal policy, and a limited role for monetary policy. It is assumed that there is a feasible 'equilibrium rate' of interest[6] which will secure a level of aggregate demand equal to the capacity level of output (which itself is compatible with constant inflation). It is pertinent to think about the effectiveness of fiscal and monetary policy in the context of a major shift in the coefficients of the model formed in this section. Suppose, for example, there is a change in 'animal spirits' or technological opportunities for investment, which leads to a reduction in d_3 of Δd. For monetary policy alone to be able to offset that reduction (to maintain demand at Y^*) would require a change in the real rate of interest of $-\Delta d/(\alpha + \beta)$. For fiscal policy alone to offset the reduction would require a change in government expenditure of Δd. It should be noted that here there would be no 'crowding out' due to a change in the rate of interest, which is under the control of the central bank, or due to output being constrained to be at the capacity level. This leads back to the question of whether there can be a feasible interest rate change which is sufficient to do the job. We think the answer is likely to be no. Let us take some illustrative numbers. If the value of $\alpha + \beta$ were equivalent to a semi-elasticity (that is, percentage change in demand divided by change in interest rate) of 0.33, it would require a change of three percentage points in the real rate of interest. This can be compared with an historic average of the real rate of interest of the order of 3 per cent. Note that a fall in investment would have multiplier effects on the level of output, and similarly a reduction in interest rates would have multiplier effects.

In the simulations surveyed in Chapter 4, the largest effect of interest rate on investment was that a one percentage point change in the rate of interest generated a 3 per cent change in investment (and generally the numbers were very much lower). Investment is 15 to 20 per cent of GDP, and hence a one percentage point change in the rate of interest was associated with a 0.45 to 0.6 per cent change in GDP (at the most). Given the bounds within which interest rates can be changed, falls in the autonomous components of aggregate demand equivalent to, say, 1 per cent would require interest rate reductions of, say, three percentage points. It is of little surprise that, when interest rate is held constant and output is well below any capacity output, fiscal policy will stimulate economic activity. Yet, in the context of endogenous money, a fall in autonomous demand would lead to precisely the position where fiscal policy would work.[7] On the other hand, interest rate changes would have little impact in offsetting the fall in autonomous demand.

In the context of equation (2.1″), a similar question can be asked with regard to a change in the capacity output Y^*, and this is the third line of enquiry.[8] If there was a change in Y^*, fiscal and monetary policy would be required to change to ensure that output attains the new Y^*. The estimates for the NAIRU showed major changes during the 1970s, 1980s and into the 1990s, particularly in Europe. The NAIRU, of course, refers to a rate of unemployment, but it is likely that there would be a corresponding shift in capacity output (corresponding to constant inflation). A change in the capacity output could be managed by a change in government expenditure of $[(1 - d_2)(1 - t) + d_4]$ times the change in capacity output (and not surprisingly this would imply a simple multiplier relationship between change in government expenditure and change in output). A monetary policy response would require a change in real interest rates of $[d_2(1 - t) + (d_4 - 1)/(\alpha + \beta)]$ times the change in capacity output. A change for whatever reason in the level of capacity output, compatible with constant inflation, does not lead in any automatic way to a change in demand corresponding to the change in capacity output. It is rather that changes in fiscal and monetary policies would be required to move demand in the relevant direction. It is again argued here that monetary policy is not an effective mechanism for generating such changes in demand. By contrast, fiscal policy can be an effective means of influencing aggregate demand.

6　SUMMARY AND CONCLUSIONS

In the context of endogenous money, the key decision to be made by the central bank relates to the discount rate, with the general structure of interest rates resting on the discount rate and the stock of money endogenously determined outside the control of the central bank. The use of interest rates as the key element of monetary policy raises the issue of effectiveness of monetary policy. It has to be recognized that there are clear limits on interest rates, notably that nominal interest rates cannot go negative, and the level of international interest rates constrain domestic interest rates.

The effectiveness of monetary policy in the case of two schools of thought that view money as endogenous has been considered. In the case of the 'new consensus', we have argued that the effectiveness of monetary policy should be judged along two lines. The first is to ask whether monetary policy is effective in the control of inflation, and in particular in quickly bringing the rate of inflation to its target level. In the simple model used to portray the 'new consensus' it is assumed that there is an 'equilibrium rate' of interest which would generate a level of aggregate demand compatible with the capacity output, and hence with a constant rate of inflation. The rate of interest is then varied with respect to the 'equilibrium rate' to influence aggregate demand and the rate of inflation, and to guide the rate of inflation to its target level. We have argued, on the basis of simulation exercises summarized in Chapter 4, that interest rates are relatively ineffective in the control of inflation. The second line along which we think monetary policy should be judged concerns the question of the ability of monetary policy to counter a major shock to the autonomous components of aggregate demand. It has been suggested that interest rate changes necessary to combat a major shift in aggregate demand are so large as to be infeasible in practice.

In terms of the Keynesian analysis of endogenous money, we have suggested that monetary policy should aim for low interest rates and, more importantly, that it should aim at directly controlling credit. Clearly, the monetary policy implications of this school of thought are very different from those of the 'new consensus'. A further important difference is in the treatment of fiscal policy. NCM downgrades fiscal policy, while the Keynesian analysis of endogenous money does not. On the contrary, it upgrades fiscal policy while recognizing a distinct role for monetary policy, as this has just been repeated. This conclusion calls for a full analysis of fiscal policy. This is precisely what is attempted in the two chapters that follow.

NOTES

1. The generic term 'central bank discount rate' is used to denote the rate of interest at which the central bank is willing to supply funds. It covers rates such as the 'repo' rate (European Central Bank), the Federal Funds rate (US, Federal Reserve System), the discount rate (UK, Bank of England), and so on. It is the rate of interest at which the central bank is willing to supply funds through its discount window.
2. For a further discussion in the specific context of the approach of the Bank of England to monetary policy, see Chapter 3.
3. It could be noted that Keynes (1930) discussed a number of these points at some length.
4. The 'natural rate' of interest could be said to be unique if there was no effect of government

expenditure on demand, which would be the equivalent of invoking Ricardian equivalence. This is further discussed in Chapters 7 and 8 below.

5. See Chapter 3 above, and Arestis and Sawyer (2002b) for our summary of the Bank of England model and its similarities to the NCM model.
6. The word 'feasible' is used in the sense of involving a positive nominal rate of interest and compatible with exchange rate targets.
7. This is the form of fiscal policy which we had in mind when we argued for the use of fiscal policy for 'coarse tuning' but not for 'fine tuning' (Arestis and Sawyer, 1998).
8. This should not be taken as suggesting that there is a well-defined and easily measured NAIRU (or capacity output) or that any inflationary barrier cannot be moved over time.

8. Reinventing fiscal policy

1 INTRODUCTION

There has been a major shift within macroeconomic policy over the past two decades or so in terms of the relative importance given to monetary policy and to fiscal policy, with the former gaining considerably in importance, and the latter being so much downgraded that it is rarely mentioned. Monetary policy has focused on the setting of interest rates as the key policy instrument, along with the adoption of inflation targets and the use of monetary policy to focus on inflation. The central bank sets its discount rate with a view to achieving the set inflation target, but the discount rate can be considered as set relative to an 'equilibrium rate' so that the problem of aggregate demand deficiency appears to be effectively dispensed with.[1] This can be seen in the operation of the Taylor rule for the setting of the discount rate (Taylor, 1993).

We critically examined the significance of this shift in terms of monetary policy in Chapters 2, 4 and 7. We also looked at the role of fiscal policy there, and argued that, within the 'new consensus', there is barely mention of fiscal policy, with the implication, presumably, that fiscal policy does not matter. This chapter aims to consider further fiscal policy (see also Arestis and Sawyer, 1998, 2003e). It begins by examining fiscal policy within the 'new consensus' macroeconomics. It then proceeds to consider whether crowding out is not inevitable, along with institutional and quantitative aspects of fiscal policy.

2 THE 'NEW CONSENSUS' MACROECONOMICS AND FISCAL POLICY

From the perspective of this chapter, equation (2.1) of the 'new consensus' model (see Chapter 2) is of particular significance. There is no explicit mention of fiscal policy, though changes in the fiscal stance could be seen as reflected in a change in the parameter a_0. But proponents of this model have produced a number of arguments that suggest that the use of discretionary fiscal policy should be seen as the exception rather than the rule (see, for example, Auerbach, 2002). The norm for fiscal policy should be to let automatic stabilizers operate in an environment of budgets balanced over the business cycle, and the operation of those stabilizers may be reflected in the coefficients a_1 and a_2. A number of arguments have been put forward to make the case against the use of discretionary fiscal policy and of long-term budget deficits. The most important, and rather more widely accepted by the proponents of the case, are those of crowding out and of the Ricardian Equivalence Theorem (RET) and, given their significance, we return to both below. Further arguments against discretionary fiscal policy relate to what has been labelled 'institutional aspects of fiscal policy' (Hemming, Kell and Mahfouz, 2002): model uncertainty, in that longer and more uncertain lags prevail than was thought previously; there is the risk of procyclical behaviour in view of cumbersome parliamentary approval and implementation; increasing taxes or decreasing government expenditure during upswings may be politically unrealistic, and this may very well generate a deficit bias; spending decisions may be subjected to irreversibility, which can lead to a public expenditure ratcheting effect; and there may be supply-side inefficiencies associated with tax rate volatility. There are also concerns that can be summarized under the heading of 'institutional aspects of fiscal policy'.

3 CROWDING OUT IS NOT INEVITABLE

There have been four distinct sets of arguments to the effect that fiscal policy will be ineffective, under the general heading of 'crowding out'. The first, in the context of the IS–LM analysis, was a 'crowding out' due to a rise in interest rates following a fiscal expansion. This was based on an exogenous money supply and the interest rate equating the demand for and supply of money. In that context, though, it was recognized that a sufficient increase in the supply of money alongside an increase in government expenditure could prevent the rise in the interest rate. In the context of endogenous money with the interest rate set by the central bank, this form of 'crowding out' would arise from the deliberate action of the central bank. That is to say, if the central bank, operating on an 'independent' policy basis, responded to a fiscal expansion by raising interest rates (say on the grounds that fiscal expansion created inflationary pressures), there would be some form of crowding out (insofar as an increase in interest rates reduces private expenditure). Its extent would depend on the size of the interest rate rise, its feed through to other interest rates, the interest rate responsiveness of expenditure and the phase of the business cycle. But the key point here is that any 'crowding out' depends on the response of the monetary authority: it does not occur through the response of the markets. Even if the rate of interest were allowed to increase, there is still the question of the investment elasticity with respect to the rate of interest. Chirinko (1993) and Fazzari (1993, 1994–5), for example, argue that the impact of the rate of interest on investment is modest at most. Sales growth (the accelerator effect) and cash flow effects are the dominant variables in the determination of investment. It is, in fact, generally recognized that activity variables, especially output, have 'a more substantial impact on investment' (Chirinko, 1993, p. 1881), so that, even if expansionary fiscal policy raised interest rates, crowding out would not materialize.

The second line of argument relates to the role of savings in fiscal policy (see also Cunningham and Vilasuso, 1994–5, and Fazzari, 1994–5). Consider the following identity in terms of outcomes:

$$DS = PI + GD + CA, \qquad (8.1)$$

where *DS* is domestic savings, *PI* is private investment, *GD* is government deficit and *CA* is current account surplus (or minus current account deficit). It is then argued that crowding out occurs because higher aggregate demand due to an increase in deficit 'absorbs' savings, which reduce investment (Cunningham and Vilasuso, 1994–5). The possibility of 'international crowding out' is also raised. This may come through the exchange rate: it is postulated that higher interest rates associated with the fiscal expansion cause capital inflows which appreciate the exchange rate and deteriorate the *CA* (smaller surplus or higher deficit), thereby offsetting the increase in aggregate demand that emanates from fiscal expansion (see Hemming, Kell and Mahfouz, 2002, for more details on international crowding out).

A related argument has been proposed. Rewrite (8.1) to read as follows:

$$DS + FS = PI + GD, \qquad (8.2)$$

where the symbols are as above, and with *FS* standing for foreign saving (equivalent to deficit in *CA*). An increase in government deficit (*GD*), then, 'signals a decline in government saving. As a result, either investment falls, foreign savings rise, or some combination of these occurs. Put differently, either crowding out occurs, international crowding out occurs or both' (Cunningham and Vilasuso, 1994–5, p. 194).[2] Clearly, both these arguments of Cunningham and Vilasuso relating to (8.1) and (8.2) are flawed. Consider the argument relating to (8.2) first. This formulation of the crowding out argument treats *DS* as exogenously given. However, *DS* should be treated as endogenous in that its size responds to changes in, inter alia, government expenditure. Then an increase in *GD* could be expected to lead to an increase in *DS*. This could also happen when we come to the argument of (8.1), for, in both cases, it is possible that, with a higher government deficit, increases in income and investment occur, as well as the economy's saving, rather than reducing investment. Consequently, expansionary fiscal policy will boost savings since it raises income and investment, rather than reducinge savings (see also Gordon, 1994). In the context of interest rates being set by the central bank, the effect of budget deficit on interest rates depends on the reactions of the central bank.

International crowding out is unlikely to materialize under the circumstances explored here. Fiscal policy influences the level of economic activity, some of which spills over into imports. The exchange rate may be affected by the change in the level of economic activity; but the precise effect is not clear. A rise in imports could be expected to depress the exchange rate, but the rise in economic activity may generate optimism about the state of the economy, thereby tending to raise the exchange rate. There may be a direct effect of fiscal policy on the exchange rate insofar as the exchange market operators react against expansionary fiscal policy and sell the currency. However, fiscal policy may very well result in increasing imports, opening up a trade deficit and thereby producing international crowding out. To the extent, however, that the rest of the world increases its appetite for the country's exports, no international crowding out need occur (see, Fazzari, 1993, for more details).

The counterargument is that all this may be true in the short run, and under conditions of excess capacity. But it is the short run in which we live (and 'in the long-run we are all dead') and conditions of excess capacity are a general (though not universal) feature of the market economy.[3] In the long run, it is argued that the dynamics of wages and prices ensure that fiscal policy crowds out private investment or increases foreign indebtedness (via its impact on *CA* in equation 8.1). This mechanism is due to the downward-sloping aggregate demand schedule (falling prices, given the money stock, raise real balance, thereby increasing aggregate demand).[4] A fiscal expansion leading to higher levels of economic activity is postulated to lead to rising prices and wages, thereby reducing private demand. A number of arguments, however, can be advanced to suggest that falling prices can go hand in hand with falling aggregate demand. Redistribution of income and wealth from debtors to creditors follows in the context of unanticipated price falls. On the assumption that debtors have a higher propensity to spend than creditors, the redistribution of real wealth caused by deflation lowers aggregate demand (see, for example, Tobin, 1993). Lower income reduces cash flows relative to debt service commitments, thereby increasing the probability of insolvency (Fisher, 1933, and Minsky, 1975, are good examples). In addition, there are the anticipated deflation effects, which may raise expected real interest rates, which dampen expenditure and prevent the occurrence of the aggregate demand effects discussed above (DeLong and Summers, 1986). More significantly, the downward-sloping aggregate demand schedule depends on the existence of 'outside money' and credit money (the dominant form in an industrialized society) is largely 'inside money'. Even when there is 'outside money' (high-powered money) and the relevant measure of the money stock is a multiple of high-powered money (determined by the size of the credit multiplier), the amount of money in existence depends on people's willingness to hold that money: the stock of money is demand-determined. If prices fall, the demand for money falls, and the stock of money falls, and there is no real balance effect. The inevitable conclusion is that it is by no means clear that the effectiveness of fiscal policy is short-lived and damaging in the long run.

The third form of 'crowding out' arose from a combination of the notion of a supply-side equilibrium (such as the 'natural rate of unemployment' or the non-accelerating inflation rate of unemployment, the NAIRU), and that the level of aggregate demand would adjust to be consistent with that supply-side equilibrium. In the context of an exogenous money supply, this came through the assertion of a 'real balance' effect, with changes in the price level generating changes in the real value of the stock of money, thereby generating changes in the level of aggregate demand (this, of course, could be a very long adjustment process indeed; what is at issue, though, is the 'automatic' adjustment invoked in the case the NAIRU). In the context of endogenous money, it would come through the adjustment of interest rate by the central bank. This would occur, as indicated above, if the central bank adopted some form of 'Taylor rule' (provided, of course, that interest rates are effective in that regard). Under such a rule the setting of the key interest rate depends on the 'equilibrium' rate of interest, deviation of inflation from target and deviation of output from trend level (Taylor, 1993). Monetary policy can guide aggregate demand to match supply provided that interest rates are effective in influencing the level of demand and provided that the central bank's calculation of the 'equilibrium rate' of interest is accurate.

Fiscal policy has an effect on the level of aggregate demand, and 'crowding out' only occurs if it is assumed that the supply-side equilibrium must be attained (in order to ensure a constant rate of inflation) *and* that the level of aggregate demand would anyway be equivalent to the supply-side equilibrium. In the absence of some powerful automatic market forces or a potent monetary policy, which can ensure that the level of aggregate demand moves quickly to be consistent with the supply-side equilibrium, fiscal policy has a clear role to play. The path of aggregate demand can itself influence the supply-side equilibrium. The size and distribution of the capital stock is a determinant of the productive capacity of the economy, and a larger capital stock would be associated with the supply-side equilibrium involving a higher level of output and employment. The level of aggregate demand (including the change in economic activity and profitability) has an impact on investment expenditure, and thereby on the size of the capital stock (as we have explored in Chapter 6). The supply-side equilibrium may form an inflation barrier at any point in time, but it is not to be seen as something immutable and unaffected by the level of aggregate demand.

The fourth route of 'crowding out' comes from the Ricardian Equivalence Theorem (RET). We may clarify RET in a bond-financed increase in household taxes, holding government expenditure constant. RET makes the assumption that there is equivalence between debt and taxes, and that consumers are forward-looking. Consumers are also assumed to be fully aware of the government's intertemporal budget constraint, and recognize that a tax increase today will be followed by lower taxes in the future imposed on their infinitely lived families. Consumers decrease their savings, in the knowledge that they will not have to pay more in the future (the debt will be less). The increase in taxes is associated with a decrease in savings. Permanent income, therefore, does not change as a result of the tax increase. In the absence of liquidity constraints and with perfect capital markets, consumption does not change (Barro, 1974).

There is, thus, equivalence between taxes and debt. This implies that an increase in government saving resulting from a tax increase is fully offset by lower private saving, so that aggregate demand is not affected. Raising taxes will have no effect; the policy is totally frustrated and the fiscal multiplier is zero. Similarly, a reduction in taxation in the present is viewed as the prospect of future taxation (which is equivalent in present value terms) leaving the public no better off in wealth terms. The reduction in present taxation may stimulate consumer expenditure but the prospect of future taxation reduces consumer expenditure by an equivalent amount. An important assumption of this process is that Ricardian behaviour implies *full* consumption smoothing to offset intergenerational redistribution imposed by government debt policy. The tax burden is redistributed among generations with families reversing the effect of this redistribution through bequests. However, the more realistic case of *partial* consumption smoothing invalidates Ricardian behaviour (Mankiw, 2002). In the event of partial consumption smoothing, a reduction in present taxation stimulates consumer expenditure to some degree, and hence fiscal policy has some effect.

A range of objections have been raised against the RET. The major proponent of the RET, Barro (1989), lists five 'major theoretical objections that have been raised against the Ricardian conclusions. The first is that people do not live forever, and hence do not care about taxes that are levied after their death. The second is that private capital markets are "imperfect" with the typical person's real discount rate exceeding that of the government. The third is that future taxes and incomes are uncertain. The fourth is that taxes are not lump sum, since they depend typically on income, spending, wealth and so on. The fifth is that the Ricardian result hinges on full employment' (p. 40). Whilst the first four listed are, in our view, significant and valid objections to RET, it is the fifth which is particularly relevant here. Given the importance of the RET we discuss it at length in the following chapter. We might actually add further objections to the list: less than perfect foresight, partial liquidity constraints and a non-altruistic desire to pass some of the current fiscal burden to future generations (Mankiw and Summers, 1984; Blanchard, 1985) are but a few of them. There may also be significant distributional effects, assumed to be negligible by the RET proponents (see below for relevant arguments). Furthermore, empirical work on the RET produces evidence that is mixed at best (Cunningham and Vilasuso, 1994–5). A more recent study comes to even more negative conclusions for the RET; clearly, 'There is little evidence of direct crowding out or crowding out through interest rates and the exchange rate. Nor does full Ricardian equivalence or a significant partial Ricardian offset get much support from the evidence' (Hemming, Kell and Mahfouz, 2002, p. 36). However, there are interest rate premia and credibility effects as well as uncertainty considerations, which can mitigate the effects to which we have just referred. With fiscal expansions and debt accumulation, risk premia that reflect the risk of default or increasing inflation risk reinforce crowding-out effects through interest rates (Miller *et al.*, 1990). They may also raise fears of future balance of payments problems, and thereby lead to foreign investment reduction and capital outflows. Similarly, to the extent that a fiscal expansion is associated with increased uncertainty (in that future deficits have a negative effect on confidence), households may accumulate precautionary savings and firms may delay irreversible investment (Caballero and Pyndick, 1996).

4   INSTITUTIONAL ASPECTS OF FISCAL POLICY

We have argued that fiscal policy appropriately applied does not lead to crowding out, and in that sense fiscal policy will be effective. This is to recognize that an attempted fiscal expansion in the context of a fully employed economy would involve 'crowding out' to some degree. The extent of the 'crowding out' would depend on how far supply can respond to increase in demand, and even at what is regarded as full employment there can be some elasticity of supply (firms hold some excess capacity, there are 'encouraged' worker effects and so on). But there may be other causes that can produce ineffectiveness in fiscal policy. These other causes have been summarized above (see the second section of this chapter) under the general title of 'institutional aspects of fiscal policy'. This section explores some of the issues that arise.

The first issue concerns what may be termed 'model uncertainty': the operation of fiscal policy requires forecasts of the future course of the economy, and uncertainty over forecasts increases the difficulties of making decisions about fiscal policy. It increases the likelihood that fiscal policy will turn out to be inappropriate. Some have argued that, in terms of model uncertainty, there is evidence that longer and more uncertain lags have prevailed recently than was thought the case previously (Hemming, Kell and Mahfouz, 2002, p. 8). Model uncertainty is, of course, not new in economics and economic policy in particular. Friedman's (1957) notion of long and variable lags in monetary policy is perhaps the most well known. This clearly shows that long and variable lags are not a reflection of fiscal policy alone. Indeed, many of the issues raised here would also apply to monetary policy: there may be model uncertainty, long and variables lags between policy announcement and effect there also. Monetary policy and fiscal policy both draw on the forecasts of macroeconometric models, and uncertainty over the models would apply with equal force to monetary policy as to fiscal policy. Further, monetary policy (in the form of interest rate decisions) involves frequent decision making (for example monthly for the Bank of England, every six weeks for the Federal Reserve) and attempts fine-tuning. Fiscal policy, in contrast, typically involves infrequent decisions (often annual), and could be described as more like 'coarse tuning'.[5] It could be argued that the 'fine-tuning' nature of monetary policy means that it suffers more from problems of model uncertainty than does fiscal policy.

The second issue relates to the argument that fiscal policy is in practice procyclical rather than countercyclical.[6] In particular, it has long been argued that the various lags of decision making, implementation and impact may mean that fiscal policy which is intended to stimulate the economy during a downturn may come into effect when the economy has already recovered (and similarly for fiscal policy designed for a boom period coming into effect when the economy has turned down). The strength of this argument depends on the relationship between the length of the business cycle and the lags of fiscal policy. For example, a four-year business cycle and a two-year fiscal policy lag would indeed lead to fiscal policy being procyclical.

The notion of the procyclical nature of fiscal policy is justified by resort to arguments relating to the cumbersome parliamentary design, approval and implementation. We may actually distinguish between inside and outside lags in this context. Inside lags refer to the time it takes policy makers to appreciate that fiscal policy action is necessary and to make the required decisions. Clearly, inside lags depend on the political process and the effectiveness of fiscal management. Outside lags refer to the time that it takes for fiscal measures to affect aggregate demand (Blinder and Solow, 1974). Discretionary policy measures, particularly when they involve policy departures, new forms of taxation and expenditure initiatives, are likely to be subject to long inside lags. Variations in tax rates and in social security benefits can potentially be made with relatively short inside lags.[7] But automatic stabilizers, by their nature, involve little by way of inside lags. Outside lags are expected to be more variable than inside lags and would vary, depending on the fiscal measure utilized, the institutional set-up of the economy in question and the period under investigation.

One difference between monetary policy and fiscal policy arises from the former being much less subject to democratic decision making than the latter. Changes in tax rates require parliamentary or congressional approval; changes in interest rates do not. But long and variable outside lags may be a feature of monetary policy as much as (or more than) fiscal policy. The inside lags of fiscal policy could be substantially reduced by the adoption of a 'fiscal policy rule' (Taylor, 2000) analogous to a 'monetary policy rule' (Taylor, 1993). To the extent that this is the right rule (that is, it places much emphasis on full employment), there could be a role for such a rule, especially so if the rule relates to the fiscal stance, leaving the issue of composition of taxation and of public expenditure to be determined through the democratic process.

The third issue is the idea that fiscal policy may entail a 'deficit bias'. This may be due to a number of factors. Increasing taxes/decreasing government expenditure during upswings may be politically unrealistic. Alesina and Perotti (1995) refer to a number of institutional factors to explain the possibility of a deficit bias. Voters and policy makers may be unaware of the government's intertemporal budget constraint,[8] and as a result favour budget deficits; they may wish to shift the fiscal burden to future generations; policy makers may wish to limit the room for manoeuvre of future governments strategically in terms of fiscal policy; political conflicts may delay fiscal consolidation in terms of sharing the burden of adjustment amongst various social groups, thereby producing a deficit bias; spending decisions may be subjected to irreversibility, which can lead to a public expenditure ratcheting effect. The presence of a deficit bias does not necessarily make fiscal policy any less effective, though it may constrain governments to engage in further deficit spending in the face of a recession.

It has been argued that large and persistent deficits may be a reflection of this deficit bias, but those deficits have to be measured against what is required. The persistence of unemployment in market economies suggests a general lack of aggregate demand, and hence a requirement for fiscal stimulus. Any tendency for savings to outrun investment also requires a budget deficit to mop up the excess net private savings. We can then distinguish those budget deficits, which are required to sustain demand and to mop up excess savings to ensure desirable levels of economic activity, which we will call necessary deficits. In contrast, unnecessary budget deficits are that part of deficits which take economic activity too high (on some criteria such as beyond full employment). This distinction clearly implies that a bias in favour of necessary deficits is consistent with the argument advanced in this chapter, whereas any bias towards unnecessary deficits is not.

The fourth issue arises from the notion that supply-side inefficiencies associated with tax rate volatility are possible. This issue is strongly related to the way in which changes in taxes affect the supply of labour, and also changes in capital taxes affect saving and investment. These considerations are expected to have a significant impact on internationally mobile labour and capital. However, ultimately, these considerations depend heavily on the empirical evidence adduced on the impact of tax changes on the supply of labour and capital, and thereby on growth. This empirical issue, however, has yet to be validated. Such limited evidence that exists has not yet provided clear-cut conclusions (see, for example, Blundell and MaCurdy, 1999; Hemming, Kell and Mahfouz, 2002). A further comment worth making is this: active monetary policy involves interest rate volatility (as compared with a passive monetary policy that changed interest rates infrequently) which would have supply-side inefficiencies. If fiscal policy was successful, demand volatility would be reduced, and demand volatility would generate supply-side inefficiencies, in that the level of supply would be continually changing, not to mention the inefficiency of excess capacity.

A final issue that belongs to the 'institutional aspects' is the level and degree of economic development. It is the case that most of the literature on the effectiveness of fiscal policy has focused on developed countries. Agénor *et al.* (1999) argue that, because the developing world is more likely to be influenced by supply shocks, fiscal policy as a tool of demand management is most likely to be used far less frequently in developing than in developed countries. A supply shock, however, is often taken to mean a cost change (for example oil price), but that has a demand dimension to it (in case of oil imports change and so on). Clearly, a supply shock change cannot affect the level of economic activity unless it causes demand to change as well. Within the AS–AD model, an adverse shift in the *AS* curve can be offset in terms of economic activity by a shift in the *AD*, albeit at the expense of a higher price level (and leaving aside the question of how the supply side would be identified). In the case of developing countries, it may be that collection of taxation is more difficult and so on, but it would also seem that there may be less call for fiscal deficits: if developing countries are characterized by low savings and high demand for investment, then $S–I$ would be negative, and hence $G–T$ would also be negative. This is the classic argument that governments in developing countries run surpluses in order to generate savings, which the private sector is unwilling or unable to undertake.

Even so, it is suggested that the availability and cost of domestic and external finance is a major constraint on fiscal policy. It follows that access to financing should determine to a large extent the size of the fiscal deficit. An increase in the fiscal deficit beyond a level that can only be financed on unacceptable terms may be associated with severe crowding out effects. Relaxing these constraints, therefore, enables fiscal policy to have significant stimulative effects (Lane *et al.*, 1999). An additional factor that enhances the effectiveness of fiscal policy in these countries is the relatively high marginal propensity to consume, which can increase the size of the impact of fiscal policy significantly. This analysis suggests that the deficit bias discussed above may be relatively higher in developing countries. In fact, Hemming, Kell and Mahfouz (2002, p. 12) provide a list of the causes of the relatively high deficit bias in developing countries. Governance, as it relates to poor tax administration and expenditure management, is probably the most important and significant item on the list. In terms of the distinction drawn above, this would be 'unnecessary' deficit bias.

5 QUANTITATIVE EFFECTS OF FISCAL POLICY

This section draws on published work on the empirics of fiscal policy. We do not offer our own empirical work but rely instead on already published evidence, and a distinction may be made between evidence adduced from developed and from developing economies. This distinction is necessary partly for the reasons alluded to at the end of the last section, but also for reasons which have to do with data deficiencies in developing countries. For all these reasons there is rather less evidence on the short-run impact of fiscal policy for developing rather than for developed countries (Hemming, Kell and Mahfouz, 2002). We begin with the available evidence on developed countries.

Following Hemming, Kell and Mahfouz (2002), we comment on three substantive components of the available evidence on developed countries. There are, to begin with, estimates of dynamic multipliers that are designed to determine the possible empirical impact of fiscal policy on economic activity. These dynamic multipliers are derived from macroeconomic model simulations and small model calibrations, as well as reduced-form equations. Studies which draw from specific episodes of fiscal contraction in an attempt to identify expansionary fiscal contractions are the second category. The third category comprises studies that attempt to assess the determinants of dynamic multipliers. Consequently, interest in this concentrates upon relationships between fiscal policy on the one hand, and other variables such as interest and exchange rates, investment, consumption and so on, on the other.

On the first issue, Hemming, Kell and Mahfouz (2002) summarize the evidence adduced from these studies. It is suggested that short-term multipliers are positive, ranging from 0.1 to 3.1, with expenditure multipliers being in the range of 0.6 to 1.4, and tax multipliers in the range of 0.3–0.8. Long-term multipliers are smaller than short-term multipliers, undoubtedly reflecting some form of crowding out. Another recent study (Hemming, Mahfouz and Schimmelpfennig, 2002) summarizes the argument along similar lines: 'Estimates of fiscal multipliers are overwhelmingly positive but small. Short-term multipliers average around a half for taxes and one for spending, with only modest variation across countries and models (albeit with some outliers). There are hardly any instances of negative fiscal multipliers, the exception being that they can be generated in some macroeconomic models with strong credibility effects' (p. 4). Small model calibrations, essentially dynamic general equilibrium models that analyse steady-state long-run effects of fiscal policy, produce results that show output to respond positively to (unanticipated) increase in government expenditure (where permanent changes have larger effects than temporary changes). Reduced-form equation results are broadly similar.

On the second category of studies, Hemming, Mahfouz and Schimmelpfennig (2002) examine fiscal policy during recessions in advanced countries to conclude that (a) fiscal policy during recessions in closed economies is effective but with a small fiscal multiplier, (b) fiscal policy is not so effective in open economies during recessions, especially when flexible exchange rates prevail and, (c) fiscal expansions can be more effective when they are expenditure-based, big government, there is excess capacity, a closed economy or an open economy with a fixed exchange rate regime, and expansionary expenditure is accompanied by monetary expansion.[9] In terms of the determinants of fiscal multipliers, the third category identified above, Hemming, Kell and Mahfouz (2002) conclude that 'There is little evidence of direct crowding out or crowding out through interest rates and the exchange rate. Nor does full Ricardian equivalence or a significant partial Ricardian offset get much support from the evidence' (p. 36).

Finally, the evidence on developing countries is not dissimilar to that obtained for developed economies. If anything, fiscal multipliers tend to be rather higher in the case of developing rather than developed economies (see, for example, Hemming, Kell and Mahfouz, 2002, p. 33).

The overall conclusion of this rather brief summary of the empirical evidence on the effectiveness of fiscal policy is encouraging. Fiscal multipliers and other tests tend to provide favourable evidence for fiscal policy, especially so in view of the argument that in most, if not all, of the studies that summarize the results reported in this chapter, there is a long-run constraint built into the models utilized for the purposes of the empirical exercises. Such constraints, labelled above 'NAIRU constraints', by their very nature and definition contain substantially the long-run values of the fiscal multipliers.

6   SUMMARY AND CONCLUSIONS

This chapter has argued that shifts in the level of aggregate demand can be readily offset by fiscal policy. Consequently, fiscal policy remains a powerful instrument for regulating the level of aggregate demand. Fiscal policy 'can and should be called upon as a key part of the remedy' when the economy needs aggregate demand boosting, and 'when the economy's resources are underutilised' (Fazzari, 1994–5, p. 247). Even when the economy's resources are fully utilized, we would still argue that, to the extent that fiscal policy can affect the capital stock of the economy, it could also have long and lasting effects in this case. In view of this significant role fiscal policy assumes within an endogenous money framework, we discuss further relevant issues in the next chapter.

NOTES

1. The 'equilibrium rate' is where savings and investment are brought into equality at full employment or some other supply-side equilibrium level of employment or output.
2. In fact Cunningham and Vilasuso (1994–5) argue strongly that 'demand management policies may be largely ineffective and, in some cases, contribute more to the problems than to the solutions' (p. 187). The main reason given is the 'structural, institutional, and regulatory changes' since the 1970s, which 'have altered the rules of the *game*, with the result that aggregate policy measures have failed to stimulate total spending' (p. 188). Fazzari (1994–5) rebuffs this proposition on both theoretical and empirical grounds.
3. If full employment (or some other desired level of economic activity) can be reached and sustained by private aggregate demand, there would be few who would advocate stimulating fiscal policy. But the advocates of fiscal policy take the view that full employment is a rare occurrence and that private aggregate demand is often insufficient to sustain full employment (Say's Law does not operate).
4. It should be noted that the extent of crowding out is, of course, affected by price flexibility. In general terms, it can be argued that 'Price flexibility, even if it is limited in the short run, will tend to narrow the range of values taken by fiscal multipliers, and in particular to limit the influence of the exchange rate regime' (Hemming, Kell and Mahfouz, 2002, p. 5).
5. This refers to discretionary fiscal policy: it could be said that the automatic stabilizers are operating all the time.
6. The operation of the 'automatic stabilizers' provides a countercyclical component of fiscal policy. The procyclical argument applies particularly to the discretionary changes in fiscal policy.
7. This is not entirely true, in that it may not be the case in all parliamentary systems. In the UK, for example, the fiscal measure of a change in the duty on alcohol, tobacco, petrol and so on is made quickly and implemented within hours (often by 6 p.m. on budget day). It is subject to retrospective approval by parliament.
8. This appears to accept the intertemporal budget constraint as a reality, which may not be

the case. In another paper (Arestis and Sawyer, 2003b), we argue that that depends on whether the rate of interest is higher or lower than the rate of growth.

9. An interesting case that has been discussed in the literature (initiated by Giavazzi and Pagano, 1990) is the case of Ireland and Denmark where, it is alleged, contractionary fiscal policy is associated with expansion in economic activity. We would dispute this result on the basis that it is other factors that explained the expansion of economic activity; it is, thus, the expansion that enabled budget deficits to be smaller than otherwise. This is a classic case of 'simultaneity bias' (Eichengreen, 1998). Also, omitted variables may very well be responsible for the results obtained in these fiscal consolidation episodes. Exchange rate depreciations that normally accompany fiscal contractions may be more responsible for the expansion in economic activity than the fiscal action itself (Hemming, Kell and Mahfouz, 2002, p. 25). More specifically in the case of Ireland, Walsh (2002) argues that a number of factors contribute to the expansion: 'a low exchange rate, the inflow of FDI to high productivity sectors, and wage moderation following the return to centralised wage agreements in 1987. Labour market reforms, including a tightening of the social welfare regime and a switch of spending from income support to active labour market policies, played a positive role' (p. 1).

9.   The case for fiscal policy

1   INTRODUCTION

Chapter 8 made the point that fiscal policy can be a powerful instrument of economic policy. This chapter strengthens that point by putting forward the case for fiscal policy. The case for the use of fiscal policy and for governments to operate with an unbalanced budget (whether in surplus or deficit) arises from the simple Keynesian proposition that there is no automatic mechanism which ensures that aggregate demand is sufficient to underpin a high level of economic activity (Kalecki, 1939; Keynes, 1936). The notion that the budget should always be in balance (or even on average in balance) is rejected on the grounds that a balanced budget is generally not compatible with the achievement of high levels of aggregate demand. Further, although interest rates may have some impact on the level of aggregate demand, there are constraints on the extent to which interest rates can be varied (whether for reasons akin to a liquidity trap in operation which prevent the reduction of interest rates below a particular level or for foreign exchange considerations) and there are doubts relating to the potency of interest rates to influence aggregate demand.

Many lines of argument have been developed to the effect that budget deficits and fiscal policy are ineffectual and/or have undesired (and undesirable) effects. This chapter starts from a 'functional finance' perspective (discussed in the next section). This views the role of fiscal policy in terms of raising the level of aggregate demand, where it would otherwise be too low, while leaving open what level of economic activity is regarded as optimum or desirable. It puts forward the view that the arguments which have been deployed against fiscal policy to the effect that it does not raise the level of economic activity do not apply when a 'functional finance' view of fiscal policy is adopted (see also Arestis and Sawyer, 2003d).

2   FISCAL POLICY AND 'FUNCTIONAL FINANCE'

The starting point is the argument that the nature and role of fiscal policy should be approached from the perspective of what has been termed 'functional finance' (Lerner, 1943). The general proposition is that the budget position should be used to secure a high level of economic activity in conditions where otherwise there would be a lower level of economic activity. Lerner put the case for Functional Finance (capitalized in the original), which 'rejects completely the traditional doctrines of "sound finance" and the principle of trying to balance the budget over a solar year or any other arbitrary period' (p. 355). 'Functional finance' supports the important proposition that total spending should be adjusted to eliminate both unemployment and inflation.

In a similar vein, Kalecki (1944a) argued that sustained full employment 'must be based either on a long-run budget deficit policy or on the redistribution of income' (p. 135). He based his argument on the assumption that there would be a tendency for the level of aggregate demand to fall short of that required for full employment. Then there was a need for either a budget deficit to mop up the difference between full employment savings and investment or for full employment savings to be reduced through a redistribution of income (from rich to poor).

He also argued that 'although it has been repeatedly stated in recent discussion that the budget deficit always finances itself – that is to say, its rise always causes such an increase in incomes and changes in their distribution that there accrue just enough savings to finance it – the matter is still frequently misunderstood' (Kalecki, 1944b). He then set out for a closed economy the equality:

$$G + I = T + S \qquad (9.1)$$

where G is government expenditure, T tax revenue, I investment expenditure and S savings, and hence

$$G - T = S - I, \qquad (9.2)$$

which can be readily modified for the open economy as

$$G + I + X = T + S + Q, \qquad (9.3)$$

where X stands for exports and Q for imports.

From this perspective, the budget deficit is to be used to mop up 'excess' private savings (over investment), and the counterpart budget surplus used when investment expenditure exceeds savings (at the desired level of economic activity). It follows, though, that a budget deficit is not required when there is a high level of private aggregate demand such that investment equals savings at a high level of economic activity (and a surplus would be required when investment exceeds savings at the desired level of economic activity).

This can be expressed by saying that the government budget position should be set so that

$$G - T = S(Y_f) - I(Y_f) + Q(Y_f) - X(WY), \qquad (9.4)$$

where Y_f is the intended level of income (which may be thought of as equivalent to full employment or to some supply-side constraint), WY is world income (taken as given for the purposes of this equation). A tendency for savings to run ahead of investment leads to the view that a budget deficit is required (in the absence of any tendency for balance of trade surplus). But it is a shortfall of investment over savings that creates the requirement for a budget deficit: in the absence of any such shortfall (in ex ante terms) there is no need for a budget deficit. The analysis of budget deficits should then be undertaken in a context which at least allows for the emergence of an excess of (ex ante) savings over (ex ante) investment. In the absence of any such excess, the 'functional finance' view would not see any cause for a budget deficit.[1]

The case for fiscal policy rests on the proposition that the equality between ex ante savings and ex ante investment at full employment income (or indeed at any target level of income) cannot be assured.[2] If there were some automatic tendency, as expressed in Say's Law, for that equality to be assured, then any case for fiscal policy in the form of unbalanced budgets would disappear. Further, if the relevant rate of interest can be manipulated through monetary policy in such a way as to ensure this equality, then again there would be little room for fiscal policy. The basic Keynesian (Kaleckian) argument is that there is no assurance that this equality will be satisfied, and hence the need for fiscal policy and for an unbalanced budget.

The general presumption of Keynesians and others has been that there is likely to be a deficiency of ex ante investment relative to ex ante savings, rather than the reverse. This does not rule out that there will be occasions (as in the late 1990s in the UK and the USA with conditions of low unemployment) when investment runs ahead of savings. In the former case, a budget deficit is required to mop up the excess savings, while in the latter case a budget surplus results. However, the presumption that budget deficits are the more frequent outcome under the use of 'functional finance' does raise the problem of cumulative budget deficits and rising government debt. Lerner (1943) and others acknowledge this possibility but saw that 'No matter how much interest has to be paid on the debt, taxation must not be applied unless it is necessary to keep spending down to prevent inflation. The interest can be paid by borrowing still more' (p. 356). He summarized the answers to arguments against deficit spending by saying that the national debt does not have to keep on increasing, and that even if it does the interest does not have to be paid from current taxes. Furthermore, interest payments on bonds are an internal transfer. This question of the sustainability of budget deficits is considered further below.

Fiscal policy is often viewed in terms of the determination of government expenditure and taxation as undertaken without specific regard to the state of private aggregate demand. The 'crowding out' argument after all assumes that there is something to be crowded out. That approach to fiscal policy suggests either that fiscal policy has no effect on the level of economic activity (since there is crowding out) or that there is a positive link between government expenditure (budget deficit) and the level of economic activity. The investigation of fiscal policy through the means of simulation of macroeconometric models is concerned (usually) with the question of what happens if government expenditure is increased, other things being equal. The results of such simulations, generally, suggest that an increase in government expenditure does have a positive effect on the level of economic activity (see Chapter 8). Indeed, in the context in which these simulations are undertaken, it is somewhat surprising that positive results are obtained since such macroeconometric models generally build in a variety of ways, which impose crowding out, the most notable being when some form of supply-side equilibrium is assumed.

The approach to fiscal policy just described is not one that underlies the approach of this chapter. Indeed, this approach has been implicit in most recent discussion of fiscal policy and 'crowding out', but does not correspond to the way in which fiscal policy should be viewed. The effects of fiscal policy (especially when that takes the form of a budget deficit) from a 'functional finance' perspective start from the position that budget deficits are applied when there would otherwise be a deficiency of aggregate demand (below that required for the target level of economic activity) and, conversely, budget surpluses are applied when there would otherwise be an excess of aggregate demand. This is not to say that fiscal policy has been always (or even usually) applied in this manner. But it is to argue that fiscal policy and its effects should be evaluated against this background. The evaluation of fiscal policy should not start from the presumption that there would otherwise be adequate effective demand, in that all would agree that in the context of adequate private effective demand there is no requirement for budget deficits. There have been three distinct sets of arguments to the effect that fiscal policy will be ineffective, under the general heading of 'crowding out', and these are now considered in turn.

3   CROWDING OUT MARK 1: INTEREST RATES

The first form of crowding, discussed in the context of the IS–LM analysis, was a partial 'crowding-out' due to a rise in interest rates following a fiscal expansion which shifted the *IS* curve outwards. This was based on the assumption that the money supply was exogenous and fixed by government (or the central bank), and that the interest rate equated the demand for and supply of money. In that context, though, it was recognized that a sufficient increase in the stock of money alongside an increase in government expenditure could prevent the rise in the interest rate and allow the full effect on the level of economic activity of the increase in government expenditure to come through.

This argument relies on the view that monetary policy (in the form of an increase in the stock of money) does not accommodate fiscal policy, and that investment and other forms of private expenditure are sensitive to the rate of interest. It is also the case that this argument assumes that the stock of money is exogenously determined (outside of the private sector). It is clear that in industrialized economies most of what is counted as money takes the form of credit money (bank deposits). In that context, the stock of money is eventually determined by the demand for money and the level of interest rates is not set by the interaction of the supply and demand for money. In the context of endogenous credit money with the key interest rate set by the central bank, and as argued in Chapter 8, any 'crowding out' comes from the discretionary actions of the central bank. The effect of a budget deficit on the general level of interest rates then depends on the reactions of the central bank to the budget deficit (or more generally to changes which are stimulated by the budget deficit). A 'conservative' central bank which viewed a budget deficit as being to some degree inflationary (whether through a direct effect on inflation or through stimulating aggregate demand which was perceived as inflationary) would respond to a budget deficit by raising interest rates. In contrast a 'Keynesian' central bank whose policy decisions were coordinated with the fiscal policy decisions would respond by making no change to the key interest rate. It is then possible that a budget deficit will be accompanied by increased interest rates, but that would be a discretionary policy decision of the central bank and not the operation of some 'iron law'.[3]

Others would argue that the (long-term) rate of interest is settled in the market for loanable funds, and further that the budget deficit, being the government's demand for loanable funds, will increase demand for loanable funds and thereby the rate of interest. But the 'functional finance' approach views the budget deficit as filling the gap between ex ante savings and investment (at the desired level of economic activity). In the absence of the budget deficit, savings and investment would adjust, notably through changes in the level of economic activity. The budget deficit is required since (by assumption) the rate of interest cannot adjust sufficiently to bring ex ante savings and investment into line at an acceptable level of economic activity. The general expectation of the 'functional finance' approach is that budget deficits have no effect on interest rates (when the budget deficit is designed to 'mop up' excessive savings) and ironically this is the conclusion which is reached by the Ricardian equivalence literature.

4 CROWDING OUT MARK 2: SUPPLY-SIDE EQUILIBRIUM

This second form of 'crowding out' arises from a combination of the notion of a supply-side equilibrium and the theory that the level of aggregate demand would adjust to that supply-side equilibrium. If the representation of the economy (economic model) is such that there are self-contained subsets of equations from which equilibrium solutions can be derived, it is possible to speak of equilibrium positions relating to each of the subsets of equations. In particular, if there is a subset of equations which can be viewed as relating to the supply-side of the economy, it is possible to speak of a supply-side equilibrium: and similarly for a demand-side equilibrium. The 'natural rate of unemployment' and the NAIRU fall into the category of supply-side equilibrium positions. In this context, the supply-side equilibrium seems to place a constraint on the level of output or employment (more generally the level of economic activity). In the present context, the supply-side equilibrium would appear to limit any role for fiscal policy (acting on the demand side of the economy) in that economic activity cannot be raised above the supply-side equilibrium for any length of time. However, this notion of supply-side equilibrium and the dichotomy (separation) between the supply side and demand side of the economy (which sometimes corresponds to the separation between the real side and the monetary side of the economy as in the classical dichotomy) raises three issues.

First, what, if any, are the mechanisms on the supply side of the economy which take the economy to the supply-side equilibrium position? Second, are there mechanisms which bring compatibility between the supply side and the demand side of the economy? Third, are there interactions between the supply side and the demand side of the economy which are generally overlooked? We now look at these issues in turn.

On the first issue, it could be said, little attention has been given to this. However, when the supply side is viewed as akin to a competitive (labour) market (with the 'natural rate of unemployment' as the supply-side equilibrium), an adjustment mechanism appears to be changes in real wages. In the expectations-augmented Phillips curve, changes in real wages (expressed in terms of changes in nominal wages minus expected inflation) are linked with unemployment as a (negative) proxy for excess demand for labour. Real wages continue to adjust until the 'natural rate of unemployment' is attained. This approach implicitly assumes that the cause of unemployment (and indeed overemployment) arises from real wages differing from the equilibrium level. No attention is given to the level of aggregate demand, and implicitly it is assumed that the level of aggregate demand underpins the level of employment as set by the level of real wages. In the more general NAIRU approach, based on imperfect competition and wage bargaining (see, for example, Layard *et al.*, 1991), there is no obvious supply-side adjustment mechanism. Wages and prices change in response to the level of demand, but there is no mechanism at work which guides the level of real wages to its equilibrium level (see, Sawyer, 1999, for further discussion). The adjustment in this NAIRU approach comes from the demand side alone.

With regard to the second issue, one proposed mechanism has been the operation of the real balance effect. The general price level is assumed to respond to the excess of the demand position over the supply-side equilibrium (for example current demand-determined level of unemployment relative to the 'natural rate of unemployment'), and the change in the general price level leads to a change in the real value of the money stock which then has an impact on the level of aggregate demand. The level of aggregate demand is (eventually) brought into line with the supply-side equilibrium. But it is well known (at least since Kalecki, 1944c) that the real balance effect relies on 'external' money with net worth to the private sector and to the stock of money remaining unchanged in the face of price changes. In a world of largely bank credit money, the amount of 'external' money is relatively small: for example, in the UK, the ratio of M0 to GDP is less than 4 per cent; a price fall of 10 per cent would increase real value of M0 by the equivalent of 0.4 per cent. With a wealth effect on consumption of the order of 0.02 to 0.05 (OECD, 2000, p. 192), aggregate demand would change by the order of 0.01 per cent (for a decline of 10 per cent in the price level). But with endogenous money the stock of money is determined by the demand for money. As prices fall, the demand for M0 would fall and hence the stock of M0 would also fall. In sum, the empirical relevance of the real balance effect can be readily dismissed.

The other adjustment mechanism postulated relates to the operation of interest rate policy by the central bank. The adoption of something akin to the Taylor rule would envisage the central bank discount rate being varied in response to the rate of inflation and to the output gap. The 'equilibrium' rate of interest is then seen to be that which brings aggregate demand in line with available supply (and a constant rate of inflation). This is clearly not an automatic market mechanism, but rather arises from the discretionary operation of monetary policy (in the form of interest rates), as discussed above. In this context, the adjustment mechanism arises from an act of government (albeit in the form of the actions of the central bank) and fiscal policy could (and perhaps does) also act as an adjustment mechanism.

Turning now to the third issue, the relationship between the demand side and the supply side of the economy in the sense of changes on one side having a long-lasting impact on the other side (rather than just an adjustment process) is often seen as non-existent. However, there are reasons for thinking that is not the case. The most cited example comes under the label of 'hysteresis effects' in the labour market: periods of low demand and high levels of unemployment are viewed as having 'scarring' effects on the workforce and the effective supply of labour. Without dismissing such effects, in the context of the present chapter a more significant effect may come through the effects of aggregate demand on investment, and of investment on productive capacity (and hence the supply side of the economy). Fiscal policy of the 'functional finance' type boosts aggregate demand, and thereby has a stimulating impact on investment, which raises the future productive capacity of the economy. Further, some advocates of 'functional finance' have viewed public sector investment as a form of expenditure, which can be varied according to the state of private demand, and to the extent to which the budget deficit permits additional public investment there can also be a boost to future productive capacity (this, of course, would depend on the nature of the investment, for example investment in roads or in defence equipment, and the productivity of that investment). The growth rate of the economy may thereby be favourably enhanced by fiscal policy. Keynes (1980) argued for public investment to be set such that Private Investment plus Public Investment equals Savings, and hence that the budget deficit appeared to finance public investment. Keynes also advocated

> in peace-time budgets through the Chancellor making a forecast of capital expenditure under all heads, and comparing this with prospective savings, so as to show that the general prospective set-up is reasonably in accordance with the requirement of equilibrium. The capital budget will be a necessary ingredient in this exposition of the prospects of investment under all heads. If, as may be the case, something like two-thirds or three-quarters of total investment will be under public or semi-public auspices, the amount of capital expenditure contemplated by the authorities will be the essential balancing factor. This is a very major change in the presentation of our affairs and one which I greatly hope we shall adopt. It has nothing whatever to do with deficit financing. (Keynes, 1980, p. 352)

5   CROWDING OUT MARK 3: RICARDIAN EQUIVALENCE

The 'Ricardian equivalence' proposition is that the future prospect of taxation to pay for a bond-financed budget deficit reduces consumer expenditure (and increases savings) which may exactly offset the boost to expenditure arising from the budget deficit. The overall level of savings (public savings plus private savings) remains unchanged.

The Ricardian equivalence proposition has been derived in the context of full employment (or at least a level of income set on the supply side of the economy) and the implicit assumption that private sector aggregate demand will underpin that level of income. Thus the Ricardian equivalence proposition is essentially irrelevant in the context of functional finance. The proposition relates to the question of what happens if a budget deficit is introduced into a situation where ex ante investment and savings are equal at full employment (or equivalent). Functional finance is concerned with the policy recommendation of introducing a budget deficit into a situation where there is a difference between ex ante savings and ex ante investment (usually an excess of savings over investment) at full employment.

The 'Ricardian equivalence' proposition clearly indicates that the level of aggregate demand is invariant to the budget deficit position. But it does not indicate what that level of private demand will be, though there is perhaps the presumption that some form of Say's Law will operate, and that aggregate demand will be sufficient to underpin full employment. However, there is no particular reason for this level of aggregate demand to correspond to any supply-side equilibrium. Specifically, in the event of a shift in the supply-side equilibrium, there is no assurance that there will be a corresponding shift in the level of private demand. Estimates of the supply-side equilibrium NAIRU vary over time and across country, but there would be little reason to think that private aggregate demand would be shifting to correspond to the shifting NAIRU.

Now consider the approach of Barro (1974) which could be seen to revive interest in the Ricardian equivalence proposition under the heading of 'are government bonds net wealth?' (we retain the same notation in what follows). Generation 1 inherits a bequest of A_0^0 from generation 0, and acquires assets of (save) A_1^y while they are young; during their old age they consume c_1^0 and leave a bequest of A_1^0. Their budget constraint in this retirement period is

$$A_0^0 + A_1^y = c_1^0 + (1-r)A_1^0, \tag{9.5}$$

where r is the rate of interest. The assets bequested are assumed to be acquired at beginning of period and yield interest during the period.

Generation 2 receives labour income of w, and saves A_2^y (on which it receives interest), and consumes c_2^y and its budget constraint is

$$c_2^y + (1-r)A_2^y = w. \tag{9.6}$$

In this economy, there is net savings to provide for an increase in the capital stock which yields interest at rate r, hence it is required that

$$A_1^0 + A_2^y - A_0^0 - A_1^y = DK, \tag{9.7}$$

where DK is the change in the capital stock set by the desire to invest. This is equivalent to

$$c_1^0 + c_2^y + DK = w + r(A_1^0 + A_2^y) = y, \tag{9.8}$$

where y stands for income.

But there is nothing which ensures that this equality will hold when the variables are in notional (ex ante) form: ex post there would (of course) have to be equality. Consider the case in notional (ex ante) terms where:

$$c_1^0 + c_2^y + DK < w + r(A_1^0 + A_2^y); \tag{9.9}$$

that is, intended expenditure falls short of income, and equivalently

$$A_0^0 + A_1^y + DK < A_2^y + A_1^0. \tag{9.10}$$

This would be a deflationary situation with (intended) expenditure falling short of (intended) income. Consider the case where income adjusts to bring equality between income and intended expenditure. We assume that consumption is a function of income (labour and capital income) and that return on capital varies proportionally with labour income (through utilization effects). Write w^* as the labour income which would result at full employment, and r^* as the rate of return at full employment, and the income and rate of return which results from a lower level of income as $m.w^*$ and $m.r^*$; then

$$c_1^0(m) + c_2^y(m) + DK = m \cdot w^* + m \cdot r^* \cdot (A_1^0 + A_2^y), \tag{9.11}$$

to give a solution for m $(m < 1)$.

By 'assumption', in this context, the intention to save will have adjusted so that

$$A_0^0 + A_1^y + DK = A^{\wedge y}_2 + A^{\wedge 0}_1 \tag{9.12}$$

where a variable followed by ^ refers to the ex post value of that variable. In equation (9.12) the left-hand side is treated as a given, and the right-hand side has adjusted to the indicated level.

Now introduce functional finance such that the budget deficit can 'mop up' excess private savings; this would mean that

$$c_1^0 + c_2^y + DK + B = w^* + r^*(A_1^0 + A_2^y), \qquad (9.13)$$

where B is the budget deficit and the other variables are at the level which corresponds to full employment. Income is higher by $(1 - m^*)$, net private savings are equal to $DK + B$, and hence

$$A_0^0 + A_1^y + DK + B = A_2^y + A_1^0, \qquad (9.14)$$

with

$$A_2^y + A_1^0 - (A^{\wedge y}_2 + A^{\wedge 0}_1) = B. \qquad (9.15)$$

In this model, generation 2 are able to save what they wish and do so in the form of assets and bonds. Their overall saving is higher than it would have been in the absence of functional finance.

What about next period's budget constraint for generation 2? In the absence of functional finance this is

$$A^{\wedge y}_2 + A_1^0 = c_2^0 + (1 - r)A_2^0. \qquad (9.16)$$

With functional finance it is

$$A_2^y + A_1^0 = c_2^0 + (1 - r)A_2^0. \qquad (9.17)$$

When fiscal policy is approached in 'functional finance' terms, which is a budget deficit run by the government because there is a difference between savings and investment at the desired income level, the Ricardian equivalence approach is scarcely relevant. In the absence of a budget deficit, the excess of savings over investment cannot occur (and the discrepancy is dealt with through a fall in income reducing savings until brought into line with income).

Thus the Ricardian equivalence theorem relies on the assumption of Say's Law. We now suggest that, when fiscal policy acts as an automatic stabilizer, the data may suggest support for the proposition that budget deficits 'crowd out' private savings even though that is not the underlying mechanism. One aspect of the 'functional finance' approach is a recognition that the expenditure/tax system can act as a (partial) automatic stabilizer, with government expenditure tending to rise and tax revenue tending to fall when output slows, thereby limiting the extent of the slowdown in output. This does not mean that these automatic stabilizers are sufficient since economic cycles still occur and employment is often far from being equivalent to full employment. The operation of the automatic stabilizer also indicates that the budget deficit can be an endogenous response to changes on the demand side of the economy.

Consider the case where there are demand shocks to the economy emanating from savings, investment and the foreign sector, which lead to fluctuations in the level of economic activity and the budget position. When fiscal policy is essentially passive (that is, the automatic stabilizers operate but there is no active discretionary policy), the budget deficit varies cyclically. However, this can give rise to the appearance of Ricardian equivalence, generated from the national income link between net private savings and the budget deficit (an equality in the simple context of a closed economy).

Next, consider a simple model in which savings are a simple function of post-tax income:

$$S = a + s(1-t)Y \qquad (9.18)$$

and investment is autonomous, that is,

$$I = b. \qquad (9.19)$$

Fluctuations in demand come from fluctuations in a and b, and these are simulated below as random variables. Tax revenue is a simple linear function of income:

$$T = tY \qquad (9.20)$$

and government expenditure moves countercyclically:

$$G = g = hY, \qquad (9.21)$$

with g also subject to random fluctuations. All variables are written so as to be positive. The current account is CA and treated as a constant (with respect to income) but subject to random fluctuations. Then

$$G - T + CA = S - I, \qquad (9.22)$$

from which

$$g - hY - tY + CA = a + s(1-t)Y - I, \tag{9.23}$$

so that income is given by

$$[h + t + s(1-t)]Y = g + I + CA - a. \tag{9.24}$$

Fluctuations in the savings and investment behaviour lead to fluctuations in the budget deficit, as well as in the level of income. The movement of income as calculated from equation (9.24) was generated through taking values of $s = 0.2$, $h = 0.1$ and $t = 0.4$, and applying random shocks to the values of g, I, a and CA. In Table 9.1 we indicate the range within which the values of these variables lay: for example, in the first experiment, a took values in the range 10 to 20 (15 ± 5) on a randomly determined basis. For each value of these variables the values of income, savings and budget deficit were calculated. Each run was based on 100 observations: the regression of savings : income ratio on the budget deficit to GDP ratio was then estimated, and we also calculated the response of budget deficit to change in income. For each range of values of g, I, a and CA, 100 runs (each based on 100 observations) were undertaken. The average outcomes are reported in Table 9.1 for the results of the regression,

$$S/Y = m + n(BD/Y), \tag{9.25}$$

and the responsiveness of the budget deficit to variations in GDP.

The results from this simple model serve to illustrate two features. First, variations in budget deficit with changes in output are of the same order of magnitude as those observed (references) in the range 0.4 to 0.7.[4] Second, the estimated coefficient on the budget deficit (relative to GDP) in a savings ratio equation is fairly close to unity (though in most cases differing significantly from unity) and hence gives the appearance of a Ricardian equivalence even

Table 9.1   Results of simulation exercise

a	I	g	CA	N	Responsiveness
15 ± 5	22.5 ± 7.5	32.5 ± 2.5	0 ± 5	-0.745 (0.0524)	0.398
				-0.755 (0.0519)	0.408
25 ± 5	22.5 ± 7.5	32.5 ± 2.5	0 ± 5	-1.020 (0.0391)	0.706
				-0.9959 (0.402)	0.666
15 ± 5	22.5 ± 7.5	30.0 ± 5	0 ± 5	-0.790 (0.0591)	0.473
				-0.778 (0.0591)	0.550

though no wealth effects have been included. The relationship between savings and the budget deficit here reflects the national income accounts relationship between private savings minus investment and the budget deficit. Thus these experiments indicate that the operation of fiscal policy as an automatic stabilizer (which partly reflects a functional finance approach) could generate (through the relationship between budget deficit, current account and net private savings) results which mimic those associated with the Ricardian equivalence approach.

6   THE INTERTEMPORAL BUDGET CONSTRAINT

The 'functional finance' approach takes the view that budget deficits (or surpluses) occur as and when required to ensure high levels of economic activity. However, the 'functional finance' view is that a budget deficit is not an occasional occurrence (for example arising from the operation of automatic stabilizers during a recession), but rather may need to be a quasi-permanent feature arising from a tendency of private savings to run ahead of investment. Indeed, the experience of the industrialized economies in the postwar period has involved budget deficits in most years (see, for example, Dwyer and Hafer, 1998, p. 43, in the case of the USA).[5]

The argument is put that long-term budget deficits are unsustainable: one year's budget deficit adds to the public debt, leading to future interest payments. The continuation of a primary budget deficit (that is, deficit excluding interest payments) involves the build-up of interest payments, and further borrowing to cover those interest payments and the continuing primary deficit. Although the budget deficit is growing (when interest payments are included) and the public debt is also growing, their relationship with GDP depends on the growth of the economy as well as the level of interest rates. Domar (1944) provided an early analysis of this and saw 'the problem of the debt burden [as] essentially a problem of achieving a growing national income' (p. 822), though when his analysis used numerical values for key variables rates of interest of 2 per cent and 3 per cent were assumed. Kalecki (1944b) argued that an increasing national debt did not constitute a burden on society as a whole since it is largely an internal transfer, and he further noted that, in an expanding economy, the debt to income ratio need not rise if the rate of growth is sufficiently high (as further discussed below). But in the event that there was a problem of a rising debt to income ratio (and hence of interest payments to income), Kalecki (1944b) advocated an annual capital tax, which would be levied on firms and individuals, which would cover interest payments on the national debt, which would affect 'neither capitalists' consumption nor the profitability of investment' (p. 363).

It is well-known that a continuing primary budget deficit equivalent to a proportion d of GDP will lead to a debt to GDP ratio stabilizing at $b = d/(g - r)$ (where g is the growth rate and r the interest rate, either both in real terms or both in nominal terms).[6] It is evident that the stabilization of the debt to income ratio (with a given primary deficit) requires that $g > r$. In a similar vein, a continuing budget deficit of d' (including interest payments) leads to a debt to GDP ratio stabilizing at d'/g where here g is in nominal terms. But this implies that $d + rb = gb$, that is, $d = (g - r)b$ and hence, if g is less than r, the primary budget deficit is negative (that is, primary budget is in surplus). However, in the functional finance approach, the budget deficit which is relevant is the overall budget position rather than the primary deficit (or surplus). To the extent that a budget deficit is required to offset an excess of private savings over investment, it is the overall budget deficit which is relevant (see below for some caveats). Bond interest payments are a transfer payment and add to the income of the recipient, and are similar in many respects to other transfer payments. In terms of sustainability, then, of a fiscal deficit, the condition under 'functional finance' is readily satisfied (with the requirement of growth being positive).

If a budget deficit (of a particular size relative to GDP) is run for a number of years, it is clear that the interest payments component of the deficit will increase, and the appearance is given that interest payments are 'crowding out' other forms of public expenditure and/or leading to higher levels of taxation. However, in the case in which it is the overall budget deficit which is relevant, a constant deficit (relative to GDP) will lead to a debt to GDP ratio which converges on the ratio deficit/nominal growth rate.[7]

This simple analysis of the budget deficit makes no allowance for any reaction in the willingness of the private sector to hold the public debt. If the public debt becomes an increasing part of the wealth portfolio, the (marginal) attractiveness of holding public debt diminishes. This could have the effect of diminishing the appeal of savings, which has the beneficial effect of stimulating aggregate demand. Further, a higher rate of interest may have to be paid on public debt. The analysis of Godley and Rowthorn (1994) incorporates aspects of that notion and includes a (pre-determined) wealth to income ratio for the private sector and a bond to wealth ratio which depends on the (exogenous) interest rate and the rate of inflation: hence there is a desired bond to income ratio. There is a sense in which the deficit of the public sector is then constrained by that bond to income ratio, and hence the non-monetized debt to income ratio. But this constraint may be of little relevance in the sense that the government is not seeking to run a deficit for the sake of it. It is more significant whether there is a constraint on the level of public expenditure and whether there are other constraints on the economy. On the former, we can note that, in the Godley and Rowthorn model, an expansion in the level of public expenditure sets off an expansion of output and hence of tax revenue (and other changes) such that there is not an explosion in the debt to GDP ratio (and this does not rely on the rate of growth being greater than the rate of interest). This would suggest that there may be reactions from the private sector (arising from a reluctance to hold ever increasing amounts of government debt) which make the conditions for the sustainability of a deficit position less constraining than at first appeared.

The contrasting approach is one based on the notion that the government faces an intertemporal budget constraint of the general form: the present value of current government debt and future budget positions should sum to zero. There has then to be some future primary surpluses on the budget to offset the initial existing government debt. It can alternatively be put that the present value of current and future budget deficits including interest payments sums to zero, and in a sense future budget positions average zero. This arises when it is not possible to service debt forever by rolling it over, and 'Ponzi finance' is ruled out when the current value of outstanding government debt is equal to the discounted future current and budget surpluses (Buiter, 2001, p. 3). Further, 'Ponzi finance is ruled out if the present discounted value of the terminal public debt goes to zero, that is, if the long-run growth rate of the public debt is less than the long-run interest rate' (ibid., p. 3, n.3). With a constant interest rate of r this becomes

$$\lim_{s \to \infty} e^{-r(s-t)} \cdot B(s) = 0, \tag{9.26}$$

where B is the volume of outstanding government bonds. If the growth rate of the bonds outstanding is h with an initial level of $B(0)$, this gives

$$\lim_{s \to \infty} e^{-r(s-t)} \cdot B(0)e^{hs} = B(0)e^{rt}e^{(h-r)s} = 0 \tag{9.27}$$

and this requires $h < r$. A constant bond to GDP ratio would then imply that g $(= h) < r$ (g is the growth of GDP), whereas a declining bond to GDP ratio would result from $g > h$.

These two approaches obviously stand in some contrast. The first indicates that a government can run a perpetual budget deficit of any size and that is sustainable, and the debt to GDP ratio will eventually stabilize (at a finite value), provided that $r < g$. The second indicates that a government must, in effect, clear its debts: a government which starts with outstanding debt (as all do) must then run a primary budget surplus in future, in effect to pay off that debt, conditioned on $r > g$. In the 'functional finance' case, as indicated above, the case of $r > g$ would lead to a stable debt to income ratio but whilst there would be an overall budget deficit, there would be a primary surplus (when the debt ratio had stabilized).

A first response to this contrast is to turn to the empirical evidence on the relationship between interest rate and growth, recalling that here the relevant interest rate is the post-tax rate of interest on government debt.[8] In Table 9.2 we report some comparisons for four major countries between post-tax rate of interest and the rate of growth. The rate of growth reported is the average annual growth rate achieved over the period considered (rather than being an estimate of some underlying trend). The original source for the data provides estimates of pre-tax rate of interest, and a 25 per cent tax rate has been assumed in order to calculate the post-tax rate of interest.

Table 9.2   Comparison of growth rates and interest rates

	Nominal long-term rate	Post-tax rate of interest	Rate of inflation	Post-tax real rate of interest	Pre-tax real rate of interest	Rate of growth
1951–97						
UK	8.45	6.34	6.22	0.12	2.21	2.31
US	7.12	5.34	3.99	1.35	3.16	2.83
France	7.46	5.60	5.57	0.03	1.80	3.36
Germany	7.22	5.42	3.01	2.41	4.15	3.87
1969–79						
UK	11.53	8.65	11.1	−2.45	0.85	2.42
US	7.86	5.90	6.5	−0.61	1.65	3.66
France	8.33	6.25	8.21	−1.96	0.49	3.50
Germany	8.18	6.14	4.56	1.58	3.72	2.93
1980–97						
UK	9.65	7.24	5.68	1.56	3.67	2.62
US	9.84	7.38	4.4	2.98	5.21	3.44
France	10.07	7.55	4.88	2.67	4.87	1.95
Germany	7.43	5.57	2.86	2.71	4.48	2.38

Source: Based on Chadha and Dimsdale (1999), with growth rate calculations based on figures from OECD (2002) and OECD, *Historical Statistics*, various issues.

It is apparent that there is a tendency for the (post-tax) rate of interest to fall below the rate of growth, though not universally and less in the past two decades than formerly. Further, the difference between the rate of interest and the rate of growth is often small. Our own calculations using figures from OECD (2002) for long-term interest rates (on 10-year government bonds) and nominal GDP growth, with again an assumed 25 per cent tax rate, indicate that, for the 20 OECD countries for which data were complete, over the period 1985 to 2001, the growth rate and post-tax interest rate were close on average, but (averaged across countries) the growth rate exceeded the post-tax rate of interest rate in most years, with the period 1990 to 1993 seeing the main exceptions.[9]

The use of the interest rate on bonds may overstate the average cost of borrowing by government in that a government funds part of its budget deficit by the issue of the monetary base (cash and notes held by the public and reserves of the commercial banks with the central bank, which the literature labels as M0). As the demand by the public to hold M0 rises with nominal income growth this is satisfied by the government. Base money bears a zero rate of interest, and to that extent part of the budget deficit is funded at zero cost. Although this is not a substantial part of the budget deficit, nevertheless it has the effect of reducing somewhat the average cost of funding the budget deficit. An M0:GDP ratio of around 5 per cent (which is not untypical) and nominal growth of 5 per cent per annum would lead to an increase of M0 equivalent to 0.25 per cent of GDP.

It can be noted that, in the literature on the Taylor rule, it has been asserted that the equilibrium real rate of interest (central bank discount rate) is approximately equal to the real rate of growth.[10] The rate of interest relevant for the present discussion is the post-tax rate of interest on (long-term) bonds. The interest rate on bonds can generally be expected to be above the discount rate, but after allowing for taxation the post-tax rate on bonds could well be below the rate of growth. This may suggest that the relevant r and g may be close.

The payment of interest on bonds (and the replacement of other forms of public expenditure in the context of a given budget deficit) changes the composition of transfer payments and of disposable income, insofar as these interest payments accrue to the rich rather than the poor. They can be expected to raise the propensity to save and hence raise the excess of savings over investment and the required budget deficit.

The size of the budget required by 'functional finance' is equal (for the closed economy) to savings minus investment (at full employment). Both savings and investment depend on the composition of income (wages versus profits for example) and on the structure of taxation and of transfer payments. As Laramie and Mair (2000) have shown, manipulation of the tax structure can be undertaken such that the tax system has a less deflationary role, and hence full employment (or any desired level of income) achieved with a lower budget deficit (than otherwise). This result can alternatively be seen as saying that the excess of savings over investment can be lowered through the adoption of an appropriate tax structure.

The second consideration also concerns the relationship between savings and investment (again considering a closed economy or modifying savings to include capital inflow from overseas). The counterpart to an intertemporal government budget constraint is an intertemporal private sector budget constraint, of the form that the present value of difference between private savings and investment summed over the future would also be zero (noting that the same discount rate would have to be used for both constraints). The fulfilment of the intertemporal private sector budget constraint requires the equality (over time) between savings and investment. It is possible that savings and investment would be equal at a rate of interest linked with the rate of discount used and compatible with a high level of economic activity. But unless some equivalent of Say's Law is invoked there is little reason to think that such a happy outcome will transpire. In other circumstances, the adjustment between savings and investment occurs through variations in the level of economic activity. Hence the intertemporal government budget constraint imposes on the private sector a requirement (over time) of 'savings equals investment', and that may require relatively low levels of economic activity.

One solution to the path of budget deficits in the face of intertemporal budget constraint is to balance budget in each accounting period. Another is to balance budget over the business cycle. Why is the first regarded (generally) as inferior to the latter? It is presumably because it is recognized that fiscal policy has some automatic stabilizer properties in the face of demand shocks, which arise from fluctuations in savings and investment functions. If the rate of interest could be used to ensure the equality between savings and investment, there would be no requirement for a budget deficit. The deficit is a recognition that the interest rate is not available and/or impotent. The automatic stabilizer dampens fluctuations in private aggregate demand.

The intertemporal budget constraint is consistent with a number of different fiscal policy regimes: for example, balance budget each year, or balance budget over the course of each business cycle. Although this does not appear to be discussed, the implicit assumption appears to be that the course of the economy (and specifically the growth rate and the rate of interest) is independent of the fiscal policy rule which is adopted (provided that the rule conforms to the intertemporal budget constraint).

Consider the case where the cause of movements from year to year in the budget position emanates from movements in the balance between savings and investment. In the absence of countervailing movements in the budget position, the movements in the propensity to save and to invest would generate variations in the level of economic activity, and further variations in the actual volume of savings and of investment. The time path followed by the level of economic activity may have hysteresis effects from a range of causes. One of these would be when variability of key economic variables affects economic decisions on savings and investment. Another would come from asymmetries: economic activity above average would have different size of effects as compared with economic activity below average. When there is some supply-side barrier to the level of economic activity, upswings in aggregate demand may not be able to lead to increases in economic activity, whereas downswings in aggregate demand lead to decreases in economic activity.

When there are variations and differences in intended savings and investment over time (and in the absence of such variations and differences there would be no need for fiscal policy), fiscal policy (of the 'functional finance' type) can be seen to lead to higher levels of economic activity, of savings and of investment. When investment expenditure is sensitive to the level of economic activity, fiscal policy leads to a higher level of investment, and thereby a larger capital stock. A number of views of the growth process (for example endogenous growth, demand-led growth), envisage that higher rates of capital formation are associated with faster growth of productivity. Thus it may be argued that fiscal policy (of the 'right sort') raises the growth rate of the economy. The intertemporal budget constraint, as usually portrayed, takes the growth rate of the economy as given, and unaffected by savings and investment. However, when consideration is given to the variations in savings and investment, and the role which fiscal policy can play in setting the level of economic activity, the growth rate cannot be taken as predetermined. Thus, even if there is some intertemporal budget constraint, there is still a role for fiscal policy.

The sustainability of a primary budget deficit (of given size relative to GDP) requires that the rate of growth exceed the post-tax rate of interest. We have suggested that it is often the case that that condition holds empirically. Tight monetary policy (in the form of relative high interest rates) both directly (through impact on interest rate on bonds) and indirectly (through impact on investment and growth) harms the prospect of sustainability being achieved. It points in the direction of ensuring appropriate monetary policy rather than being too concerned over the precise size of the budget deficit. We have also argued that it is the size of the overall budget deficit which is relevant in the context of functional finance, rather than the size of the primary budget deficit, since it is the impact of the deficit on aggregate demand and the ability of the deficit to mop up excess savings which are relevant. For the overall budget deficit the issue of sustainability does not arise (provided that the growth rate of GDP is positive).

7 SUMMARY AND CONCLUSIONS

The levels of taxation and public expenditure and the balance between them vary for many reasons. Writing this at a time when the proposals of the US administration for tax cuts for the rich are introduced and implemented, it is not possible to forget that the fiscal stance may change for reasons far removed from the application of the ideas of 'functional finance'. The case we have set out in this chapter is that fiscal policy *should* be operated to secure the desired level of economic activity (and that it is a potent instrument for doing so). This 'functional finance' view means that any budget deficit should be seen as a response to the perceived excess of private savings over investment at the desired level of economic activity. We have maintained that the 'crowding out' arguments which have been advanced do not take into account this view of 'functional finance'. The assessment of fiscal policy should relate to the circumstances in which it is intended to be employed, and then we find that the 'crowding out' arguments do not apply.

NOTES

1. One caveat to that statement is the following. A growing economy generally requires an increase in the stock of money, and within that an increase in the monetary base (M0) for which there is an increasing demand as income rises. The provision of M0 comes from a budget deficit.
2. This discussion is cast in terms of a closed economy: adjustments to account for an open economy can be readily made without undermining the basic approach pursued here.
3. In the reverse direction, the reported agreement between Clinton and Greenspan, whereby the latter would reduce interest rate if the former reduced budget deficit, is an example of the policy nature of links between budget deficit and interest rates. This is a clear example of monetary and fiscal policies coordination.
4. The European Commission has, for example, estimated that the sensitivity of the budget balance to output is around 0.5 per cent for the EU; that is, a 1 per cent fall in GDP will increase the budget deficit by 0.5 per cent (Buti *et al.*, 1997, p. 7).
5. Figures in OECD, *Economic Outlook*, December 2002, reveal that there was no year in the 17 years since the mid-1980s for which data are given when the OECD area as a whole had a budget surplus (and one year, 2000, when the deficit was zero).
6. Let the outstanding public sector debt be D; then the budget deficit is dD/dt and is equal to $G + rD - T$, where r is the post-tax rate of interest on public debt, G is government expenditure (other than interest payments) and T is taxation (other than that based on receipt of interest from government). With Y as national income, we have:

$$d(D/Y)/dt = (1/Y)dD/dt - (D/Y)(1/Y) \cdot dY/dt = (G + rD - T)/Y - (D/Y)g,$$

    where g is the growth of national income. The debt to income ratio rises (falls) if $(G - T)/Y > (<) (D/Y)(g - r)$.
7. In that context, the Stability and Growth Pact requirements (for the operation of the European single currency; see Chapter 10) of a maximum budget deficit of 3 per cent of GDP with a balance to small surplus in the budget over the business cycle and debt to GDP ratio of 60 per cent are not compatible. An average 3 per cent deficit and 60 per cent debt ratio would be compatible with a 5 per cent nominal growth rate.
8. The conditions discussed immediately above relate to the actual rate of interest which is paid, and does not in any way relate to what would be the appropriate rate of discount to be applied to government decisions.
9. In 1990, the average difference of $r - g$ was calculated at 0.46 per cent, rising to 2.17 and 2.68 in 1991 and 1992, respectively, then falling back to 1.71 per cent in 1993. In those years there were some particularly large gaps, for example, Finland had a decline in

nominal GDP of 4.5 per cent and pre-tax interest rate of 11.9 per cent. The average for the whole period across all countries was –0.16 per cent (that is, on average, g exceeded r, and, excluding the four years of the early 1990s, the average was –0.75 per cent.

10.   Taylor (1993), for example, postulates a 2 per cent 'equilibrium' real rate of interest which he says 'is close to the assumed steady-state growth rate of 2.2 per cent'.

10. Macroeconomic policies of the European economic and monetary union

1 INTRODUCTION

In this chapter we turn our attention to material of a more applied nature. What it is meant to imply by this is that the theoretical underpinnings put forward in the book are utilized either to analyse real world phenomena or to study further certain features of the real world. The macroeconomic policies of the European economic and monetary union (EMU) are the subject matter of this chapter. More concretely, this chapter seeks to decipher the type of economic analysis and macroeconomic policies of the EMU. It argues that the challenges to the EMU macroeconomic policies lie in their potential to achieve full employment and low inflation in the euro area. It is concluded that these policies as they currently operate have not performed satisfactorily since the inception of the EMU and are unlikely to operate any better in the future. The chapter presents some alternatives, which are based on a different theoretical framework (akin to that put forward in Chapter 6) and institutions.

We begin with the theoretical underpinnings of the EMU model, and deal with the nature of the economic model surrounding the EMU and suggest that it is essentially of what has been termed in this book and elsewhere (see Chapter 2) the 'new consensus' in macroeconomics. The macroeconomic policies that emanate from this model are then deciphered. We suggest that the key challenge is whether in the EMU these policies are adequate to deal with the problems of unemployment and inflation, and thus help to achieve and maintain a framework of full employment. Monetary policy and fiscal policy are then considered within the EMU context. They are both found unable to steer the euro area to a non-inflationary full-employment environment. We argue that the institutional and policy arrangements surrounding the EMU, and the euro, desperately need to be changed, in that they are quite inadequate to deal with problems of unemployment and inflation. We propose alternative policies and institutional arrangements.

2 THEORETICAL UNDERPINNINGS OF THE EMU MODEL

It is unlikely that economic policy pursued by any government or institution is fully consistent either internally or with some theoretical paradigm. However, in view of the approach adopted by the EMU, and the theoretical positions put forward by its officials (see, for example, Issing, 2003b; European Commission, 2000, for recent expositions), it can be thought of as embedded in the 'new consensus' economics paradigm. We argue that the approach can be viewed as 'new consensus' through its emphasis on the supply side-determined equilibrium level of unemployment (the 'natural rate' or the non-accelerating inflation rate of unemployment, the NAIRU), its neglect of aggregate or effective demand, and of fiscal policy, and the elevation of monetary policy at the expense of fiscal policy. We postulate that the economics of the EMU can be understood as based on the elements listed below, which we would argue justify the description of a 'new consensus' variety:

1. The market economy is viewed as essentially stable, and that macroeconomic policy (particularly discretionary fiscal policy) may well destabilize it. Markets, and particularly the financial markets, make well-informed judgments on the sustainability of economic policies, especially so in the current environment of open, globalized, capital and financial markets.
2. Monetary policy is taken as the main instrument of macroeconomic policy, with the view that it is a flexible instrument for achieving medium-term stabilization objectives: it can be adjusted quickly in response to macroeconomic developments. Indeed, monetary policy is the most direct determinant of inflation, so much so that in the long run the inflation rate is the only macroeconomic variable that monetary policy can affect (see, for example, ECB, 2003c). Fiscal policy is no longer viewed as a powerful macroeconomic instrument (in any case it is hostage to the slow and uncertain legislative process). It has a passive role to play, in that the budget deficit position varies over the business cycle in the well-known manner. The budget (at least on current account) can and should be balanced over the course of the business cycle. Fiscal policies 'based on clear mandates and rules reflect a macroeconomic policy design that is generally preferable to the ad-hoc discretionary coordination of day-to-day policy action in the face of shocks' (ibid., p. 37). Monetary policy has thus been upgraded and fiscal policy has been downgraded. It is recognized that the budget position will vary over the course of the business cycle in a countercyclical manner (that is, deficit rising in downturn, surplus rising in upturn), which helps to dampen the scale of economic fluctuations (that is, act as an 'automatic

stabilizer'). But these fluctuations in the budget position take place around a balanced budget on average over the cycle.

3. Monetary policy can be used to meet the objective of low rates of inflation (which are always desirable in this view, since low, and stable, rates of inflation are conducive to healthy growth rates).[1] However, monetary policy should not be operated by politicians but by experts (whether banks, economists or others) in the form of an 'independent' central bank (ibid., pp. 40–41). Indeed, those operating monetary policy should be more 'conservative', that is place greater weight on low inflation and less weight on the level of unemployment than the politicians do (Rogoff, 1985). Politicians would be tempted to use monetary policy for short-term gain (lower unemployment) at the expense of long-term loss (higher inflation). An 'independent' central bank would also have greater credibility in the financial markets and be seen to have a stronger commitment to low inflation than politicians do.

4. Credibility is recognized as paramount in the conduct of monetary policy to avoid problems associated with time inconsistency.[2] This is an argument that reinforces the requirement of central bank independence. It is argued that a policy which lacks credibility because of time inconsistency is neither optimal nor feasible (Kydland and Prescott, 1977). The only credible policy is the one that leaves the authority no freedom to react to developments in the future, and even if aggregate demand policies matter in the short run in this model, a policy of non-intervention is preferable. It is precisely because of the time inconsistency and credibility problems that monetary policy should be assigned to a 'credible' and independent central bank. Such a central bank should be given price stability as its sole objective.

5. The inflation objective is preferred to a money supply objective. The inflation objective is neither a simple rule that inflation is the only target, nor is it discretionary: it is rather a framework for monetary policy whereby public announcement of official inflation objectives, or ranges, is undertaken along with explicit acknowledgment that low and stable inflation is monetary policy's primary long-term objective. This improves communication between the public and policy makers and provides discipline, accountability, transparency and flexibility in monetary policy. The inflation objective has been described as 'constrained' or 'enlightened' discretion, in that an inflation objective serves as a nominal anchor for monetary policy. Thus monetary policy imposes discipline on the central bank and the government within a flexible policy framework. For example, even if monetary policy is used to address short-run stabilization objectives, the long-run inflation objective must not be compromised; this imposes consistency and rationality in policy choices (in this way,

monetary policy focuses the public's expectations and provides a reference point to judge short-run policies). Although the ECB allegedly does not pursue an 'inflation targeting policy' of the type described in Chapter 2 (Duisenberg, 2003a; Issing, 2003b; see also our discussion below), it does, nonetheless, pursue a monetary policy strategy with 'the clear commitment to the maintenance of price stability over the medium term' which 'implies a stable nominal anchor to the economy in all circumstances' (ECB, 2001b, p. 49; see also ECB, 2001c, p. 6; 2001d, p. 6).

6.   The level of economic activity fluctuates around the NAIRU, and unemployment below (above) the NAIRU would lead to higher (lower) rates of inflation. The NAIRU is a supply-side phenomenon closely related to the workings of the labour market. The March 2003 issue of the ECB's Monthly Bulletin puts it as follows: 'the outlook for the euro area economy could be significantly improved if governments strengthen their efforts to implement structural reforms in labour and product markets. Such reforms are important to ultimately raise the euro area's production potential, improve the flexibility of the economy and make the euro area more resilient to external shocks' (ECB, 2003b, p. 6), a point repeated in the April 2003 issue of the Monthly Bulletin. Domestic inflation (relative to the expected rate of inflation) is seen to arise from unemployment falling below the NAIRU, and inflation is postulated to accelerate if unemployment is held below the NAIRU. However, in the long run there is no trade-off between inflation and unemployment, and the economy has to operate (on average) at the NAIRU if accelerating inflation is to be avoided. In the long run, inflation is viewed as a monetary phenomenon, in that the pace of inflation is aligned with the rate of interest. Monetary policy is thus in the hands of central bankers. Control of the money supply is not an issue, essentially because of the instability of the demand for money that makes the impact of changes in the money supply a highly uncertain channel of influence.

7.   The essence of Say's Law holds, namely that the level of effective demand does not play an independent role in the (long-run) determination of the level of economic activity, and adjusts to underpin the supply side-determined level of economic activity (which itself corresponds to the NAIRU). Shocks to the level of demand can be met by variations in the rate of interest to ensure that inflation does not develop (if unemployment falls below the NAIRU).[3]

Most of these general ideas can be seen as formalized (explicitly or implicitly) in what has become known as the 'new consensus' of macroeconomics, and a simple three-equation model describing the 'new consensus' has been set out in Chapter 2. The three relationships that summarize the 'new consensus' contain all the essential elements of the theoretical framework of the EMU (see also ECB, 2003a). There are, however, two important differences worth highlighting. The first is that the ECB does not pursue 'inflation targeting'. We discuss this issue below, in the section entitled 'Monetary Policy', but here it suffices to quote Duisenberg (2003a), who is adamant that the ECB approach does not entail an inflation target: 'I protest against the word "target". We do not have a target ... we won't have a target.' The second is that, in the ECB view, the demand for money in the euro area is a stable relationship in the long run; most central banks would suggest the opposite in the case of their economies.[4] This is also an issue we pursue further below.

3   EMU MACROPOLICIES

The launch of the euro as a 'real' currency (since January 2002), rather than as a 'virtual' currency (since January 1999), took place in an economic environment where there is the prospect of slowing growth and rising unemployment across the world and the euro area, adding to the already high levels of unemployment. Table 10.1 illustrates this point. Since the second quarter of 2000, there has been a continuous slowdown in real GDP growth rate in the euro area. The forecasts for the years 2003 and 2004 and the European Central Bank (ECB) projections for the same years are that this slowdown will continue in 2003, with some recovery expected in 2004. A similar pattern is evident in the cases of the US economy and Britain (where the situation does not appear to be as bad). However, it is the US growth rate, expected at 3.4 and 3.6 per cent in 2003 and 2004, respectively, against the euro area's 1.0 and 2.3 per cent, respectively, which might lead the world economy out of the present slowdown, though the recent rise in the value of the euro may knock the rate of growth down further. In terms of unemployment and inflation the situation is no better. The euro area unemployment is already high at 8.9 per cent (October 2003) and is forecast to be 8.8 per cent for 2003 as a whole and for 2004, and, though the rate is much lower in the USA and Britain, it is now increasing in all three countries (and quite rapidly in the US case).[5] Inflation may not be a problem in the USA and Britain (though some forecasts indicate that inflation may hit the upper limit of the inflation target range of 1.5 per cent to 3.5 per cent) but in the euro area it is above the 2 per cent limit set by the ECB. The forecasts for inflation and the ECB projections relating to inflation tell a similar story: the situation may improve by the year 2004, although it may still be above the 2 per cent ECB inflation target.

Table 10.1(a) Real GDP growth rates (per cent)

	1999				2000				2001				2002				GDP Forecasts	
	1Q	2Q	3Q	4Q	1Q	2Q	3Q	4Q	1Q	2Q	3Q	4Q	1Q	2Q	3Q	4Q	2003	2004
Euro area	1.7	1.8	2.6	3.3	3.5	3.7	3.2	2.8	2.5	1.6	1.3	0.5	0.3	0.7	0.8	0.7	1.0	2.3
USA	4.0	3.9	4.2	4.3	4.2	4.9	3.7	2.3	1.5	−0.1	−0.4	0.1	1.4	2.2	3.3	2.9	3.4	3.6
Britain	2.2	1.9	2.4	3.2	3.4	3.6	3.0	2.3	2.6	2.0	1.9	1.9	1.2	1.6	2.2	2.2	2.2	2.6

Notes: Growth rates = $100 [X_t/X_{t-1} - 1]$, where X_t is value in quarter t, and X_{t-1} is value in quarter of a year ago. Inflation is defined as the overall harmonised index of consumer prices (HICP) for the Euro area and the UK; consumer price index (CPI) for the USA.

Sources: Euro area, ECB *Monthly Bulletin*, various issues; USA, Bureau of Labor Statistics (CPI and Unemployment, April 2003), Bureau of Economic Analysis (GDP, March 2003); UK, National Statistics (March 2003). FORECASTS: European Commission Spring Forecasts (2003) for the Euro area and the UK. The Economic Report of the President for the USA (February, 2003).

Table 10.1(b) *Inflation rates (per cent)*

| | 1999 | | | | 2000 | | | | 2001 | | | | 2002 | | | | Inflation Forecasts | |
	1Q	2Q	3Q	4Q	1Q	2Q	3Q	4Q	1Q	2Q	3Q	4Q	1Q	2Q	3Q	4Q	2003	2004
Euro area	0.8	1.0	1.1	1.5	2.1	2.1	2.5	2.7	2.6	3.2	2.7	2.2	2.6	2.1	2.0	2.3	2.1	1.7
USA	1.7	2.1	2.4	2.6	3.2	3.3	3.5	3.4	3.4	3.4	2.7	1.9	1.3	1.3	1.6	2.2	2.0	2.1
Britain	1.0	1.5	1.3	1.2	0.8	0.6	0.9	1.0	0.9	1.5	1.5	1.0	1.6	1.0	1.0	1.5	1.9	1.8

Sources: As in Table 10.1(a).

Table 10.1(c) *Unemployment rates (per cent)*

| | 1999 | | | | 2000 | | | | 2001 | | | | 2002 | | | | Unemployment Forecasts | |
	1Q	2Q	3Q	4Q	1Q	2Q	3Q	4Q	1Q	2Q	3Q	4Q	1Q	2Q	3Q	4Q	2003	2004
Euro area	10.3	10.1	10.0	9.7	9.5	9.2	9.0	8.6	8.5	8.4	8.4	8.0	8.1	8.2	8.3	8.5	8.8	8.8
USA	4.3	4.3	4.2	4.0	4.0	4.0	4.0	4.0	4.2	4.5	4.8	5.6	5.6	5.8	5.8	5.9	5.7	5.5
Britain	6.3	6.1	6.0	5.9	5.9	5.6	5.5	5.3	5.2	5.1	5.2	5.3	5.2	5.2	5.4	5.2	5.1	5.1

Sources: As in Table 10.1(a).

The challenges to the EMU macropolicies surrounding the euro arise from the extent to which they can tackle the problems just summarized. These are embedded in the monetary policy operated by the ECB, and in the Stability and Growth Pact (SGP).[6] Can they deliver full employment without inflationary pressures? We now attempt to answer this question and begin by briefly locating the key economic policy ingredients of the EMU system.

Monetary policy has been removed from national authorities and from political authorities and placed with the ECB, and fiscal policy will be permanently constrained by the SGP. The ECB and the national central banks are linked into the European System of Central Banks (ESCB) with a division of responsibility between them. The ECB has the responsibility for setting interest rates in pursuit of the inflation objective and the national central banks have responsibility for regulatory matters. Central banks are viewed as having no discernible effects on the level or growth rate of output in the long run, but do determine the rate of inflation in the long run. Thus inflation is still viewed as a monetary phenomenon and ultimately it is central banks that determine the inflation rate.

The ECB is set up to be independent of the European Union (EU) Council and Parliament and of its member governments. There is, thus, a complete separation between the monetary authorities, in the form of the ECB, and the fiscal authorities, in the shape of the national governments comprising the EMU. It follows that there can be little coordination of monetary and fiscal policy. Indeed, any attempt at coordination would be extremely difficult to implement, for, apart from the separation of the monetary and fiscal authorities, there is also the constitutional requirement that national governments (and hence the fiscal authorities) should not exert any influence on the ECB (and hence the monetary authorities). Any strict interpretation of that edict would rule out any attempt at coordination of monetary and fiscal policies.

The ECB is the only effective federal economic institution, and it has the one policy instrument of the 'repo' rate to pursue the main objective of low inflation. The ECB is very clear on this issue. For example, in ECB (2003a), it is stated that 'In the field of monetary–fiscal policy coordination, the emphasis has shifted away from the joint design of short-term policy responses to shocks towards the establishment of a non-discretionary, rule-based regime capable of providing monetary and fiscal policy-makers with a time-consistent guide for action and thus a reliable anchor for private expectations …. Therefore there will generally be no need for further coordination of day-to-day policy moves' (p. 38).

National fiscal policy is subject to the requirements of the SGP (with no fiscal policy at the level of the EU with a balanced budget requirement and EU expenditure set at 1.24 per cent of EU GDP). The official rationale for the SGP is twofold. The first is that a medium-term balanced budget rule secures the scope for automatic stabilizers without breaching the limits set by the SGP (see below for more details). Second, since a balanced budget explicitly sets the debt ratio on a declining trend, it reduces the interest burden and improves the overall position of the government budget. Underlying the approach to SGP, though, is the notion of sound public finances. The European Commission (2000) is emphatic on this issue:

> Achieving and sustaining sound positions in public finances is essential to raise output and employment in Europe. Low public debt and deficits help maintain low interest rates, facilitate the task of monetary authorities in keeping inflation under control and create a stable environment which fosters investment and growth ... The Maastricht Treaty clearly recognizes the need for enhanced fiscal discipline in EMU to avoid overburdening the single monetary authority and prevent fiscal crises, which would have negative consequences for other countries. Moreover, the loss of exchange rate instrument implies the need to create room for fiscal policy to tackle adverse economic shocks and smooth the business cycle. The stability and growth pact is the concrete manifestation of the shared need for fiscal discipline. (European Commission, 2000, p. 1; see also ECB, 2001a, p. 6)

It is further argued that these views spring from experience, in that both emphases on fiscal prudence and stability in the founding Treaty of the EMU spring from the firm conviction that

> the deterioration of public finances was an important cause behind the poor economic performance of many EU countries since the early 1970s. The subsequent decades taught Europe a salutary lesson of how economic prosperity cannot be sustained in an unstable economic policy environment. Inappropriate fiscal policies frequently overburdened monetary policy leading to high interest rates. On the supply-side, generous welfare systems contributed to structural rigidities in EU economies and fuelled inappropriate wage behaviour. The net effect was a negative impact on business expectations and on investment, thus contributing to a slower rise in actual and potential output. As a result, employment stagnated. (European Commission, 2000, p. 9)

The level of NAIRU is viewed as being favourably affected by a 'flexible' labour market, but is unaffected by the level of aggregate demand or by productive capacity.

We may turn our attention next to the EMU policy framework, and discuss first monetary policy as implemented by the ECB, followed by the fiscal policy aspects.

4   MONETARY POLICY

4.1   Institutional and Policy Arrangements

ECB monetary policy has been assigned a quantitative definition of price stability in the form of a 0–2 per cent target for the annual increase in the harmonised index of consumer prices (HICP) for the euro area (preferably hovering in the lower range of 0–2 per cent). The ECB, however, announced at a press conference on 8 May 2003 its intention to maintain inflation 'close to but below 2 per cent' over the medium term (insisting that neither was this a change in policy, nor should it be interpreted as a target; it should be viewed as a 'clarification' of policy). Issing (2003b) insists on the 'clarification' aspect as being 'totally different from what is normally seen as inflation targeting'. Furthermore, the 'close to but below 2 per cent' inflation 'is not a change, it is a clarification of what we have done so far, what we have achieved – namely inflation expectations remaining in a narrow range of between roughly 1.7 per cent and 1.9 per cent – and what we intend to do in our forward-looking monetary policy'.[7] This 'clarification' may have become necessary in view of 'deflation' fears in the euro area, in that the ECB would worry about deflation if it were to arise. The president of the ECB at the press conference on 8 May 2003 expressed 'the ECB's commitment to provide a sufficient safety margin to guard against the risks of deflation', although he insisted that 'We do not share this fear for the euro area as a whole' (Duisenberg, 2003a). Issing (2003b) concurs when he suggests that 'it is clear enough that we are not blind in the eye which identifies deflationary problems. We have both eyes … watching deflationary as well as inflationary developments'.

The official doctrine of the ECB is based on a 'two-pillar' monetary strategy. The 'first pillar' is a commitment to analyse monetary developments for the information they contain about future price developments. This is the quantitative reference value for monetary growth, where a target of 4.5 per cent of M3 has been imposed. Being a reference level, there is no mechanistic commitment to correct deviations in the short term, although it is stated that deviations from the reference value would, under normal circumstances, 'signal risks to price stability'. The 'second pillar' is a broadly based assessment of the outlook of price developments and the risks to price stability. This broad range of indicators includes the euro exchange rate; labour market indicators, such as wages and unit labour costs; fiscal policy indicators; and financial market indicators, such as asset prices.

The rationale of the 'two-pillar' approach is based on the theoretical premise that there are different time perspectives in the conduct of monetary policy that require a different focus in each case. There is the short- to medium-term focus on price movements that requires economic analysis. In this analysis a 'broad range of economic/financial developments are analysed, to assess economic shocks, dynamics and perspectives and the resulting risks to price stability over the short to medium term' (Issing, 2003b). There is also the focus on long-term price trends that requires monetary analysis. It is for this reason that the ECB 'decided to discontinue the practice of conducting the review of the reference value for M3 on an annual basis' (ECB, 2003d, p. 5). There is, thus, a strong belief in the long-term link between money (M3 in this case) and inflation. Issing (2003b) leaves no ambiguity about the ECB belief in this relationship when he argues that there is 'no evidence that long-run link between money and prices has broken down in euro area; many studies show good leading indicator properties'; and that 'excess money/credit may provide additional information for identifying financial imbalances and/or asset price bubbles, which ultimately may impact on price developments'. The ECB also conducts 'cross checking' between the two analyses so that consistency is ensured (ibid.). The ECB has recently stressed this argument when stating that what the cross-checking implies is that its editorial 'will first present the economic analysis, which identifies short- to medium-term risks to price stability, and then turns to the monetary analysis, which assess medium- to long-term trends in inflation. It will conclude by cross-checking the analyses conducted under these two pillars' (ECB, 2003d, p. 5).

4.2   Policy Defects of the ECB Monetary Policy Arrangements

These policy arrangements just discussed suffer from a number of defects. First, if inflation is induced by a demand shock (that is, a higher level of demand pushes up inflation) then a policy to influence aggregate demand and thereby, it is hoped, inflation may have some validity. But such a policy is powerless to deal with cost inflation or supply shock inflation. A supply shock would lower (raise) output while raising (lowering) inflation. Further, the extent to which the domestic interest rate can be changed is circumscribed by exchange rate considerations and these are likely to take some time to have any impact on aggregate demand (and then the impact may be rather small). Indeed, the British monetary authorities (and others) talk in terms of a two-year lag between the change in interest rates and resulting impact of changes in aggregate demand on the rate of inflation. Interest rates are likely to influence investment expenditure, consumer expenditure, market interest rates and asset prices, expectations and the exchange rate. These changes in turn influence domestic and external demand, and then inflationary pressures. In addition, interest rate changes can also have distributional effects, whether between individuals (Arestis and Howells, 1991) or between economic regions (Arestis and Sawyer, 2002a).

Second, changes in interest rates have only a limited impact on aggregate demand, but insofar as interest rates do have an impact this comes through effects on investment and on the exchange rate. High interest rates have long-term detrimental effects through reducing future productive capacity and through the impact of foreign trade. The results of simulations of the effects of monetary policy using macroeconometric models were surveyed in Chapter 4. The conclusion of that survey is that the effects of interest rate changes on inflation tend to be rather small: typically, a one percentage point change in interest rates may dampen inflation by 0.2 to 0.3 per cent after two years.

Third, monetary policy is a 'one policy fits all' approach. Within the euro area there is a single central bank discount rate. It is well-known that the setting of that single interest rate poses difficulties: the rate which is appropriate for a country experiencing high demand and perhaps inflationary pressures is not the same as that appropriate for one facing low demand. Indeed, monetary policy may address the average inflation picture but cannot address differences in inflationary experience across the euro area countries. At the time of writing, there is evidence of significant disparities in inflationary experience despite the convergence of inflation that was required by the Maastricht criteria (and indeed a number of countries would not now satisfy the inflation convergence conditions of the Maastricht Treaty).[8] Further, the impact of interest rate changes is likely to differ markedly across countries.

Fourth, the ECB assessment of the level of economic activity is completely impervious to the behaviour of interest rates. Bibow (2003) puts it very aptly: 'Ex ante interest rate policies never seem to conflict with economic growth in ECB policy communications and assessments. Ex post economic developments do not appear to have been related to interest rate developments either' (p. 5). The ECB rationale is that monetary tightening would not pose any risk to economic activity. Such policy keeps inflationary expectations under control, thereby sustaining confidence in price stability, which stimulates economic activity. This is rather surprising in view of the work undertaken on the transmission mechanism in the euro area (ECB, 2002e), which shows that monetary policy has strong real effects, especially so, in that 'investment is a main driving force, with a contribution of more than 80 percent to the total response of gdp after three years' (p. 47). Further confirmation of the limited effects of interest rates is clear from the work we have surveyed in Chapter 4.

4.3 Problems with the ECB Monetary Policy

The management, operation, communication and potential efficacy of monetary policy within these institutional arrangements by the ECB have entailed many problems. In terms of the management aspect, the response of monetary policy decisions to evolving events has been slow. It is of some interest to note in this context the reluctance of the ECB to reduce the rate of interest when a downturn in economic activity in 2001, not just in the euro area, became rather obvious. In particular, the ECB is faulted for underestimating the impact of the US recession on the euro area, and for not reacting in time in terms of reducing interest rates. After signalling in April 2001 an imminent cut in interest rates, it never implemented it; however, when in May it signalled no change, the ECB subsequently cut interest rates. It is of considerable importance to note that ECB (2001b) in March 2001 was claiming that

> The general outlook for this year and next remains positive. Economic activity in the euro area is mainly determined by domestic factors. The conditions on the domestic side ... have remained favourable .... This notwithstanding, an element of uncertainty with regard to the outlook for euro area continues to be the world economy and its potential impact on euro area developments. However, at this juncture there are no signs that the slowdown in the US economy is having significant and lasting spillover effects on the euro area. (ECB, 2001b, p. 5)

By May, the ECB (2001d) was declaring that 'economic growth, supported by domestic demand, will be broadly in line with estimates of potential growth in 2001' (p. 5). As mentioned above, the ECB cut its key interest rate on 10 May 2001, thereby throwing the financial markets into widespread confusion (see also Bibow, 2002a). In the June *Monthly Bulletin* (ECB, 2001e), the scenario changed to one that suggested, 'Real GDP growth in the euro area in 2001 is expected to come down from the high level reached in 2000 ... primarily as a result of the less favourable external environment' (p. 5). However, 'the contribution to real GDP growth from domestic demand is expected to remain robust. This is consistent with the favourable economic fundamentals of the euro area' (p. 5). In November 2001, the ECB (2001g) reverts: 'The conditions exist for a recovery to take place in the course of 2002 and economic growth to return to a more satisfactory path. The economic fundamentals of the euro area are sound and there are no major imbalances, which would require prolonged adjustment. The uncertainty currently overshadowing the world economy should diminish over time' (p. 6). This ought to be contrasted to the Bank of International Settlement (BIS) *Annual Report* (2002) statement that, 'On balance, it seems that the synchronised downturn in 2001 mainly represented the effects of common shocks, reinforced by the high trade intensity of the demand components most severely affected' (p. 16).

ECB monetary policy since then has been no less confusing. In January 2002, the ECB (2002a) was stating that 'no fundamental economic imbalances have built up in recent years in the euro area which would require a long correction process' (p. 5), thereby attempting to let the financial markets believe that there was no need for further interest rate cuts. If anything, increases in interest rates were implied. In April 2002, the 'thread' of interest rate increase was evident enough: 'the persistence of excess liquidity in the economy could become a concern once the economic recovery in the euro area gathers pace' (ECB, 2002b, p. 5). Similarly, in May 2002, the ECB (2002c) was more explicit about 'the prospects for price stability', which 'appear to be somewhat less favourable than they were towards the end of last year' (p. 5). In the meantime, in the USA, the Federal (Reserve) Open Market Committee (FOMC) kept lowering interest rates aggressively. It took the ECB until December 2002 to lower interest rates on the premise that 'the evidence has increased that inflationary pressures are easing, owing in particular to the sluggish economic expansion. Furthermore, the downside risks to economic expansion have not vanished' (ECB, 2002d, p. 5).

The Federal Reserve System had already reduced interest rates on no fewer than 12 occasions. Still, in March 2003, a 25 basis point reduction in the 'repo' rate prompted ECB to argue that 'Overall, ECB interest rates have reached very low levels. On the basis of currently available information, this policy stance, while contributing to the preservation of price stability over the medium term, provides some counterbalance to the factors which are currently having an adverse effect on economic activity' (ECB, 2003b, p. 6). However, the sharp euro appreciation since April 2002 would suggest the opposite: relative interest rates have not reached very low levels; so much so that 'The euro area's immediate problem is overly tight monetary and fiscal policy' (*The Economist*, 3 May 2003, p. 71). And yet the ECB president at a press conference on 8 May 2003, declared that 'the euro at the moment – is about at the level which ... better reflects the fundamentals and it is roughly at average historical levels. So, there is not yet anything excessive about the level' (Duisenberg, 2003a). As a result, the euro jumped to its highest level against the dollar and the pound sterling for four years (Duisenberg, 2003a).[9]

The ECB's methods of operation and communication have been confusing to the financial markets. In the 'two-pillar' strategy, there is uncertainty as to the value attached to the M3 reference value. The target has rarely been met, and yet this does not seem to have an impact on official strategy. As Fitousi and Creel (2002) have put it, 'In its communication with the public, the ECB consistently highlights its "reference value" for inflation and – often in a confusing way – its monetary policy target. This may well have undermined the ECB's credibility, rather than added to it' (p. 67). The 'clarification' offered on 8 May 2003 appears to play down the importance of the money stock, and yet it reaffirmed its long-run importance (see the relevant discussion above).

There is, indeed, the further question of whether the aim of inflation being 'close to 2 percent' is not too restrictive, and it suffers from not being symmetrical. Not to mention the confusion it has created with the statement 'close to but below 2 percent'; is there no change, as the ECB suggested, or is it a move to a 2 per cent mid-point target (flatly denied by the ECB, as noted above)? The ECB has been reluctant to manipulate the rate of interest sufficiently and for other purposes, when it is abundantly clear that such a move is paramount. In practice most central banks do not concentrate on inflation to the exclusion of any other policy objective (they usually take unemployment into account). In any case, it actually becomes more and more obvious that the 'close to 2 percent' formulation is by far too low, especially so currently, when it is apparent that this policy stance 'provides an inadequate cushion against the risk of deflation in the event of a serious slump in demand' (*The Economist*, 28 September, 2002, p. 11). Clearly, the ECB believes that it is an adequate cushion, as evidenced by the 8 May 2003 'clarification' of monetary policy by its officers (Duisenberg, 2003a; Issing, 2003b; see also the relevant discussion above).

The problem with the ECB's methods of operation is partly the bank's secretiveness, for it does not publish minutes of its meetings. This is compensated to some extent by the ECB president's news conference once a month after the monetary policy meetings, by the president's testimony to the European parliament on a regular basis, by the monthly publication of the ECB bulletin, and by the ECB's GDP growth and inflation projections twice a year. The trouble is that the ECB has not learned to communicate its methods of operation, essentially because it does not publish minutes of the monetary policy meetings.

A further problem is that of the voting behaviour of the ECB Governing Council, and the real possibility of the ECB policy decisions being affected by national loyalties.[10] Meade and Sheets (2001) argue that they are affected. They formulate a hypothesis that each council member would vote on the basis of the differential between national and euro area inflation rates in the month prior to the monetary policy meeting. They also hypothesize that, if the national inflation rate of a country is higher than the euro area average in the given month by more than a threshold value, then the council member from that country will vote for monetary tightening or against monetary easing; and conversely if national inflation is below the euro area average. They investigate all the ECB policy changes since January 1999, and calculated the aggregate number of Governing Council members who would have dissented from the actual policy change, given the authors' voting rule and different threshold values. They concluded that voting behaviour reflects their hypothesis. There is thus national bias in the ECB policy making, and reform of the ECB's structure appears inevitable.[11]

4.4   Reservations Regarding the Efficacy of ECB Monetary Policy

A number of reservations may be raised in terms of the efficacy of this monetary policy. First, there is the problem of the 'one-size-fits-all' monetary policy, a point raised by the governor of the Bank of England. He argued, in an interview on German television on the 20 December 2001, that such policy is risky and that 'The same monetary policy is not necessarily the best for every country at the same time' in such a diverse economic area. The governor also suggested in an interview on BBC radio on 21 December 2001 that, unlike monetary policy in a single country where 'mitigating factors' exist, such as labour migration and fiscal redistribution, these factors 'are not present to any significant degree at the euro area level'. There is thus no way a country can offset undesirable effects of a too high or a too low rate of interest imposed by the ECB.

The second issue impinges crucially on the problem of the transmission mechanism of monetary policy in the euro area since, as Duisenberg (1999) concedes, 'Relatively little is known as yet' about it. Consequently, 'One important challenge for the Eurosystem is to obtain better knowledge of the structure and functioning of the euro area economy and the transmission mechanism of monetary policy within it, so that policy actions can be implemented accordingly' (p. 189).

Third, considerable doubt may be cast on the effectiveness of monetary policy in terms of responding to recession and as a means of controlling inflation. There has been a reluctance to cut interest rates in the face of recession (with the USA a notable exception in this regard). The ECB has failed to meet its inflation target of below 2 per cent for three years (and has presided over widely differing inflation rates within the euro area).

Fourth, the inflation target of below 2 per cent can be argued to be too low. The consequence is that deflationary policy is continuously pursued. This has a number of implications, of which two stand out here. The first is that it is very difficult to see how full employment with no inflation can be achieved. The deflationary thrust to the policies not only ensures that unemployment rises in the present but it also serves to depress investment and capital formation, thereby harming future prospects for employment. The second raises a serious concern about the distributional effects of contractionary policies. Moderate rates of inflation improve the relative position of low-income groups, and deflationary policies deteriorate it (Nordhaus, 1973). Blinder (1987) concurs with the contention that contractionary monetary policies distort income distribution against low-income groups (see also Forder, 2003).

Fifth, in terms of the impact of interest rates on expenditure, there are questions relating to the magnitude of the impact, timing and variability of the time lags involved. Sixth, since interest rate policy has a range of effects, such as on aggregate demand and on the exchange rate, and also has distributional effects, the objectives of monetary policy should reflect that, and should therefore be recast to include growth and high levels of employment alongside inflation. Seventh, exchange rate changes are expected to have small effects on the EMU economy. Its relatively closed nature in terms of international trade (with imports and exports amounting to less than 10 per cent of GDP) means that variations in the exchange rate of the euro will have much less impact on prices than they do in more open economies.

4.5 Further Critique

Despite all these problems and criticisms, the ECB president went to new lengths in early October 2002, when testifying before the European Parliament, to defend the prevailing high level of interest rates in the euro area despite its economic problems (see Table 10.1 above). He defended his decision, arguing that if 'I, perhaps unkindly, compare the euro area economy with the other major economies in the world, which have followed, what I would call a more-aggressive interest rate policies. If one looks at the results of these policies, then I am positively convinced that our policy stance, which implies historically low real interest rates and nominal interest rates, but also presents an image of stability, forward-looking and creating no hindrance whatsoever to the resumption of growth in both investment and consumption; with a liquidity situation which can be described as ample and a monetary policy stance which can be characterized as accommodative, is one which deserves to be greatly valued' (Duisenberg, 2002). The policy stance the ECB president was referring to relates to the reduction of the key euro-area interest rate by 1.5 percentage points, to 3.25 per cent, since the beginning of 2001 (when the global slowdown began). By contrast, the US Federal Reserve System cut its equivalent rate by 4.75 percentage points, to 1.75 per cent, during the same period. The results of the ECB policy as compared to the Federal Reserve System's are not complimentary to the president's argument, to say the least: compare the GDP annualized growth rates in the first three quarters of 2002, with 0.3 per cent, 0.7 per cent and 0.8 per cent respectively, in the case of the euro area, and 1.4 per cent, 2.2 per cent and 3.3 per cent in the USA; and also the annualized unemployment rate of 8.1. 8.2 and 8.3 per cent, respectively, in the euro area, as compared to 4.0, 4.0 and 5.8 per cent, respectively, in the USA.[12] Furthermore, the dollar did not suffer over the period the kind of decline suggested by the ECB president's comparisons. On the contrary, following his statement, referred to above, the dollar moved higher than the euro at that time.[13] Clearly, the claims of the ECB president could not have been sustained.

Worst still is the insistence of the ECB that the current level of interest rate in the euro area is the 'right' one (see Duisenberg, 2003b, for a recent statement). The euro has appreciated substantially since October 2002 and three of its major countries, Germany, Italy and the Netherlands, are now in recession (and Portugal has already experienced two quarters of negative growth). Recent data, see European Commission (2003), reveal that Germany contracted by 0.03 per cent in the last quarter of 2002, and by 0.2 per cent in both the first and second quarters of 2003, thus experiencing three consecutive quarters of negative growth. Italy reported 0.1 per cent contraction in the first quarter of 2003, and 0.4 in the second quarter of 2003 (although it had expanded by 0.4 per cent in the fourth quarter of 2002); and the Netherlands shrunk by 0.3 per cent in the first quarter and by 2.1 in the second quarter of 2003, having contracted by 0.2 per cent in the fourth quarter of 2002. France experienced a 0.1 per cent contraction in the fourth quarter of 2002, a positive growth rate in the first quarter of 2003 (1.1), but a negative 1.3 growth rate in the second quarter of 2003. The whole euro area growth, in the meantime, was near zero (actually 0.1) in the first quarter and zero growth in the second quarter of 2003, following growth of 0.1 per cent in the fourth quarter of 2002. The dangers of 'deflation' in the euro area were very clear indeed, and yet the ECB (2003d) argued that 'the monetary policy stance remains consistent with the preservation of price stability in the medium term' (p. 5) and also 'a gradual strengthening of real GDP growth in the course of 2003 and 2004, supported by both external and domestic factors' (ECB, 2003e, p. 5) is expected. At the time of writing (early 2004) neither deflation nor the expected strengthening of real GDP had materialized.

5   FISCAL POLICY

5.1   Institutional and Policy Arrangements

The core elements of SGP are three: (a) to pursue the medium-term objectives of budgetary positions close to balance or in surplus, (b) the submission of annual stability and convergence programmes by the member states, and (c) the monitoring of the implementation of the stability and convergence programmes. The main feature of the core elements is the requirement that the national budget deficit does not exceed 3 per cent of GDP, and failure to meet that requirement could lead to a series of fines depending on the degree to which the deficit exceeds 3 per cent. It is also necessary for national budgetary policies to 'support stability oriented monetary policies. Adherence to the objective of sound budgetary positions close to balance or in surplus will allow all Member States to deal with normal cyclical fluctuations while keeping the government deficit within the reference value of 3 percent of GDP' (Resolution of the European Council on the Stability and Growth Pact, Amsterdam 17 June 1997). Furthermore, 'Member States commit themselves to respect the medium-term budgetary objective of positions close to balance or in surplus set out in their stability of convergence programmes and to take the corrective budgetary action they deem necessary to meet the objectives of their stability or convergence programmes, whenever they have information indicating actual or expected significant divergence from those objectives.'

A country's budgetary data become available for the Commission to scrutinize on 1 March each year when the stability programmes are submitted. Each programme contains information about the paths of the ratios of budget deficit to GDP and national debt to GDP. The Council (ECOFIN) examines the stability reports and delivers an opinion within two months of the report's submission. If the stability programme reveals that a country is significantly diverging from its medium-term budgetary objective, the council will make relevant recommendations to strengthen the stability programme. If the situation persists, the member state is judged to have breached the reference values. The pact details 'escape' clauses which allow a member state that has an excessive deficit to avoid sanction. If there is an economic downturn and output has fallen by more than 2 per cent, the member state will escape sanction automatically but the deficit should be corrected once the recession has finished. If output falls by between 0.75 and 2 per cent, the Council can use discretion when making a decision on an 'excessive' deficit, other factors will be taken into account, such as the abruptness of the downturn, the accumulated loss of output relative to past trends and whether the government deficit exceeds government investment expenditure.[14] If a country is found to have breached the reference values, it has four months to introduce the corrective measures suggested by the Council. If the country follows the Council's recommendations, the 'excessive' deficit can continue, but the budget deficit must be corrected within a year of its identification. A country which chooses not to introduce corrective measures will be subject to a range of sanctions; one or more must be imposed, of which one must be in the form of a non-interest-bearing deposit lodged by the national government. In this instance, it will fall upon EMU members, excluding the member country under consideration, to reach a decision on sanctions. The non-interest-bearing deposit consists of a fixed component (0.2 per cent of GDP) and a variable component (one tenth of the difference between the deficit ratio and the 3 per cent reference value). If the budget deficit is not corrected within two years, the deposit is forfeited and becomes a fine, whereas, if the deficit is corrected within two years, the deposit is returned and the penalty becomes the forgone interest.

5.2 Flaws of the SGP

These SGP institutional arrangements point to a general deflationary bias in the operation of the SGP. It is illustrated by the response of the ECB president at a press conference on 6 December 2001, after the ECB's policy-making council, to an Italian request to delay target dates for budget balance in view of the projected downturn in economic activity. He argued that 'it is of the greatest importance to enhance confidence with both consumers and investors if governments stick to their medium-term strategy, whatever happens' (Duisenberg, 2001). The ECB president was more forthcoming at a similar press conference on 8 May 2003, when he argued that, 'Looking ahead, it is crucial to underpin the fiscal policy framework with decisive action, strong peer pressure and consistent implementation of the rules of the Treaty and of the Stability and Growth Pact. Countries should maintain budgetary positions close to balance or in surplus over the cycle, and, where this is not the case, take the required structural consolidation measures' (Duisenberg, 2003a); similar arguments are repeated in the August 2003 issue of the ECB (2003e, p. 6).

There are serious flaws in the management of the SGP. One illustration of this is the predictions made in January 2002 by the European Commission for the year 2002 relating to budget deficits under the terms of the SGP. Those predictions prompted the possibility of the 'early warning' mechanism in the case of Germany and Portugal in particular. ECOFIN ignored the European Commission's recommendation for Germany and Portugal to be censured in view of the size of their deficits, which were creeping close to the SGP 3 per cent ceiling (it stood at 2.7 per cent of GDP in the case of Germany and 2.2 per cent in the case of Portugal, though it later transpired that the figure for 2001 was 4.2 per cent). ECOFIN chose, instead, to strike a deal whereby no formal warning was issued, but the two countries made pledges to keep within the rules of the SGP.[15] This accord raises questions about the governance of the euro area, and provides fertile ground for financial markets to question the credibility of the EMU institutions. Furthermore, it could substantially weaken the credibility of the fiscal constraints that are imposed on the prospective new EU entrants in the period leading to their accession. It also supports the charge that the EMU does not keep to its rules and pledges. The comparison with the episode of the application of the Maastricht criteria in the period leading to the introduction of the virtual euro, when the criteria were fudged to ensure that a large number of countries could join the euro, is telling (Arestis, Brown and Sawyer, 2001).

5.3   More Flexible SGP Fiscal Rules?

In September 2002, the European Commission admitted for the first time that the SGP fiscal rules relating to the single currency need to be changed. They would be more flexible in the future in view of the euro area economic weaknesses. The European Commission actually relaxed the deadline of 2004 by which Germany, Portugal and France should balance their budgets. These countries were given until 2006 to do so. In return the Commission demanded that the members reduce their deficit by 0.5 per cent a year, starting in 2003. It was at the 2002 summer summit in Seville of the 15 European Union members that they all signed a commitment 'to achieve budgetary positions close to balance or in surplus as soon as possible in all Member States and at the latest by 2004' (Council of the European Union, 2002, p. 8). The European Commissioner for Economic and Monetary Affairs admitted at the time that it was of great concern to them that the original political commitment of national governments to uphold the SGP was substantially weakening.

The Commission also said that they would pay more attention to structural deficits, so that a country's fiscal deficit would be judged in relation to cyclical conditions. Those changes took place alongside Germany, Portugal and France showing evidence of having breached the conditions of the SGP. Portugal became the first country to breach the 3 per cent rule, and admitted in July 2002 to a budget deficit in excess of the 3 per cent of GDP upper limit in 2002. Germany and France followed soon afterwards. Italy's 2002 budget deficit was also criticized by the European Commission for reaching 'dangerous proportions'. The charge was made that the Italian government was massaging the figures. France, too, was criticized by the European Commissioner for Economic and Monetary Affairs, for the 2003 tax and spending plans of this country; and he expressed concern that France may not be able to meet the new deadline of 2006. In fact, in October 2002, France refused to adhere even to the 2006 deadline, arguing that its expenditure plans were affordable, and also claiming that 'other priorities' were in place.

The ECB president, in his early October 2002 testimony to the European Parliament, actually blamed France, Germany and Italy for being responsible for the uncertainty surrounding the economic recovery in the euro area; he argued that 'Three of the larger countries have not used the time when there were good economic conditions ... to consolidate their budgets. Now they bear the burden of it' (Duisenberg, 2002). In fact, the SGP has been the focus of growing controversy within the euro area member countries. There is still the argument, mainly from the ECB, that reforming the SGP, especially relaxing its rules, would damage the euro's credibility. It can be argued, though, that the opposite may be nearer to reality. In any case, the relaxation that has been implemented is far too small to create any serious problems of credibility. It is our view that a great deal more is needed if fiscal policy is to help the euro area to head speedily towards a real recovery. Under these circumstances, credibility might be enhanced rather than reduced.

Germany was told in January 2003 by the European Commission to draw up plans urgently to bring deficit below 3 per cent. In June 2003, Germany announced plans to bring forward 15.5 billion euros of tax cuts, and admitted that it may break the SGP in 2004 for a third successive year. In April 2003, it became apparent that all three countries could very well be fined. In fact the Commission was of the opinion that 'an excessive government deficit' had already existed in France. It recommended that France should eliminate the deficit by the end of 2004, 'at the latest' and, also by 2004, France should bring back to a declining path its government to GDP ratio. France was asked to have relevant measures in place to achieve those objectives by October 2003. France did not adhere to that dictum by October 2003, claiming that that the deficit was justified by economic circumstances, but pledging to bring the budget deficit below 3 per cent by 2005, thereby showing cooperation.

According to the SGP rules, France should have been penalized, but instead was offered an extra year to comply. France even refused to abide by the European Commission's 'flexible' interpretation of the SGP, which was asking that country to cut its structural deficit by 1 per cent in 2004, instead of the 0.7 per cent planned by France, and by 0.5 in 2005; instead France vowed to make fresh spending cuts in 2004. Germany by that time was also predicted to violate the 3 per cent fiscal rule for the third successive year in 2004; the European Commission expectation was that this country, too, would be treated in the same way as France. Germany responded by proposing that countries that show 'cooperation' in reducing their deficits should be exempted from the SGP's sanctions mechanism, regardless of 'success'. Sanctions would only apply to those countries that refuse to cooperate. In the event, the European Finance Ministers (ECOFIN) at their meeting on the 24 November 2003, decided not to penalize France and Germany. A compromise solution, in effect suspending the SGP, required Germany and France to cut their deficit by 0.6 per cent and 0.77 per cent, respectively, of GDP in 2004 and by 0.5 per cent and 0.6 per cent, respectively, in 2005. This was under the proviso that those reductions would not be required if economic growth was not solid. The European Commission and the ECB governing council responded, showing grave concerns. The Governing Council of the ECB in a press release (25 November 2003), said that it 'deeply regrets these developments and shares the views made public by the Commission on the ECOFIN Council conclusions' (the European Commission expressed their deep regret at the decision); 'The conclusions adopted by the ECOFIN Council carry

serious dangers. The failure to go along with the rules and procedures foreseen in the Stability and Growth Pact risks undermining the credibility of the
institutional framework and the confidence in sound public finances of Member States across the euro area.'

These incidents raised the question of the validity of the use of a 'one-size-
fits-all' approach to fiscal policy, without accounting for the different
circumstances of the countries involved and the differential impact which
recession can have. They also illustrated that the SGP serves to operate in a
deflationary manner. Furthermore, these incidents provided additional evidence of the fragility and exposure of the SGP; the once feared instrument of
EMU fiscal policy has become in effect completely paralysed. The *Economist*
(1 November 2003) is very clear on the matter: 'the euro area's stability and
growth pact is plain daft. It insists on deficits of less than 3% of GDP
virtually all the time, even when, as now, the zone is flirting with recession.
Today the pact looks more of a nonsense than ever, with France and Germany
both in breach and the French in virtual contempt of it' (p. 16).

It became apparent that the slowdown in economic growth brought about
the deterioration in the scale of budget deficit; the latter could readily be
predicted from the size of the slowdown in growth. This was largely due to
the 'automatic stabilizers' rather than discretionary fiscal policy. Buti *et al.*
(1997) had found that a 1 per cent change in GDP produced on average a 0.5
per cent change in the average budget deficit in the EU countries. The economic slowdown in the eurozone also showed clearly that the fiscal rules of
the SGP are counterproductive during a slowdown and that the budget rules
cannot cope with the effects of recession. Moves to enforce the fiscal rules
will inevitably add further deflationary pressures.

5.4   Flaws Relating to the Balanced Budget Requirement

Further reservations relate to the requirement of a balanced budget over the
cycle. Even if it is accepted that the budget should be balanced over the cycle,
there is little reason to think that the extent of the swings in the budget
position will be similar across countries. What reason is there to think that a
swing in the deficit to a maximum of 3 per cent of GDP is relevant for all
countries? Countries will differ in the extent to which their GDP varies in the
course of a business cycle and in the extent to which the budget position is
sensitive to the business cycle. Buti *et al.* (1997) found that the budget
balance is negatively linked to GDP growth, but in a way that varies between
countries, with estimates of changes in the deficit to GDP ratio of up to 0.8
per cent and 0.9 per cent for the Netherlands and Spain, respectively, for a 1
per cent slowdown in growth. The notable feature is the differences amongst
countries.

The next question is whether there is any reason to think that an (on average) balanced budget is compatible with high levels of employment – indeed, whether it is compatible with any level of employment (including the NAIRU). A well-known identity (though one generally forgotten by advocates of the SGP) drawn from the national income accounts tells us that (Private Savings minus Investment) plus (Imports minus Exports) plus (Tax Revenue minus Government Expenditure) equals zero:

$$(S - I) + (Q - X) + (T - G) = 0. \tag{10.1}$$

Individuals and firms make decisions on savings, investment, imports and exports. For any particular level of employment (and income), there is no reason to think that those decisions will lead to

$$(S - I) + (Q - X) = 0. \tag{10.2}$$

But if they are not equal to zero, then $(G - T)$, the budget deficit, will not be equal to zero, since

$$(G - T) = (S - I) + (Q - X). \tag{10.3}$$

The SGP in effect assumes that any level of output and employment is consistent with a balanced budget $(G - T = 0)$, and hence compatible with a combination of net private savings and the trade position summing to zero. But no satisfactory justification has been given for this view. Two possible arguments could be advanced. First, it could be argued that budget deficits cannot be run for ever as the government debt to income ratio would continuously rise and that would be unsustainable. Hence governments eventually have to run balanced (on average) budgets. However, that depends on whether the post-tax rate of interest (on government bonds) is greater or less than the growth rate, the debt to income ratio being unsustainable in the former case but not in the latter. Further, it relates to the size of the primary deficit, which is the deficit that excludes interest payments. It is the overall budget deficit which is the target of the SGP, and it can be readily shown that an *average* 3 per cent budget deficit and a 60 per cent debt ratio are compatible and sustainable, if the rate of growth of money GDP is 5 per cent (which is not an unreasonable assumption and could arise from, for example, 2.5 per cent inflation and 2.5 per cent real growth).[16] In general, a 3 per cent budget deficit would be compatible with a sustainable debt ratio of $3/g$, where g is nominal growth rate.

Second, some form of Say's Law could be invoked to the effect that intended savings and investment are equal at full employment (or, modified for foreign trade, domestic savings plus trade deficit equals investment). Even if Say's Law held (which we would dispute), what is required here is that the level of private demand could sustain the supply-side equilibrium, that is the non-accelerating inflation rate of unemployment, and the NAIRU does not correspond to full employment. In particular, there is no reason to think that a balanced budget position is compatible with employment at the level given by the NAIRU.

This equality can be viewed in another way. Suppose that the condition of balanced budget is imposed; it then follows that

$$(S - I) + (Q - X) = 0. \tag{10.4}$$

If (as is likely) $S > I$, then $Q < X$. Hence a country would be required to run a trade surplus (and hence run a capital account deficit with the export of capital to other countries). A budget in balance would imply that net private savings $(S - I)$ is equal to the trade surplus $(X - Q)$, which in turn is equal to the capital account deficit. It can first be noted only some countries can run a trade surplus, and that must be balanced by others which run a deficit. This would then imply that some countries would have positive net private savings and others negative private savings. Countries that are able to run a trade surplus (at high levels of employment) can, in effect, export their 'excess' savings, but that cannot be the case for all countries.

The imposition of an upper limit of 3 per cent of GDP on the size of the budget deficit and the declaration of the aim of a balanced budget over the cycle represented a significant tightening of the fiscal position as compared with the 3 per cent of GDP target for the budget deficit in the Maastricht Treaty convergence conditions. In those conditions, the 3 per cent was to be achieved at a particular point in time: under the SGP the 3 per cent limit is to be exceeded only under extreme conditions. Although no justification was ever given by the European Union for the choice of 3 per cent in the convergence conditions, others advanced two arguments. Buiter *et al.* (1993), for example, suggested that the choice of the 3 per cent figure for the deficit to GDP ratio arose from a combination of advocacy of the so-called 'golden rule' (that current expenditure should be covered by current revenue) and that 'EC public investment averaged almost exactly 3% of EC GDP during 1974–91' (ibid. p. 63). Others have suggested that the 3 per cent figure corresponded to the range of deficits run by a number of countries, notably Germany, and was achievable.[17] These possible justifications remind us of two points. The first is that, typically, governments have run budget deficits. The imposition of a balanced budget requirement represents a major departure from what governments have done in the past. The second is that governments invest, and it is generally accepted that governments can and should borrow to fund their investment programmes. The SGP imposes the requirement that governments generally fund their investment programmes from current tax revenue.

A balanced budget (on average) means, of course, that current government expenditure will be much less than tax revenue since that tax revenue would also need to cover interest payments on debt and to pay for capital expenditure. In the UK, this has been cast in terms of the so-called 'golden rule' of public finance, which is taken to be that 'over the economic cycle the Government will borrow only to invest and not to fund current expenditure' (Treasury, 1997, p. 1), though capital consumption (depreciation) is regarded as current spending so that it is net capital formation which can be financed by borrowing. The 'public debt as a proportion of national income will be held over the economic cycle at a stable and prudent level' (ibid.). Furthermore, 'The fiscal rules focus on the whole of the public sector, because the debts of any part of the public sector could ultimately fall on the taxpayer. Looking at the whole public sector also removes incentives to reclassify activities simply to evade prudent constraints on borrowing' (ibid., p. 16). Thus the use of fiscal policy to regulate aggregate demand in the economy is much reduced, if not entirely removed, especially in the direction of stimulating the economy. It is therefore argued that 'Discretionary fiscal changes should only be made if they are demonstrably consistent with achievement of the Government's fiscal rules over the economic cycle' (ibid.).

The general stance of the SGP with its requirement of an overall balanced budget and maximum deficit of 3 per cent of GDP is a deeply flawed one. There is no reason to think that a balanced budget position is consistent with high levels of employment (or indeed with any particular level of employment). Furthermore, there is little reason to think that the 3 per cent limit can permit the automatic stabilizers to work, and striving to reach the 3 per cent limit in times of recession is likely to push economies further into recession. The balanced budget requirement does not allow governments even to borrow to fund capital investment projects. Additional reservations include the separation of the monetary authorities from the fiscal authorities. The decentralization of the fiscal authorities inevitably makes any effective coordination of fiscal and monetary policy difficult. Since the ECB is instructed to focus on inflation, while the fiscal authorities will have a broader range of concerns, there will be considerable grounds for conflict. A serious implication of this is that the SGP is in danger of becoming the 'instability' pact. This suggests a need for the evolution of a body which would be charged with the coordination of EMU monetary and fiscal policies. In the absence of such a body, tensions will emerge in the real sector when monetary policy and fiscal policy pull in different directions. The SGP in effect resolves these issues by establishing the dominance of the monetary authorities (ECB) over the fiscal authorities (national governments).

The SGP seeks to impose a 'one size (of straitjacket) fits all' fiscal policy, namely that, over the course of the cycle, national government budgets should be in balance or slight surplus with a maximum deficit of 3 per cent of GDP. It has *never* been shown (or even argued) that fiscal policy should be uniform across countries. The SGP imposes a fiscal policy which in the end fits nobody. For, actually, there is no reason to think that what is in effect a single fiscal policy (balanced budget over the cycle) is appropriate for all. The April 2003 *Monthly Bulletin* of the ECB is, nonetheless, very explicit. It clearly, and forcibly, suggests that 'the Stability and Growth Pact provides a robust and flexible framework within which any strains on public finances can be addressed and budgetary discipline is secured .... It remains essential that both the commitments made in the stability programmes and the requests to further improve fiscal positions, as subsequently agreed in the ECOFIN Council, be implemented in full. This will help to build confidence in the fiscal framework and anchor expectations about the future macroeconomic environment' (ECB, 2003c, p. 6).[18] This argument has been repeated time and time again in the ECB *Monthly Bulletin* since then; even after the event described in subsection 5.3 above, which led to the SGP being discredited.

6   POLICIES FOR FULL EMPLOYMENT AND LOW INFLATION

If current EMU policy arrangements cannot produce full employment and low inflation within the euro area, the obvious question is the extent to which necessary changes to the existing framework are required to achieve this objective. The present section attempts to answer this question.

6.1   Institutional Changes

The slowdown in economic activity in the euro area has exposed the serious fault lines in the SGP. The present policy stance would seem to be untenable in the longer term. As detailed above, for fiscal policy, the 3 per cent budget deficit limit and (on average) balanced budget remain in place, but as countries approach the 3 per cent limit, in practice the limit has been relaxed. Some countries now have four years to meet the balanced budget requirements with a resulting lack of clarity over the operation of the SGP. One response has been to call for some slackening of the restraints of the SGP; for example, modifying the limits to permit borrowing for capital investment.

Another response has been to decry the 'flexibility' that there has been in the interpretation of the SGP, and to seek ways of making the balanced budget requirement really bite. This would simply be a disaster, and would turn the SGP into the 'Instability and No Growth Pact'.

The response of the ECB is worrying when they argue that 'It is natural for an economic slowdown to have adverse effects on member countries' budget position. However, for countries with a budget position still not close to balance or in surplus, it is important to adhere to their medium-term consolidation plans. A short-lived slowdown should not significantly change the scope for reaching the targets set in the countries' stability programmes.' Further, 'as adjustment needs are likely to become more visible in periods of less vigorous economic growth, policy makers must now step up the reforms rather than allowing efforts to abate' (ECB, 2001g, p. 6; see also ECB 2001h, p. 6).

The draft of the European Convention (2003a, 2003b) does not indicate any proposals for change in the fiscal and monetary policies of the eurozone (confirmed in the final draft as agreed by the intergovernmental conference, 17/18 June 2004). Working Group IV, in their preliminary publication, begin by suggesting 'the Union's economic and social objectives should be included in a new constitutional treaty' (European Convention, 2003a, p. 2). Indeed, 'Some members of the group have emphasized the importance of including a reference to sustainable growth and productivity. Others attach more importance to highlighting full employment, social and regional cohesion, and a better balance between competition and public services in a social market economy' (ibid.). The final draft proposals stipulate that 'The Union shall work for a Europe of sustainable development based on balanced economic growth, with a social market economy aiming at full employment and social progress' (ibid., p. 3). Furthermore, some of the members felt that the objectives of growth and development should be included in the mandate of the ECB, although 'A large number of the group considers that the tasks, mandate and statute of the European Central Bank should remain unchanged, and should not be affected by any new treaty provisions' (ibid.). Transparency and accountability of the ECB, enhancing the reporting of the ECB to the European Parliament and the publication of the ECB minutes are further recommendations. In the event, the proposals in the final EU draft constitution confirm the current objective of the ECB without further recommendations. It merely restates the previous Treaty agreements when it says that 'The primary objective of the Bank shall be to maintain price stability. Without prejudice to the objective of price stability, it shall support general economic policies in the Union with a view to contributing to the achievement of the Union's objectives' (ibid., p. 20).

In terms of the SGP, the European Convention (2002) does not offer much of a change:

as far as the Treaty provisions on excessive deficit procedures (Article 104) are concerned, a majority of the Group wish to see these amended in order to allow the Commission to issue first warnings of excessive deficits directly to the Member State concerned. In the subsequent phases, the Council should take decisions by QMV (Qualified Majority Voting) on the basis of a Commission proposal, always excluding from voting the Member State concerned. (European Convention, 2002, p. 4)

The Convention goes on to suggest that 'some propose that the deficit criteria should take into account structural elements, as well as the "golden rule" on public investments' (p. 4). Another assessment of the situation, and a set of proposals, come from the Centre for European Reform. Fitousi and Creel (2002) suggest that

Meanwhile, the Growth and Stability Pact is in crisis. While the European economy is grinding to a halt, euro area governments are less and less willing to comply with the strict fiscal limits of the Pact. Their attempts to evade its rules have undermined the Pact's credibility. There can now be no doubt that a thorough overhaul is necessary ... For the European policy mix, this 'liberation' of fiscal policy would be a breath of fresh air. It would ease the constant pressure on the ECB to adopt a more active style of macro-economic management, and remove many of the constraints that are currently inhibiting economic policy coordination in the EU. (p. 68)

The UK Treasury has published a set of proposals to reform EMU fiscal policy. Treasury (2003) proposes to endow fiscal policy with a stabilization objective along with a trigger point for discretionary action. This would be a rule whereby discretionary fiscal policy was undertaken when the output gap exceeded a certain percentage of GDP, or when expected inflation deviated from the target. Credibility and transparency would be ensured through the publication of a 'stabilization report' along the lines of the current 'inflation report' of the Bank of England. However pertinent this proposal may be, it does not tackle the serious constraint of the SGP and the 3 per cent ceiling on fiscal deficit.

Svensson (2003a) calls for the ECB to modify its monetary policy strategy in the manner of some other central banks. It is argued that the ECB should abandon completely the two-pillar strategy and 'just adopt the much superior international-best-practice strategy of flexible inflation strategy, as it is demonstrated by the Reserve Bank of New Zealand, the Bank of England, the Riksbank and the Bank of Norway' (p. 5). The 'clarification' arguments rehearsed above may very well constitute an attempt towards this objective, although by no means does it address entirely the Svensson (2003a) recommendation. The problem with this particular proposal is whether the premise of its argument is acceptable. It is rather debatable whether the 'international-best-practice strategy' is represented by flexible 'inflation targeting'. Ball and

Sheridan (2003) provide evidence that suggests that this need not be the case. They conclude that there is 'no evidence that inflation targeting improves a country's economic performance' (p. 29).

Some of these proposals, especially the one by Fitousi and Creel (2002), do open the way to improve the institutional set-up of the euro area, but they are incomplete in a serious sense. Although they begin to address the issue of institutional revisions, they do not go far enough to cure the fundamental problem of inherent deflationary bias in the current institutional system. The problems identified above with the operation and management of the ECB remain, save for attempts at accountability and transparency. The objectives of the ECB and, thus, the deflationary bias in its operation remain intact. Similarly, in the case of the SGP, the stance taken is essentially to accept the current arrangements, other than making the point that 'budgetary and financial coordination of the Member States with the objective of monetary stability as a basis for sound economic growth is of utmost common concern' (p. 4). It is essentially the failure of the European Convention to address the issue of the deflationary bias of the euro area institutional arrangements.

Our own response is to say 'scrap the SGP'. In other words, remove these artificial limits on budget deficits and stop seeking to impose a 'one size fits all' policy on all countries. A substantial EU budget (of the order of 5 per cent or more of GDP), which could be used to provide fiscal stimulus (as recommended in the MacDougall report, 1977) with coordinated national fiscal policies, would be a good way of addressing problems of low demand in the euro area. But, in the absence of a significant EU budget capable of providing automatic stabilizers and stimulating the EU economies, active fiscal policy must remain in the hands of national governments. An interesting case was made by Stiglitz in the *Guardian* (8 May 2003) under the title 'Don't trust the bankers' homilies: the EU stability pact destabilises by cutting spending in a downturn', saying that 'The lesson for Europe is clear: the EU should redefine the stability pact in terms of the structural or full employment deficit – what the fiscal deficit would be if the economy were performing at full employment. To do otherwise is irresponsible.'

It is often argued that the budget position of each country has to be restrained, for there are in effect externalities or spillover effects. This sometimes takes the form that a national government's spending puts upward pressure on interest rates (more specifically on bond rates) that is perceived to raise the cost of borrowing for other governments. It can take the form that government expenditure pushes up demand, which pushes up inflation at least in the country concerned. This may then spill over into other countries and/or lead the ECB to raise interest rates to damp down inflation. Without accepting that government expenditure would have these effects, we would observe that the expansion of private sector expenditure could be expected to have similar effects to those of public expenditure. The fluctuations in the overall level of expenditure come, in practice, predominantly from fluctuations in private expenditure and, particularly, investment. The logic of imposing limits on public sector expenditure (budget deficit) would also apply to imposing limits on private sector expenditure. Perhaps there should be limits on the size of the private sector deficit or on the trade account!

The objectives and mode of operation of the ECB must also be changed. The objectives of the ECB should conspicuously include growth and employment variables, and not merely the problem of inflation. The reformulated ECB should be required to act as lender of last resort and not merely possess the potential to act as such. Moreover, the ECB should adopt a more proactive stance regarding bank surveillance and supervision. The proposal for the reformulation of objectives readily follows from what has been previously said: the ECB should be charged with setting interest rates in a manner that encourages growth and full employment, rather than merely addressing inflation. Further, EMU institutional arrangements are required for the operation of an EMU fiscal policy, and to ensure that monetary authorities do not dominate economic policy making; serious coordination of monetary and fiscal policies is paramount, just as the European Convention suggests, but it would have to go hand in hand with the other changes to which we have just alluded. These are important institutional changes. In terms of economic policy, further changes are required.

6.2   Economic Policy Changes

The achievement of full employment does require an appropriate high level of aggregate demand. This translates into some combination of increased demand for consumption, for investment, for public expenditure and for exports. Whether such a level of aggregate demand would require a substantial budget deficit inevitably depends on what happens to the other sources of demand in the equation. But a high level of aggregate demand is only one condition for the achievement of full employment. In the context of the euro area, there are further significant obstacles to the achievement of full employment. The first is the lack of productive capacity in many regions to provide high levels of employment. Estimates by the OECD of the 'output gap' for the European Union for 2002 are −0.8 per cent, which is actual output, slightly below potential output; yet this is combined with over 8.2 per cent unemployment. In a similar vein, the OECD's estimates of the Non Accelerating Wage Rate of Unemployment (NAWRU) average of 8.1 per cent for the European Union is again close to the actual experience of 8.25 per cent.[19] Interpreting the NAWRU as an indicator of a capacity constraint suggests capacity problems.[20] In this context, higher levels of aggregate demand would

place pressure on capacity and could well have some inflationary consequences. The second obstacle is the disparity of unemployment, in that a
general increase in demand would push some regions to or even above full
employment. The third problem is that there has been incomplete convergence of business cycles across euro area countries, suggesting the need for
differentiated policies across countries (and specifically differentiated fiscal
policies). But even if there were convergence of business cycles, the cyclical
movements would be around with quite different levels of unemployment.

These considerations suggest that the restoration of full employment in the
euro area will take much more than a level of aggregate demand. It will
require the creation of sufficient capacity to support full employment, and the
substantial reduction of regional disparities. But the creation of high levels of
aggregate demand remains a necessary, though not sufficient, condition for
the creation of full employment. At the present time, the euro area lacks any
significant policies which address the unemployment issue: it lacks the power
to create high levels of aggregate demand to promote investment or to reduce
regional disparities.

The achievement of high levels of economic activity without inflationary
pressures then requires three elements, in addition to high levels of aggregate
demand. The first is institutional arrangements for collective wage determination and price setting which are conducive to low inflation. Wage determination
within the EU is currently undertaken on a decentralized and fragmented
basis, even where it is (or has been) centralized within a particular national
economy. The institutional arrangements for collective wage determination at
the EU level do not exist currently, and this effectively rules out any possibilities for the operation of incomes policy or similar for the next few years.
There are a number of examples in Europe (within and outside the EU) of
centralized institutional arrangements which have been conducive to relatively low inflation: for example, Austria, Germany, Norway and Sweden.
The idea of a state-funded 'buffer fund' to stabilize employment in cases of
difficulties is a relevant suggestion. The trade union movement in Sweden
has proposed this idea recently. Finland has already been operating such a
'buffer fund', but it is not state-funded and it is only a tenth of the one
suggested in the case of Sweden.

Second, in addition to the construction of the relevant institutional arrangements discussed so far, it is necessary to construct a well functioning real
economy which is also conducive to combining low inflation with high levels
of economic activity. We take the view that a major element of that would be
the construction of a level and location of productive capacity which is
capable of providing work to all that seek paid employment. This would
require not only that the general level of productive capacity is raised, but
also that much of that increase is directed towards the less prosperous regions

of the EMU. This would require the enhancement of the functions of the European Investment Bank (EIB), or a similar institution, to ensure high rates of capital formation, appropriately located across the EMU.

Third, the present disparities in regional unemployment levels (and also in labour market participation rates) within the EU would suggest that, even if full employment were achieved in some regions, there would still be very substantial levels of unemployment in many others. In the presence of such disparities in unemployment, the achievement of a low level of unemployment overall (not to mention full employment) would be difficult. This problem is compounded by the fact that, within the EMU, not only is there high unemployment on average, but there is at the same time a severe shortage of highly qualified labour in many member countries. On top of all these problems, there is still very low or even negligible mobility within the EMU (Fertig and Schmidt, 2002). Inflationary pressures would build up in the fully employed regions even when the less prosperous regions were still suffering from significant levels of unemployment. Interest rates would then rise to dampen down the inflationary pressures in the prosperous regions without consideration for the continuing unemployment in other regions.

Therefore a further recommendation would be to have a revamped EIB to supplement the activities of the ECB, with the specific objective of enhancing investment activity in those regions where unemployment is acute. Enhanced investment activity will thus aim to reduce the dispersion of unemployment within the framework of reducing unemployment in general. This could be achieved through encouraging long-term investment whenever this is necessary by providing appropriate finance for it.

7   SUMMARY AND CONCLUSIONS

In this chapter we have examined the theoretical foundations of the EMU model. We have examined the policy implications of the EMU, along with its theoretical and institutional dimensions surrounding monetary and fiscal policies. The real challenges to EMU macro policies lie in their ability to move the euro area to a full-employment situation with low inflation. They are actually unsatisfactory to withstand the challenge. They are overtly deflationary. We have proposed a number of changes that would include the following elements. First, any political constraints on national budget positions should be removed, and national governments set fiscal policy as they deem appropriate. Second, institutional arrangements for the coordination of national fiscal policies should be strengthened. Third, EU institutional arrangements are required for the operation of an EU fiscal policy, and to ensure that monetary authorities do not dominate economic policy making. Fourth, serious coordination of monetary and fiscal policies is paramount. Above all, though, the current mix of fiscal and monetary tightening, along with currency appreciation, cannot deliver a healthy macroeconomic landscape: especially so in an environment that is geared to stagnation,[21] not to say deflation, in some of its major economies (Germany and France).[22] The analysis and suggestions we have initiated in this chapter fall squarely within the theoretical premises and policy implications of the theoretical framework we have been building throughout this study.

NOTES

1. Issing (2003a) puts it in the following way: 'Widespread consensus: even low inflation entails significant costs'. This statement should be judged against evidence provided by Ghosh and Phillips (1998), as shown in Chapter 2.
2. See Forder (2000) for an extensive discussion and critique of the notion of credibility.
3. More details on the euro area theoretical framework may be found in Duisenberg (1999), Issing (2003a), Arestis, Brown and Sawyer (2001), Tsakalotos (2001) and Bibow (2003), to mention only a few relevant examples.
4. Our own empirical work (Arestis *et al.*, 2003) suggests that the demand for money differs between the component countries of the EMU and that the demand for money is unstable in a number of those countries.
5. Forecasts from European Commission Spring Forecasts, 2003.
6. For more details on the EMU institutional macroeconomic framework, see, for example, ECB (1999, 2001b, 2001f, 2003a, pp. 37–49).
7. It can, though, be noted that the inflation rate in the eurozone has generally been above the 2 per cent level.
8. In the year to November 2002, inflation in Ireland was 4.7 per cent, Portugal 4.1 per cent and Spain and Greece both at 3.9 per cent, whereas inflation in Germany was 1.0 per cent and in Belgium 1.1 per cent.
9. The euro exchange rate jumped to 1.1506 against the dollar. It had been at 1.1360 against the dollar ahead of the ECB's decision.
10. The Governing Council comprises 18 members, as follows: six policy makers based in Frankfurt (they are from Finland, France, Germany, Italy, the Netherlands and Spain) and 12 heads of national central banks (members of the EMU) in the euro area. All 18 members have equal say. There are, thus, six countries with two representatives on the Governing Council.
11. In the same paper, Meade and Sheets (2001) provide evidence that enables them to conclude that, in the case of the US Federal Reserve System, policy makers' regional unemployment plays a significant role in monetary policy decisions. Thus regional factors play an important role in monetary policy decisions.
12. The US also had fiscal stimulus first from the Bush tax cuts of mid-2001 and then the increased expenditure on security measures in the aftermath of 11 September.
13. The *Financial Times* (Wednesday 9 October 2002) explained that dollar rise as 'traders expressing disappointment at the outlook for euro area growth'; this was essentially due to 'Comments by ... the president of the European Central Bank' which 'dampened tentative hopes that the ECB had been braced to support growth with a cut in interest rates'.
14. Note the severity of the downturn which would be involved if the 'escape clauses' are to be invoked.
15. On 30 January 2002, the European Commission issued for the first time a recommendation with a view to giving an early warning to Germany and Portugal in an attempt to avoid excessive budgetary deficits. On 12 February 2002, ECOFIN decided to abrogate

the early warning in view of the commitment by Germany and Portugal to take action to avoid the occurrence of an excessive deficit.

16. The general formulation is $d = b/g$, where b is budget ratio, d debt ratio and g the rate of nominal growth.

17. In the decade up to 1992 the German general government financial balance averaged 1.8 per cent deficit, and the euro area as a whole averaged 4.45 per cent deficit (calculated from OECD *Economic Outlook*, various issues).

18. A further disturbing, and highly objectionable, implication of the monolithic focus on price stability and on the 3 per cent SGP rule is the manner in which it is thought appropriate 'to address the fiscal challenges of population age' (ECB, 2003c, p. 46). The ECB (2003c) paper actually warns that free health care, as for example in many euro area countries, will have to be restricted to emergency services only. This is so in view of the high and rising 'ratio between the number of pensioners and the number of contributors'; for 'otherwise the cost would overwhelm economies and lead to rising inflation' (p. 39). Although the report recognizes that raising the retirement age should produce large gains, funded-pension arrangements are thought to carry potentially larger benefits for economic growth. These relate to the beneficial effects on the labour market (social security contributions would thereby be perceived as savings for retirement rather than as taxes) and the capital market (higher capital accumulation of capital). This absurd suggestion is not unrelated, of course, to the SGP ideas, to which we have objected vehemently in this study.

19. The figures in this and the preceding sentence are derived from OECD *Economic Outlook* databank (accessed June 2003).

20. In this context it is worth quoting the ECB chief economist, who suggested at a press conference in Berlin on 16 April 2002, that the return in 2002 of the euro area to its average growth after the 2001 economic slowdown 'is an indication that the euro area and Europe in general still have low potential growth' (reported in the *Financial Times*, 18 April 2002).

21. Interestingly enough, the OECD (2003) cut sharply its forecasts for the euro area growth for 2003 (from 1.8 per cent in its December 2002 forecasts to 1.0 per cent in its April 2003 forecasts), and for 2004 (from 2.7 per cent in its December 2002 forecasts to 2.4 per cent in its April forecasts). This while trimming its forecasts for the US in 2003 only to 2.5 per cent in its April 2003 forecasts (from 2.6 per cent in its December 2002 forecasts) and raising expected GDP growth for 2004 to 4 per cent in its April 2003 forecasts (from 3.6 per cent in its December 2002 forecasts).

22. A relevant table published in the *Economist* (3 May 2003, p. 70) clearly indicates that forecasts for core inflation (inflation that excludes energy, food and tobacco) for the period March 2003 to June 2004 portray Germany moving into deflation, with France being on the margin.

References

Agénor, P.-R., C.J. McDermott and E.S. Prasad (1999), 'Macroeconomic fluctuations in developing countries: some stylised facts', IMF Working Paper 99/35, International Monetary Fund, Washington, DC.

Akerlof, G.A., W.T. Dickens and G.L. Perry (1996), 'The macroeconomics of low inflation', *Brookings Papers on Economic Activity*, **1**, 1–76.

Alesina, A. and R. Perotti (1995), 'The political economy of budget deficits', *Staff Papers*, International Monetary Fund, **42**(2), 1–31.

Alesina, A.F., O. Blanchard, J. Gali, F. Giavazzi and H. Uhlig (2001), *Defining a Macroeconomic Framework for the Euro Area: Monitoring the European Central Bank*, *3*, London: Centre for Economic Policy Research.

Alexiou, C. and C. Pitelis (2003), 'On capital shortages and European unemployment: a panel data investigation', *Journal of Post Keynesian Economics*, **25**(4), 613–31.

Ando, A. and F. Modigliani (1965), 'The relative stability of monetary velocity and the investment multiplier', *American Economic Review*, **55**, September.

Angeloni, I., A. Kashyap, B. Mojon and D. Terlizzese (2002), 'Monetary transmission in the euro area: where do we stand?', European Central Bank Working Paper Series, no. 114.

Arestis, P. (1986), 'Wages and prices in the UK: the post Keynesian view', *Journal of Post Keynesian Economics*, **8**(3), 339–58; reprinted in M.C. Sawyer (ed.) (1988), *Post-Keynesian Economics*, Aldershot, UK and Brookfield, US: Edward Elgar Publishing, pp. 456–75.

Arestis, P. and I. Biefang-Frisancho Mariscal (1997), 'Conflict, effort and capital stock in UK wage determination', *Empirica*, **24**(3), 179–93.

Arestis, P. and I. Biefang-Frisancho Mariscal (1998), 'Capital shortages and asymmetries in UK unemployment', *Structural Change and Economic Dynamics*, **9**(2), 189–204.

Arestis, P. and I. Biefang-Frisancho Mariscal (2000), 'Capital stock, unemployment and wages in the UK and Germany', *Scottish Journal of Political Economy*, **47**(5), 487–503.

Arestis, P. and P.G.A. Howells (1991), 'Financial innovations and the distributional effects of interest rate changes in the UK', *Eastern Economic Journal*, **17**(3), 263–71.

Arestis, P. and M. Sawyer (1998), 'Keynesian policies for the new millennium', *Economic Journal*, **108**, 181–95.

Arestis, P. and M. Sawyer (2002a), 'Can monetary policy affect the real economy?', Working Paper Series, no. 355, Levy Economics Institute of Bard College (September).

Arestis, P. and M. Sawyer (2002b), 'The Bank of England macroeconomic model: its nature and implications', *Journal of Post Keynesian Economics*, **24**(4), 529–45.

Arestis, P. and M. Sawyer (2003a), 'Does the stock of money have any causal significance?', *Banca Nazionale Del Lavoro Quarterly Review*, **LVI**(225), 113–36.

Arestis, P. and M. Sawyer (2003b), 'On the effectiveness of monetary policy and of fiscal policy', Working Paper Series, no. 369, Levy Economics Institute of Bard College (January).

Arestis, P. and M. Sawyer (2003c), 'The nature and role of monetary policy when money is endogenous', Working Paper Series, no. 374, Levy Economics Institute of Bard College (March).

Arestis, P. and M. Sawyer (2003d), 'The case for fiscal policy', Working Papers Series, no. 382, Levy Economics Institute of Bard College (May).

Arestis, P. and M. Sawyer (2003e), 'Reinventing fiscal policy', *Journal of Post Keynesian Economics*, **26**(1), 3–25.

Arestis, P. and M. Sawyer (2003f), 'Aggregate demand conflict and capacity in the inflationary process', paper presented to the International Conference, '100 Years of Cambridge Economics', held at the University of Cambridge, 17–19 September 2003.

Arestis, P., A. Brown and M. Sawyer (2001), *The Euro: Evolution and Prospects*, Cheltenham, UK and Northampton, MA, USA: Edward Elgar Publishing.

Arestis, P., G.M. Caporale and A. Cipollini (2002), 'Is there a trade-off between inflation and output gap?', *The Manchester School of Economic and Social Research*, **70**(4), 528–45.

Arestis, P., K. McCauley and M.C. Sawyer (2001), 'An alternative stability and growth pact for the European Union', *Cambridge Journal of Economics*, **25**(1), 113–30.

Arestis, P., I. Biefang-Frisancho Mariscal, A. Brown and M. Sawyer (2003), 'Asymmetries of demand for money functions amongst EMU countries', *Investigación Económica*, **LXII**(245), 15–32.

Auerbach, A. (2002), 'Is there a role for discretionary fiscal policy?', paper prepared for the Federal Reserve Bank of Kansas City conference on 'Rethinking Stabilization Policy', 29–31 August.

Baddeley, M.C. (2003), *Investment: Theories and Analysis*, Basingstoke: Palgrave Macmillan.

Baker, D., A. Glyn, D. Howell and J. Schmitt (2002), 'Labour market institutions and unemployment: a critical assessment of the cross-country evidence', Working Paper 2002–17, Center for Economic Policy Analysis, New School University, New York: USA.

Ball, L. and N. Sheridan (2003), 'Does inflation targeting matter?', NBER Working Paper Series, no. 9577, National Bureau of Economic Research, Cambridge, MA.

Bank of England (1999), *Economic Models at the Bank of England*, London: Bank of England.

Bank of England (2000), *Economic Models at the Bank of England*, London: Bank of England (September update).

Bank of England Quarterly Bulletin (BEQB) (2004), 'The new Bank of England Quarterly Model', **44**(2), 188–93.

Bank of International Settlements (BIS) (2002), *Annual Report*, Basle: Switzerland.

Barro, R.J. (1974), 'Are government bonds net wealth?', *Journal of Political Economy*, **82**(6), 1095–117.

Barro, R.J. (1989), 'The Ricardian approach to budget deficits', *Journal of Economic Perspectives*, **3**(2), 37–54.

Barro, R.J. and D.B. Gordon (1983), 'A positive theory of monetary policy in a natural rate model', *Journal of Political Economy*, **91**(3), 589–619.

Bernanke, B.S. (2003a), '"Constrained discretion" and monetary policy', remarks before the Money Marketeers of New York University, 3 February, New York.

Bernanke, B.S. (2003b), 'A perspective on inflation targeting', Remarks at the Annual Washington Policy Conference of the National Association of Business Economists, 25 March, Washington, DC.

Bernanke, B.S. (2003c), 'The legacy of Milton and Rose Friedman', Remarks at the Federal Reserve Bank of Dallas Conference on 'The Legacy of Milton and Rose Friedman's Free to Choose', 24 October, Dallas, Texas.

Bernanke, B.S. and A.S. Blinder (1988), 'Credit, money and aggregate demand', *American Economic Review*, Papers and Proceedings, **78**(2), 435–9.

Bernanke, B.S. and M. Gertler (1989), 'Agency costs, net worth and business fluctuations', *American Economic Review*, **79**(1), 14–31.

Bernanke, B.S. and M. Gertler (1999), 'Monetary policy and asset price volatility', in *New Challenges for Monetary Policy*, Proceedings of the Symposium Sponsored by the Federal Reserve Bank of Kansas City, Jackson Hole, Wyoming, 26–8 August, pp. 77–128.

Bernanke, B.S. and F.S. Mishkin (1997), 'Inflation targeting: a new framework for monetary policy?', *NBER Working Paper*, no. 5893, NBER, Cambridge, MA.

Bernanke, B.S., M. Gertler and S. Gilchrist (1996), 'The financial accelerator and the flight to quality', *Review of Economics and Statistics*, **78**, 1–15.

Bernanke, B.S., M. Gertler and S. Gilchrist (1999), 'The financial accelerator in a quantitative business cycle framework', in J. Taylor and M. Woodford (eds), *Handbook of Macroeconomics*, vol. 1, Amsterdam: North-Holland.

Bernanke, B.S., M. Gertler and M. Watson (1997), 'Systematic monetary policy and the effects of oil price shocks', *Brookings Papers on Economic Activity*, no. 1, 91–142.

Bernanke, B.S., T. Laubach, F.S. Mishkin and A. Posen (1999), *Inflation Targeting: Lessons from the International Experience*, Princeton: Princeton University Press.

Bhadhuri, A. and S. Marglin (1990), 'Unemployment and the real wage: the economic basis for contesting political ideologies', *Cambridge Journal of Economics*, **14**(4), 375–93.

Bibow, J. (2002a), 'The monetary policies of the European Central Bank and the euro's (mal-) performance: a stability oriented assessment', *International Review of Applied Economics*, **16**(1), 31–50.

Bibow, J. (2002b), 'Keynes on central banking and the structure of monetary policy', *History of Political Economy*, **34**(4), 749–87.

Bibow, J. (2003), 'Is Europe doomed to stagnation? An analysis of the current crisis and recommendations for reforming macroeconomic policymaking in Euroland', mimeo, University of Hamburg, Germany.

Blanchard, O.J. (1985), 'Debt, deficits and finite horizons', *Journal of Political Economy*, **93**, 223–47.

Blanchflower, D.G. and A.J. Oswald (1994), *The Wage Curve*, Cambridge, MA: MIT Press.

Blinder, A. (1987), *Hard Heads, Soft Hearts*, Reading, MA: Addison-Wesley.

Blinder, A. and R. Solow (1974), 'Analytical foundations of fiscal policy', in A. Blinder, R. Solow, G. Break, P. Steiner and D. Netzer (eds), *The Economics of Public Finance: Essays*, Washington: The Brookings Institution.

Blinder, A.S. (1998), *Central Banking in Theory and Practice*, Cambridge, MA: MIT Press.

Blundell, R. and T. MaCurdy (1999), 'Labour supply: a review of alternative approaches', in O. Ashenfelter and D. Card (eds), *Handbook of Labour Economics*, vol. 3A, Amsterdam and New York: Elsevier.

Bodkin, R.G. and A.E. Neder (2003), 'Monetary policy targeting in Argentina and Canada in the 1990s: a comparison, some contrasts and a tentative evaluation', *Eastern Economic Journal*, **29**(3), 339–58.

Boivin, J. and M. Giannoni (2002a), 'Assessing changes in the monetary transmission mechanism: a VAR approach', *Federal Reserve Bank of New York Economic Policy Review*, **8**(1), 97–111.

Boivin, J. and M. Giannoni (2002b), 'Has monetary policy become less powerful?', Federal Reserve Bank of New York Staff Report, no. 144, March.

Brown, G. (1999), 'The conditions for full employment', Mais Lecture, 19 October, City University London.

Brunner, K. and A.H. Meltzer (1993), *Money and the Economy: Issues in Monetary Analysis*, Cambridge: Cambridge University Press for the Raffaele Mattioli Foundation.

Buiter, W., G. Corsetti and N. Roubini (1993), 'Excessive deficits: sense and nonsense in the Treaty of Maastricht', *Economic Policy*, **16**, 58–90.

Buiter, W.H. (2001), 'Notes on "A code for fiscal stability"', *Oxford Economic Papers*, **53**, 1–19.

Buti, M., D. Franco and H. Ongena (1997), *Budgetary Policies During Recessions: Retrospective Application of the 'Stability and Growth Pact' to the Post-War Period*, Brussels: European Commission.

Caballero, R. and R.S. Pyndick (1996), 'Uncertainty, investment, and industry evolution', *International Economic Review*, **37**(3), 641–62.

Calvo, G. (1978), 'On the time consistency of optimal policy in the monetary economy', *Econometrica*, **46**(4), 1411–28.

Cecchetti, S. and M. Ehrmann (2000), 'Does inflation targeting increase output volatility? An international comparison of policymakers' preferences and outcomes', working paper 69, Central Bank of Chile: Santiago.

Chadha, J.S. and N.H. Dimsdale (1999), 'A long view of real rates', *Oxford Review of Economic Policy*, **15**(2), 17–45.

Chirinko, R.S. (1993), 'Business fixed investment spending: modeling strategies, empirical results, and policy implications', *Journal of Economic Literature*, **31**(4), 1875–911.

Church, K.B., P.R. Mitchel, J.E. Sault and K.F. Wallis (1997), 'Comparative performance of models of the UK economy', *National Institute Economic Review*, **161**, 91–100.

Clarida, R., J. Galí and M. Gertler (1999), 'The science of monetary policy: a new Keynesian perspective', *Journal of Economic Literature*, **37**(4), 1661–707.

Clifton, E.V., L. Hyginus and C.-H. Wong (2001), 'Inflation targeting and the unemployment–inflation trade-off', IMF Working Paper 01/166, International Monetary Fund: Washington, DC.

Congressional Budget Office (1994), *The Economic and Budget Outlook: Fiscal Years 1996–2000*, Washington: Congressional Budget Office.

Corbo,V., M.O. Landerrretche and K. Schmidt-Hebbel (2001), 'Assessing inflation targeting after a decade of world experience', mimeo, Central Bank of Chile, Santiago.

Corbo,V., M.O. Landerrretche and K. Schmidt-Hebbel (2002), 'Does inflation targeting make a difference?', in N. Loayza and R. Saito (eds), *Inflation*

Targeting: Design, Performance, Challenges, Santiago: Central Bank of Chile.

Cottrell, A. (1994), 'Post-Keynesian monetary economics', *Cambridge Journal of Economics*, **18**(6), 587–606.

Council of the European Union (2002), 'Council Recommendation of 21 June 2002 on the Broad Guidelines of the Economic Policies of the Member States and the Community', Brussels.

Cunningham, S.R. and J. Vilasuso (1994–5), 'Is Keynesian demand management policy still viable?', *Journal of Post Keynesian Economics*, **17**(2), 231–48.

Debelle, G. and S. Fischer (1994), 'How independent should a central bank be?', in J.C. Fuhrer (ed.), *Goals, Guidelines, and Constraints Facing Monetary Policymakers*, Boston: Federal Reserve Bank of Boston, pp. 195–221.

DeLong, J.B. and L. Summers (1986), 'Is increased price flexibility stabilizing?', *American Economic Review*, **76**, 1031–44.

Domar, E.D. (1944), 'The "burden of the debt" and the national income', *American Economic Review*, **34**(4), 798–827.

Dow, J.C.R. (1998), *Major Recessions: Britain and the World, 1920–1995*, London and New York: Oxford University Press.

Duisenberg, W.F. (1999), 'Economic and monetary union in Europe: the challenges ahead', in *New Challenges for Monetary Policy*, Proceedings of the Symposium Sponsored by the Federal Reserve Bank of Kansas City, Jackson Hole, Wyoming, 26–8 August, pp. 185–94.

Duisenberg, W.F. (2001), 'Introductory statement, and questions and answers', ECB Press Conference, 6 December, Frankfurt.

Duisenberg, W.F. (2002), 'Testimony to the European Parliament', October, Brussels.

Duisenberg, W.F. (2003a), 'Introductory statement, and questions and answers', ECB Press Conference, 8 May, Frankfurt.

Duisenberg, W.F. (2003b), 'Introductory statement, and questions and answers', ECB Press Conference, 5 June, Frankfurt.

Dwyer Jr., G.P. and R.W. Haffer (1998), 'The Federal Government's budget surplus: cause for celebration?', *Federal Reserve Bank of Atlanta*, **83**(3), 42–51.

Eichengreen, B. (1998), 'Comment on "The Political Economy of Fiscal Adjustments"', *Brookings Papers on Economic Activity*, **1**, 255–62, Brookings Institution, Washington.

Elsmeskov, J.M. and S. Scarpetta (1998), 'Key lessons for labour market reforms: evidence from OECD countries' experience', *Swedish Economic Policy*, **5**(2), 205–52.

European Central Bank (ECB) (1999), 'The institutional framework of the

European system of central banks', *Monthly Bulletin*, July, Frankfurt, pp. 55–63.

European Central Bank (ECB) (2001a), *Monthly Bulletin*, January, Frankfurt.

European Central Bank (ECB) (2001b), *Monthly Bulletin*, March, Frankfurt.

European Central Bank (ECB) (2001c), *Monthly Bulletin*, April, Frankfurt.

European Central Bank (ECB) (2001d), *Monthly Bulletin*, May, Frankfurt.

European Central Bank (ECB) (2001e), *Monthly Bulletin*, June, Frankfurt.

European Central Bank (ECB) (2001f), 'Issues Related to Monetary Policy Rules', *Monthly Bulletin*, October, Frankfurt, pp. 37–50.

European Central Bank (ECB) (2001g), 'The Economic Policy Framework in EMU', *Monthly Bulletin*, November, Frankfurt, pp. 51–65.

European Central Bank (ECB) (2001h), *Monthly Bulletin*, December, Frankfurt.

European Central Bank (ECB) (2002a), *Monthly Bulletin*, January, Frankfurt.

European Central Bank (ECB) (2002b), *Monthly Bulletin*, April, Frankfurt.

European Central Bank (ECB) (2002c), *Monthly Bulletin*, May, Frankfurt.

European Central Bank (ECB) (2002d), *Monthly Bulletin*, December, Frankfurt.

European Central Bank (ECB) (2002e), 'Recent Findings on Monetary Transmission in the Euro Area', *Monthly Bulletin*, October.

European Central Bank (ECB) (2003a), 'The Relationship Between Monetary Policy and Fiscal Policies in the Euro Area', *Monthly Bulletin*, February, Frankfurt, pp. 37–49.

European Central Bank (ECB) (2003b), *Monthly Bulletin*, March 2003, Frankfurt.

European Central Bank (ECB) (2003c), 'The Need for Comprehensive Reforms to Cope with Population Ageing', *Monthly Bulletin*, April, Frankfurt, pp. 39–51.

European Central Bank (ECB) (2003d), *Monthly Bulletin*, May 2003, Frankfurt.

European Central Bank (ECB) (2003e), *Monthly Bulletin*, June 2003, Frankfurt.

European Commission (2000), 'Public Finances in EMU – 2000', *European Economy – Reports and Studies*, no. 3, Brussels.

European Commission (2003), 'Flash estimates for the first quarter of 2003', website http://europa.eu.int accessed May 2003.

European Commission (MacDougall Report) (1977), *Report of the Study Group on the Role of Public Finance in European Integration*, Brussels: European Commission.

European Convention (2002), 'Economic governance', Working Group IV, Working Document 19, 7 October, Brussels.

European Convention (2003a), *Draft Constitution*, vol. 1, 26 May, Brussels.

European Convention (2003b), *Draft Constitution*, vol. 2, 26 May, Brussels.

Fair, R. (2001), 'Estimates of the effectiveness of monetary policy', mimeo, Yale University: Cowles Foundation and International Center for Finance.

Fazzari, S. (1993), 'Monetary policy, financial structure and investment', chapter 3 in *Transforming the U.S. Financial System: Equity and Efficiency for the 21st Century*, Armonk, New York: M.E. Sharpe.

Fazzari, S. and B. Peterson (1993), 'Working capital and fixed investment: new evidence on financing constraints', *Rand Economic Journal*, **24**, 328–42.

Fazzari, S., R.G. Hubbard and B.C. Peterson (1988), 'Financing constraints and corporate investment', *Brookings Papers on Economic Activity*, **1**, 141–95.

Fazzari, S.M (1994–5), 'Why doubt the effectiveness of Keynesian fiscal policy?', *Journal of Post Keynesian Economics*, **17**(2), 231–48.

Federal Reserve Bank of New York (2002), 'Financial Innovation and Monetary Transmission', *Economic Policy Review*, **8**(1), Proceedings of a Conference Sponsored by the Federal Reserve Bank of New York.

Fertig, M. and C.M. Schmidt (2002), 'Mobility within Europe – What do we (still not) know?', IZA Discussion Paper, no. 447, March.

Fischer, S. (1994), 'Modern central banking', in F. Capie, C.A.E. Goodhart, S. Fischer and N. Schnadt (eds), *The Future of Central Banking*, Cambridge: Cambridge University Press, pp. 262–308.

Fisher, I. (1933), 'The debt–deflation theory of great depressions', *Econometrica*, **1**, 337–57.

Fitousi, J.-P. and J. Creel (2002), *How to Reform the European Central Bank*, London: Centre for European Reform.

Fontana, G. and A. Palacio-Vera (2002), 'Monetary policy rules: what are we learning?', *Journal of Post Keynesian Economics*, **24**(4), 547–68.

Fontana, G. and E. Venturino (2003), 'Endogenous money: an analytical approach', *Scottish Journal of Political Economy*, **50**(4), 1–19.

Forder, J. (2000), 'The theory of credibility: confusions, limitations, and dangers', *International Papers in Political Economy*, **7**(2), 3–40.

Forder, J. (2003), 'Central bank independence: economic theory, evidence, and political legitimacy', *International Papers in Political Economy*, **10**(3), 1–54.

Fracasso, A., H. Genberg and C. Wyplosz (2003), 'How do central banks write? An evaluation of inflation reports by inflation targeting central banks', *Geneva Reports on the World Economy, Special Report 2*, London: Centre for Economic Policy Research.

Friedman, M. (1957), *A Theory of the Consumption Function*, Princeton: Princeton University Press.

Friedman, M. (1960), *A Programme for Monetary Stability*, New York: Fordham University Press.

Friedman, M. (1968), 'The role of monetary policy', *American Economic Review*, **58**(1), 1–17.

Friedman, M. (1969), *The Optimum Quantity Theory of Money and other Essays*, Chicago: Aldine.

Friedman, M. and D. Meiselman (1963), 'The relative stability of monetary velocity and the investment multiplier in the USA, 1897–1958', in Commission of Money and Credit (ed.), *Stabilization Policies, Research Study No. 2*, Englewood Cliffs, NJ: Prentice-Hall, pp. 165–269.

Galbraith, J.K. (1999), 'The inflation obsession: flying in the face of the facts', *Foreign Affairs*, **78**(1), 152–6.

Ghosh, A. and S. Phillips (1998), 'Warning: inflation may be harmful to your growth', *IMF Staff Papers*, **45**(4), 672–710.

Giavazzi, F. and M. Pagano (1990), 'Can severe fiscal contractions be expansionary? Tales of two small European countries', in O.J. Blanchard and S. Fischer (eds), *NBER Macroeconomics Annual 1990*, Cambridge, MA: MIT Press.

Gilchrist, S. and C.P. Himmelberg (1995), 'Evidence on the role of cash flow for investment', *Journal of Monetary Economics*, **36**(3), 541–72.

Godley, W. and R. Rowthorn (1994), 'The dynamics of public sector deficits and debts', in J. Michie (ed.), *Unemployment in Europe*, London: Academic Press.

Gordon, D. (1994), 'Must we save our way out of stagnation? The investment/saving relation revisited', mimeo, New School for Social Research (March).

Gordon, R.J. (1997), 'The time-varying NAIRU and its implications for economic policy', *Journal of Economic Perspectives*, **11**(1), 11–32.

Gramlich, E.M. (2000), 'Inflation targeting', remarks before the Charlotte Economics Club, 13 January, Charlotte, North Carolina.

Greenspan, A. (2002), 'Issues for monetary policy', Remarks Before the Economic Club of New York, 19 December, New York City, paper available online at http://www.federalreserve.gov/boarddocs/speeches/2002/20021219/ (pages in the text refer to the website document).

Groshen, E.L. and S. Potter (2003), 'Has structural change contributed to a jobless recovery?', *Federal Reserve Bank of New York Current Issues in Economics and Finance*, **9**(8), 1–7.

Gross, D. (1994), 'The investment and financing decisions of liquidity-constrained firms', unpublished paper (MIT).

Hall, S. (2001), 'Credit channel effects in the monetary transmission mechanism', *Bank of England Quarterly Bulletin*, Winter, 442–8.

Hemming, R., M. Kell and S. Mahfouz (2002), 'The effectiveness of fiscal policy in stimulating economic activity: a review of the literature', IMF Working Paper 02/208, International Monetary Fund, Washington, DC.

Hemming, R., S. Mahfouz and A. Schimmelpfennig (2002), 'Fiscal policy and economic activity in advanced economies', IMF Working Paper 02/87, International Monetary Fund, Washington, DC.

Hendry, S. (1995), 'Long-run demand for M1', Bank of Canada Working Paper 95–11.

HM Treasury (2003), *Policy Frameworks in the UK and EMU: EMU Study*, available at //www.hm-treasury.gov.uk.

Hoshi, T., A.K. Kashyap and D. Scharfstein (1991), 'Corporate structure, liquidity and investment: evidence from Japanese industrial groups', *Quarterly Journal of Economics*, **106**(1), 33–60.

Howells, P. (1995), 'Endogenous money', *International Papers in Political Economy*, **2**(2): reprinted in P. Arestis and M. Sawyer (eds) (2001), *Money, Finance and Capitalist Development*, Aldershot, UK and Northampton, MA, USA: Edward Elgar Publishing.

Hubbard, R.G. (1998), 'Capital-market imperfections and investment', *Journal of Economic Literature*, **XXXVI**(1), 193–225.

Hubbard, R.G., A.K. Kashyap and T. Whited (1995), 'Internal finance and firm investment', *Journal of Money, Credit and Banking*, **27**(3), 683–701.

Ireland, P.N. (2001), 'Money's role in the monetary business cycle', National Bureau of Economic Research Working Paper 8115, February.

Issing, O. (2003a), 'Testimony before the Committee on Economic and Monetary Affairs of the European Parliament', Brussels, 24 March; paper available online at http://www.ecb.int.

Issing, O. (2003b), 'Evaluation of the ECB's monetary policy strategy', ECB Press Conference and Press Seminar, 8 May, Frankfurt: Germany.

Johnson, D.R. (2002), 'The effect of inflation targeting on the behaviour of expected inflation: evidence from an 11-country panel', *Journal of Monetary Economics*, **49**, 1521–38.

Kalecki, M. (1939), *Essays in the Theory of Economic Fluctuations*, New York: Russell & Russell.

Kalecki, M. (1943), 'The determinants of investment', in *Studies in Economic Dynamics*, London: Allen and Unwin.

Kalecki, M. (1944a), 'The white paper on employment policy', *Bulletin of the Oxford University Institute of Statistics*, **6**.

Kalecki, M. (1944b), 'Three ways to full employment', in Oxford University Institute of Statistics (ed.), *The Economics of Full Employment*, Oxford: Blackwell

Kalecki, M. (1944c), 'Professor Pigou on "The classical stationary state": a comment', *Economic Journal*, **54**.

Keynes, J.M. (1930), *Treatise on Money*, London: Macmillan (page references refer to *The Collected Writings of John Maynard Keynes*, vol. V, London: Macmillan).

Keynes, J.M. (1932), 'The monetary policy of the Labour Party', in D. Moggridge (ed.), *The Collected Writings of John Maynard Keynes*, vol. 21, London: Macmillan, pp. 128–45.

Keynes, J.M. (1936), *The General Theory of Employment, Interest and Money*, London: Macmillan.

Keynes, J.M. (1980), *Activities 1940–1946 Shaping the Post-War World: Employment and Commodities, Collected Writings*, vol. 27, London: Macmillan.

King, M. (1997), 'Changes in UK monetary policy: rules and discretion in practice', *Journal of Monetary Policy*, **39**, 81–97.

King, M. (2002), 'No money, no inflation – the role of money in the economy', *Bank of England Quarterly Bulletin*, Summer, 162–77.

Kuttner, K.N. and P.C. Mosser (2002), 'The monetary transmission mechanism: some answers and further questions', *Federal Reserve Bank of New York Economic Policy Review*, **8**(1), 15–24.

Kydland, F. and E.C. Prescott (1977), 'Rules rather than discretion: the inconsistency of optimal plans', *Journal of Political Economy*, **85**(3), 473–92.

Laidler, D. (1999), 'The quantity of money and monetary policy', Bank of Canada Working Paper 99–5.

Lane, T.D., A. Ghosh, J. Hamann, S. Phillips, M. Schulze-Ghattas and T. Tsikata (1999), 'IMF-supported programs in Indonesia, Korea, and Thailand: a preliminary assessment', IMF Occasional Paper, no. 178, International Monetary Fund, Washington, DC.

Laramie, A.J. and D. Mair (2000), *A Dynamic Theory of Taxation: Integrating Kalecki into Modern Public Finance*, Cheltenham, UK and Northampton, MA, USA: Edward Elgar.

Lavoie, M. (2000), 'A Post Keynesian view of interest rate parity theorems', *Journal of Post Keynesian Economics*, **23**(1), 163–79.

Layard, R., S. Nickell and R. Jackman (1991), *Unemployment: Macroeconomic Performance and the Labour Market*, Oxford: Oxford University Press.

Layard, R., S. Nickell and R. Jackman (1994), *The Unemployment Crisis*, Oxford: Oxford University Press.

Leahy, J.V. (2001), 'Commentary', *Federal Reserve Bank of St. Louis Review*, **83**(4), 161–3.

Lee, F.S. (1998), *Post Keynesian Price Theory*, Cambridge: Cambridge University Press.

Leiderman, L. and L.E.O. Svensson (eds) (1995), *Inflation Targets*, London: Centre for Economic Policy Research.

Lerner, A. (1943), 'Functional finance and the federal debt', *Social Research*, **10**, 38–51; reprinted in M.G. Mueller (ed.) (1971), *Readings in Macroeco-*

nomics, New York: Holt, Rinehart and Winston, pp. 353–60 (page numbers refer to the reprint).

Mankiw, N.G. (2002), 'U.S. monetary policy during the 1990s', in J.A. Frankel and P.R. Orslag (eds), *American Economic Policy in the 1990s*, Cambridge, MA: MIT Press, pp. 1–43.

Mankiw, N.G. and L.H. Summers (1984), 'Do long-term interest rates over-react to short-term interest rates?', NBER Working Paper, no. 1345, National Bureau of Economic Research, Cambridge, MA.

McCallum, B.T. (2001), 'Monetary policy analysis in models without money', *Federal Reserve Bank of St. Louis Review*, **83**(4), 145–60.

Meade, E.E. and N.D. Sheets (2001), 'Regional influences on US monetary policy: some implications for Europe', discussion paper no. 523, Centre for Economic Performance, LSE.

Meyer, L.H. (2001a), 'Inflation targets and inflation targeting', remarks at the University of California at San Diego Economics Roundtable, 17 July, San Diego, California.

Meyer, L.H. (2001b), 'Does money matter?', *Federal Reserve Bank of St. Louis Review*, **83**(5), 1–15.

Miaouli, N. (2001), 'Employment and capital accumulation in unionised labour markets', *International Review of Applied Economics*, **15**(1), 5–30.

Miller, M., R. Skidelsky and P. Weller (1990), 'Fear of deficit financing – is it rational?', in R. Dornbusch and M. Draghi (eds), *Public Debt Management: Theory and History*, Cambridge and New York: Cambridge University Press, pp. 293–310.

Minsky, H.P. (1975), *John Maynard Keynes*, New York: Columbia University Press.

Mishkin, F.S. (1999), 'International experiences with different monetary policy regimes', *Journal of Monetary Economics*, **43**, 579–605.

Mishkin, F.S. (2000), 'What should central banks do?', *Federal Reserve Bank of St. Louis Review*, **82**(6), 1–13.

Mishkin, F.S. (2002a), 'Does inflation targeting matter? Commentary', *Federal Reserve Bank of St. Louis Review*, **84**(4), 149–53.

Mishkin, F.S. (2002b), 'The role of output stabilization in the conduct of monetary policy', NBER Working Paper 9291, Cambridge, MA, NBER.

Mishkin, F.S. and A.S. Posen (1997), 'Inflation targeting lessons from four countries', *Federal Reserve Bank of New York Economic Policy Review*, **3**(1), 9–117.

Monetary Policy Committee (1999), *The Transmission Mechanism of Monetary Policy*, London: Bank of England.

Moore, B.J. (1989), 'A model of bank intermediation', *Journal of Post Keynesian Economics*, **12**(1), 10–29.

Neumann, M.J.M. and J. von Hagen (2002), 'Does inflation targeting matter?', *Federal Reserve Bank of St. Louis Review*, **84**(4), 127–48.

Nordhaus, W. (1973), 'The effects of inflation on the distribution of economic welfare', *Journal of Money, Credit and Banking*, **5**, 465–504.

OECD (1994a), *OECD Jobs Study, Evidence and Explanations, Part I: Labour Market Trends and Underlying Forces of Change*, Paris: OECD.

OECD (1994b), *OECD Jobs Study, Evidence and Explanations, Part II: The Adjustment Potential of the Labour Market*, Paris: OECD.

OECD (1994c), *OECD Jobs Study, Taxation Employment and Unemployment*, Paris: OECD.

OECD (1999), *OECD Employment Outlook*, June, Paris: OECD.

OECD (2000), *Economic Outlook*, 68, Paris: OECD.

OECD (2002), *Economic Outlook*, 72, Paris: OECD.

OECD (2003), *Trends and Underlying Forces of Change*, Paris: OECD.

Orphanides, A. (2001), 'Monetary policy rules based on real-time data', *American Economic Review*, **91**(4), 964–85.

Orphanides, A. (2002), 'Monetary policy rules and the great inflation', *American Economic Review*, **92**(2), 115–20.

Palley, T. (2000), 'Evaluating the OECD's *Job Strategy*: has it helped lower unemployment?', AFL-CIO Technical Working Paper, T024.

Palley, T. (2001), 'The role of institutions and policies in creating high European unemployment: the evidence', Working Paper Series, no. 336, Levy Economics Institute of Bard College (August).

Palley, T.I. (2003), 'A Post Keynesian framework for monetary policy: why interest rate operating procedures are not enough', paper presented to the Conference on 'Economic Policies: Perspectives from Keynesian Heterodoxy', 14–16 November 2002, Dijon, France, (revised March 2003).

Peersman, G. and F. Smets (2001), 'The monetary transmission mechanism in the euro area: more evidence from VAR analysis', European Central Bank Working Paper Series, no. 91.

Poole, W. (1970), 'Optimum choice of monetary policy instruments in a simple stochastic macromodel', *Quarterly Journal of Economics*, May.

Rogoff, K. (1985), 'The optimal degree of commitment to an intermediate monetary target', *Quarterly Journal of Economics*, **100**(4), 1169–89.

Roosa, R.V. (1951), 'Interest rates and the central bank', in *Money, Trade and Economic Growth: Essays in Honour of John Henry Williams*, New York: Macmillan, pp. 270–95.

Rotemberg, J.J. and M. Woodford (1997), 'An optimization-based econometric framework for the evaluation of monetary policy', *NBER Macroeconomics Annual 1997*, Cambridge, MA: National Bureau of Economic Research, pp. 297–346.

Rowthorn, R. (1995), 'Capital formation and unemployment', *Oxford Review of Economic Policy*, **11**(1), 26–39.

Rudebusch, G.D. and L.E.O. Svensson (1999), 'Policy rules for inflation targeting', in J.B. Taylor (ed.), *Monetary Policy Rules*, Chicago: University of Chicago Press.

Sarel, M. (1996), 'Nonlinear effects of inflation on economic growth', *Staff Papers*, International Monetary Fund, **43**(1), 199–215.

Sargan, J.D. (1964), 'Wages and prices in the United Kingdom: a study in econometric methodology', in P.E. Hart, G. Mills and J.K. Whitaker (eds), *Econometric Analysis for National Economic Planning*, London: Butterworths, pp. 25–63.

Sawyer, M. (1982a), *Macro-Economics in Question*, Brighton: Wheatsheaf Books and New York: M.E. Sharpe.

Sawyer, M. (1982b), 'Collective bargaining, oligopoly and macro-economics', *Oxford Economic Papers*, **34**(4), 428–48.

Sawyer, M. (1983), *Business Pricing and Inflation*, London: Macmillan and New York: St. Martin's Press.

Sawyer, M. (1985), *The Economics of Michal Kalecki*, London: Macmillan.

Sawyer, M. (1999), 'The NAIRU: a critical appraisal', *International Papers in Political Economy*, **6**(2), 1–40; reprinted in P. Arestis and M. Sawyer (eds) (2001), *Money, Finance and Capitalist Development*, Cheltenham, UK and Northampton, MA, USA: Edward Elgar Publishing, pp. 220–54.

Sawyer, M. (2002), 'The NAIRU, aggregate demand and investment', *Metroeconomica*, **53**(1), 66–94.

Sepehri, A. and S. Moshiri (2004), 'Inflation-growth profiles across countries: evidence from developing and developed countries', *International Review of Applied Economics*, **18**(2), 191–208.

Siebert, H. (1997), 'Labour market rigidities: at the root of the unemployment problem', *Journal of Economic Perspectives*, **11**(3), 37–54.

Stiglitz, J. (2003), 'Too important for bankers: central banks' ruthless pursuit of price stability holds back economic growth and boosts unemployment', *The Guardian*, 10 June.

Stiglitz, J. and A. Weiss (1981), 'Credit rationing in markets with imperfect information', *American Economic Review*, **71**(3), 393–410.

Stockhammer, E. (2004), 'Explaining European unemployment: testing the NAIRU hypothesis and a Keynesian approach', *International Review of Applied Economics*, **18**(1), 3–24.

Svensson, L.E.O. (1997), 'Inflation forecast targeting: implementing and monitoring inflation targets', *European Economic Review*, **41**, 1111–46.

Svensson, L.E.O. (1999), 'Inflation targeting as monetary policy rule', *Journal of Monetary Economics*, **43**, 607–54.

Svensson, L.E.O. (2003a), 'How should the eurosystem reform its monetary strategy?', briefing paper for the Committee on Economic and Monetary Affairs of the European Parliament, available at http://www.princeton.edu/~svensson.

Svensson, L.E.O. (2003b), 'What is wrong with Taylor rules? Using judgement in monetary policy through targeting rules', *Journal of Economic Literature*, **XLI**(2), 426–77.

Svensson, L.E.O. and M. Woodford (2003), 'Implementing optimal policy through inflation – forecast targeting', *NBER Working Paper Series*, No. 9747, National Bureau of Economic Research: Cambridge, MA.

Taylor, J.B. (1993), 'Discretion versus policy rules in practice', *Carnegie-Rochester Conference Series on Public Policy*, **39**(4), 195–214.

Taylor, J.B. (1999), 'A historical analysis of monetary policy rules', in J.B. Taylor (ed.), *Monetary Policy Rules*, Chicago: University of Chicago Press.

Taylor, J.B. (2000), 'Reassessing discretionary fiscal policy', *Journal of Economic Perspectives*, **14**(3), 21–36.

Tobin, J. (1993), 'Price flexibility and output stability: an old Keynesian view', *Journal of Economic Perspectives*, **7**, 45–66.

Treasury (1997), *Pre Budget Report*, Cmnd. 3804, London: HMSO.

Treasury (1999), *The New Monetary Policy Framework*, London: H.M. Treasury, October.

Treasury (2003), *Fiscal Stabilization and EMU*, London: HMSO, available at http://www.hm-treasury.gov.uk.

Tsakalotos, E. (2001), 'European employment policies: a new social democratic model for Europe?', in P. Arestis and M. Sawyer (eds), *The Economics of the Third Way: Experience from Around the World*, Edward Elgar Publishing: Cheltenham.

Van Els, P., A. Locarno, J. Morgan and J.-P. Villetelle (2001), 'Monetary policy transmission in the euro area: what do aggregate and national structural models tell us?', European Central Bank Working Paper Series, no. 94.

Volcker, P. (2002), 'Monetary policy transmission: past and future challenges', *Federal Reserve Bank of New York Economic Policy Review*, **8**(1), 7–11.

Walsh, B.M. (2002), 'When unemployment disappears: Ireland in the 1990s', CESIFO Working Paper no. 856, Category 4: Labour Markets (December).

Weller, C.E. (2002), 'What drives the Fed to act?', *Journal of Post Keynesian Economics*, **24**(3), 391–417.

Whited, T. (1992), 'Debt, liquidity constraints, and corporate investment: evidence from panel data', *Journal of Finance*, **47**(4), 1425–60.

Wicksell, K. (1898/1936), *Interest and Prices*, trans. R.F. Kahn, London: Royal Economic Society.

Woodford, M. (1999), 'Optimal monetary policy inertia', NBER Working

Paper Series, no. 7261, National Bureau of Economic Research, Cambridge, MA.

Woodford, M. (2001), 'The Taylor rule and optimal monetary policy', *American Economic Review, Papers and Proceedings*, **91**(2), 232–7.

Index